ASPEN
PUBLISHERS

Americans with Disabilities A[ct] Handbook

Fourth Edition

by Henry H. Perritt, Jr.

Litigation involving the Americans with Disabilities Act (ADA) is one of the most significant fields of discrimination-based litigation facing business and government entities today. The *Americans with Disabilities Act Handbook* provides comprehensive coverage of the ADA's employment, commercial facilities, and public accommodations provisions, as well as coverage of the transportation, communication, and federal, state, and local government requirements. Providing in-depth analysis of the statutory definition of *disability*, as well as practical guidance on all aspects of ADA litigation from complaint through jury instructions, the *Americans with Disabilities Act Handbook* provides all the information you need to successfully evaluate and litigate an ADA case.

Highlights of the 2005-2 Cumulative Supplement

The 2005-2 Cumulative Supplement brings you up to date on the latest developments, including:

- New analysis and tips on demonstrative evidence.
- New case law on "interaction with others" as a major life activity.
- New section on judicial notice.
- New material on developing evidence in amputee cases to avoid findings of not being "disabled," and not being "qualified."
- New material on pleading requirements.
- New cases on proving "substantial" limitation.
- New cases on "regarded-as" disabled.
- New cases on application of Eleventh Amendment in Title II cases.

- New case law on effect of prior statements regarding disability in subsequent ADA litigation.

- New case law on standards for admitting expert testimony.

4/05

For questions concerning this shipment, billing, or other customer service matters, call our Customer Service Department at 1-800-234-1660.

For toll-free ordering, please call 1-800-638-8437.

A WoltersKluwer Company

AMERICANS WITH DISABILITIES ACT HANDBOOK

Fourth Edition

Volumes 1 & 2

2005-2 Cumulative Supplement

This supplement supersedes all previous supplements.

AMERICANS WITH DISABILITIES ACT HANDBOOK

Fourth Edition

Volumes 1 & 2

2005-2 Cumulative Supplement

Henry H. Perritt, Jr.

ASPEN PUBLISHERS

111 Eighth Avenue, New York, NY 10011
www.aspenpublishers.com

Printed in the United States of America

ISBN 0-7355-5310-6

1 2 3 4 5 6 7 8 9 0

About Aspen Publishers

Aspen Publishers, headquartered in New York City, is a leading information provider for attorneys, business professionals, and law students. Written by preeminent authorities, our products consist of analytical and practical information covering both U.S. and international topics. We publish in the full range of formats, including updated manuals, books, periodicals, CDs, and online products.

Our proprietary content is complemented by 2,500 legal databases, containing over 11 million documents, available through our Loislaw division. Aspen Publishers also offers a wide range of topical legal and business databases linked to Loislaw's primary material. Our mission is to provide accurate, timely, and authoritative content in easily accessible formats, supported by unmatched customer care.

To order any Aspen Publishers title, go to *www.aspenpublishers.com* or call 1-800-638-8437.

To reinstate your manual update service, call 1-800-638-8437.

For more information on Loislaw products, go to *www.loislaw.com* or call 1-800-364-2512.

For Customer Care issues, e-mail *CustomerCare@aspenpublishers.com*; call 1-800-234-1660; or fax 1-800-901-9075.

Aspen Publishers
A Wolters Kluwer Company

SUBSCRIPTION NOTICE

This Aspen Publishers product is updated on a periodic basis with supplements to reflect important changes in the subject matter. If you purchased this product directly from Aspen Publishers, we have already recorded your subscription for the update service.

If, however, you purchased this product from a bookstore and wish to receive future updates and revised or related volumes billed separately with a 30-day examination review, please contact our Customer Service Department at 1-800-234-1660, or send your name, company name (if applicable), address, and the title of the product to:

Aspen Publishers
7201 McKinney Circle
Frederick, MD 21704

ABOUT THE AUTHOR

Henry H. Perritt, Jr., is Professor of Law and former Dean at Chicago-Kent College of Law, the law school of Illinois Institute of Technology. He formerly was a professor of law at Villanova University School of Law.

Mr. Perritt served as the top labor and employment lawyer for Consolidated Rail Corporation and as deputy undersecretary of labor during the Ford administration and was vice chairman of a commission appointed by Secretary of Labor Elizabeth Dole to develop measures to preserve health care for retired coal miners, resulting in recommendations subsequently enacted by Congress. He has represented and counseled a variety of employers, employees, and unions on employment law issues. He served as Secretary of the Section on Labor and Employment Law of the American Bar Association in 2000–2001. Mr. Perritt is the author of the following Aspen Publishers publications: *Employee Dismissal Law and Practice* and *Civil Rights in the Workplace*. He edits the annual *Employment Law Update*. He has written more than 80 law review articles on labor and employment law, administrative law, dispute resolution, and technology applications in law. Mr. Perritt received his S.B. and S.M. degrees from M.I.T. and his J.D. degree from Georgetown University. He is a member of the bars of Virginia, Pennsylvania, District of Columbia, Maryland, and Illinois and of the Bar of the U.S. Supreme Court.

He was the Democratic candidate for U.S. Congress from the 10th District of Illinois in 2002, while on leave from Chicago-Kent.

CONTENTS

Sections listed below appear only in the supplement and not in the main volume.

Chapter 5
GOVERNMENT OBLIGATIONS UNDER TITLE II

Chapter 6
REQUIREMENTS UNDER TITLE III FOR PUBLIC ACCOMMODATIONS AND SERVICES OPERATED BY PRIVATE ENTITIES

Chapter 7
TRANSPORTATION AND COMMUNICATIONS SYSTEM REQUIREMENTS UNDER TITLE IV

Chapter 8
REHABILITATION ACT OF 1973

Chapter 9
PROCEDURAL AND EVIDENTIARY ISSUES

Volume 1

CHAPTER 1
INTRODUCTION AND OVERVIEW OF STATUTE

§ 1.01 OVERVIEW OF THE ADA

Page 3, add at end of note 1:

See Stanley S. Herr, *Directions for Reform, Reforming Disability Non Discrimination Laws: A Comparative Perspective*, 35 U. Mich. J.L. Reform 305, 368 n. 346 (2001) (citing this book).

§ 1.07 ADA IMPACT ON OTHER LEGAL CLAIMS

[B] Claims Under 42 U.S.C. § 1983 and § 1985

Page 11, following note 43 reference, add:

In *Bryant v. City of Blackfoot*,[43.1] the Idaho Supreme Court rejected an attempt to base a Section 1983 claim on a violation of the ADA. The plaintiff filed claims under the ADA, the Rehabilitation Act, and Title VII along with her claim under 42 U.S.C. § 1983. She failed to present her ADA claim to the EEOC, and therefore it was appropriately dismissed.[43.2] The court restated the general rules applicable to Section 1983 claims premised on a federal right found in another statute:

> Bryant also alleged that she was entitled to recover under 42 U.S.C. § 1983. That statute does not confer any substantive rights. It is a vehicle for vindicating rights secured by the United States Constitution or federal law. It provides a cause of action to anyone who is deprived, by a person acting under color of state law, of rights secured by federal law. Municipalities are "persons" under the statute. Maine v. Thiboutot, 448 U.S. 1 (1980). Section 1983 encompasses violations of federal statutory law as well as constitutional law. Maine v. Thiboutot, 448 U.S. 1, 100 S. Ct. 2502, 65 L. Ed. 2d 555 (1980). However, § 1983 may not be used to enforce a right secured by a particular federal act if the remedial devices provided in that act are sufficiently comprehensive to demonstrate that congress intended to preclude the remedy of suits under § 1983. Middlesex County Sewerage Authority v. National Sea Clammers Ass'n,

> 453 U.S. 1 (1981). If a federal statute has its own comprehensive enforcement scheme, the requirements of that procedure may not be bypassed by bringing suit directly under § 1983. Id. The statute would be the exclusive remedy for the violation of its terms. This rule is limited, however, to situations in which the cause of action is based solely upon such federal statute. If the challenged conduct violates both such federal statute and the United States Constitution, the plaintiff may bring an action under § 1983 to enforce the Constitutional violation even though the conduct upon which the Constitutional violation is based would also have violated such federal statute. The § 1983 claim may be prosecuted concurrently with the claim based upon the federal statute, or the plaintiff may avoid the enforcement scheme in the statute and sue only under § 1983 to enforce the Constitutional violation. Bradley v. Pittsburgh Bd. of Educ., 913 F.2d 1064 (3d Cir. 1990); Beardsley v. Webb, 30 F.3d 524 (4th Cir. 1994); Southard v. Texas Board of Criminal Justice, 114 F.3d 539 (5th Cir. 1997); Grano v. Department of Dev., 637 F.2d 1073 (6th Cir. 1980); Wudtke v. Davel, 128 F.3d 1057 (7th Cir. 1997); Roberts v. College of the Desert, 870 F.2d 1411 (9th Cir. 1989); Polson v. Davis, 895 F.2d 705 (10th Cir. 1990); Thigpen v. Bibb County, Ga., Sheriff's Dept., 223 F.3d 1231 (11th Cir. 2000).
>
> The only circuit court of appeals to address the issue has held that the Rehabilitation Act provides an extensive, comprehensive remedial framework and that a plaintiff may not maintain a § 1983 action to recover for the deprivation of rights granted by that Act. Holbrook v. City of Alpharetta, Ga., 112 F.3d 1522 (11th Cir. 1997). Likewise, the ADA enforcement scheme is sufficiently comprehensive to bar a § 1983 action based upon the deprivation of rights granted by the ADA. Alsbrook v. City of Maumelle, 184 F.3d 999 (8th Cir. 1999); Holbrook v. City of Alpharetta, Ga., 112 F.3d 1522 (11th Cir. 1997). Because the enforcement scheme of the ADA is borrowed from Title VII, Bryant likewise may not use § 1983 to enforce rights granted solely by Title VII.[43.3]

The court went on to find, however, that discrimination based on disability or gender can violate the equal protection clause, and therefore that the plaintiff could sue under Section 1983 for deprivation of those rights.[43.4]

[43.1] 48 P.3d 636 (Idaho 2002).

[43.2] *Id.* at 642.

[43.3] *Id.* at 643.

[43.4] *Id.* at 643-44.

CHAPTER 3
WHAT IS A STATUTORY DISABILITY?

§ 3.02 ELEMENTS AND STATUTORY DEFINITIONS

[A] Actual Impairments

Page 43, add at end of page:

As § 3.07 explains, application of the impairment, substantial limitation, and major life activity criteria limit the focus of the ADA to a class of persons whose physical or mental impairments tend to exclude them from the workforce and from the enjoyment of other benefits of a modern society. Too relaxed an interpretation of these requirements opens the door to the federal courts to almost anyone who is disqualified from a job based on physical or mental limitations. Too strict an application makes it nearly impossible for one to establish protection by the ADA and also demonstrate qualification for a job or other services.

[2] Major Life Activity

Page 48, add at beginning of subsection:

In *Toyota Motor Manufacturing Kentucky, Inc. v. Williams*,[46.1] discussed also in the next subsection, the Supreme Court reversed the United States Court of Appeals for the Sixth Circuit, and unanimously held that the "substantially limited" test in the Americans with Disabilities Act definition of "disabled" must be applied to activities that are of "central importance to most people's daily lives, not [to] tasks associated with [the plaintiff's] specific job."[46.2] The definition of major life activities "is intended to cover individuals with disabling impairments regardless of whether the individuals have any connection to a workplace."[46.3]

> [T]he manual tasks unique to any particular job are not necessarily important parts of most people's lives. As a result, occupation-specific tasks may have only limited relevance to the manual task inquiry. In this case, repetitive work with hands and arms extended at or above shoulder levels for

> extended periods of time, the manual task on which the Court of Appeals relied, is not an important part of most people's daily lives. . . .

At the same time, the Supreme Court thought that the Court of Appeals disregarded the very type of evidence that it should have focused upon:

> It treated as irrelevant the fact that respondent can tend to her personal hygiene and carry out personal or household chores. Yet household chores, bathing, and brushing one's teeth are among the types of manual tasks of central importance to people's daily lives, and should have been part of the assessment of whether respondent was substantially limited in performing manual tasks.[46.4]

As of early November 2002, 96 state and federal cases had cited Toyota in applying the ADA definition of disability. This section analyzes some of the more significant opinions and their factual context.

In *Sheehan v. City of Gloucester*,[46.5] the court of appeals held that a delay in deciding an ADA case resulting in two remands to the district court, allowed application of the stricter standards of *Toyota*, resulting in a conclusion that the plaintiff did not qualify as disabled, although the court of appeals thought he might have in an earlier appeal. "Although we understand Sheehan's frustration with the delay below, there is no merit in his claim that the timing of the District Court's decision and its application of *Toyota* violated his constitutional rights. A party simply does not suffer any legally cognizable injury when a court applies the intervening precedent of a higher court which decides an issue against that party. After all, it is axiomatic that 'a court is to apply the law and effect at the time it renders its decision, unless doing so would result in manifest injustice or there is statutory direction or legislative history to the contrary.'"[46.6]

In *Rakity v. Dillon Companies*,[46.7] the court of appeals affirmed summary judgment for the employer, finding that the "manual activity of continuously shelving groceries is not centrally important to most people's daily lives."[46.8]

In *Stedman v. Bizmart, Inc.*,[46.9] the district court granted summary judgment to the employer, finding that the plaintiff had not "produced any evidence that his diabetes impeded his activities outside of the workplace in any way."[46.10] The evidence further showed that his impairment did not preclude his performing a broad class of jobs in the workplace, but only the specific job as industrial engineer.[46.11]

In *Kammueller v. Loomis, Fargo & Co.*,[46.12] the court of appeals reversed summary judgment for the employer, finding that an employee with kidney disease who was required to spend 10 hours per week in dialysis and 4 to 5 additional hours in the hospital and traveling was incapable of doing activities of central importance to a person's life, such as cleansing one's own blood cells." [46.13] It found that these limitations qualified the plaintiff as disabled under the ADA, and therefore under the less stringent "materially limits" standard of the Minnesota disability discrimination statute.

In *Rohan v. Networks Presentations LLC*,[46.14] a regarded-as case, the court of appeals, reversing judgment on a jury verdict for the plaintiff, provided an extensive analysis of "interaction with others" as a major life activity. That analysis is discussed in §§ 3.02[A][3] and 3.02[C] of this supplement.

In *EEOC v. Yellow Freight System, Inc.*,[46.15] the district awarded compensatory and punitive damages to an ADA claimant, finding that sitting is a major life activity, and that being unable to sit for more than 45 minutes without moving around constituted a substantial limitation.

In *Mickelsen v. Albertson's, Inc.*,[46.16] the district court found that "not being able to do some of the recreation that I did like running, bicycle riding," while being able to do "housekeeping, cooking, laundry, mowing her lawn, gardening, some rototilling, raking leaves, playing with great grandchildren, washing windows, shopping, driving (including four hour drives to Jackpot, Nevada), painting woodwork, computer work, taking out the garbage, and walking daily for exercise," foreclosed the plaintiff's satisfying the test for disability under *Toyota*.

In *Mack v. Great Dane Trailers*,[46.17] the Seventh Circuit applied *Toyota* to a "regarded-as" ADA claim:

> Furthermore, while Toyota did not address a claim that the employee was regarded as disabled, its analysis still controls in this case. Under the ADA, the concepts of "substantially limits" and "major life activity" are the same whether the employee is proceeding under a claim that she is actually disabled or regarded as disabled. The statute defines disability to include "being regarded as having such an impairment," 42 U.S.C. § 12102(2)(C)—the referenced impairment being that described in the definition of actual impairment. See 42 U.S.C. § 12102(2)(A). So if the condition that is the subject of the employer's belief is not substantially limiting, and the employer does not believe that it is, then there is no violation of the ADA under the "regarded as" prong of the statute. See Sutton, 527 U.S. at 489, 119 S. Ct. 2139; see also EEOC v. United Parcel Serv., Inc., 306 F.3d 794, 2002 WL 31096703, at *7 (applying Toyota's analysis to "regarded as" claim); Gordon v. E.L. Hamm & Assocs., Inc., 100 F.3d 907, 913 (11th Cir. 1996) ("As with real impairments, . . . a perceived impairment must be substantially limiting and significant.").
>
> Applying these principles, we conclude that Mack's ADA claim fails as a matter of law. The parties dispute whether the evidence showed that Great Dane regarded Mack as unable to squat to lift from the floor (Great Dane's version), or as unable to lift (Mack's version). But one thing is clear—all the direct evidence about Great Dane's knowledge of Mack's physical impairment concerned lifting restrictions related to his job and there is no evidence from which a jury reasonably could infer anything about Great Dane's belief about the extent of Mack's limitations as to tasks central to his daily life. For example, Mack relies on one of the

> neurosur-geon's reports received by Great Dane, which stated that Mack could return to work with a restriction of "no lifting" and if he wore a custom work boot. But even if the jury ignored the numerous other reports from the same doctor that identified the restriction as one on kneeling and squatting, the report itself demonstrates that the described restriction was in reference to the limitations at work and nothing more.[46.18]

In *Powdertech, Inc. v. Joganic*,[46.19] the court found the requirements of Toyota satisfied: "Here, the evidence reveals that Joganic cannot climb stairs, lift barrels, do any strenuous activity, or work in heated conditions. This evidence raises a genuine issue of material fact regarding whether Joganic is disabled, as compared to the average person, in performing activities that are central to most people's daily life."

In *Bailey v. Georgia-Pacific Corp.*,[46.20] the court of appeals affirmed summary judgment for the employer. It found that the plaintiff's alcoholism was not shown to have caused more than "isolated" problems on major life activities and thus did not constitute a statutory disability.[46.21]

In *EEOC v. United Parcel Service, Inc.*,[46.22] the court of appeals found that two monocular drivers had failed to satisfy the *Toyota* test: "Applying this standard here leaves us convinced that neither Francis nor Ligas is disabled. Despite not having fully compensated for loss of near-field vision, that impairment does not keep either one of them from using his eyesight as most people do for daily life. Both drive (including for UPS, just not its package cars), read, use tools, and play sports. Accordingly, they do not have an impairment that substantially limits the major life activity of seeing."[46.23]

46.1 534 U.S. 184 (2002).
46.2 *Id.* at 201.
46.3 *Id.*
46.4 *Id.* [internal citation and quotation omitted].
46.5 321 F.3d 21 (1st Cir. 2003).
46.6 *Id.* at 24.
46.7 302 F.3d 1152 (10th Cir. 2002).
46.8 *Id.* at 1159.
46.9 219 F. Supp. 2d 1212 (N.D. Ala. 2002).
46.10 *Id.* at 1221.
46.11 *Id.*
46.12 383 F.3d 779 (8th Cir. 2004).
46.13 *Id.* at 785.
46.14 375 F.3d 266 (4th Cir. 2004).
46.15 ___ F. Supp. 2d ___, 2002 WL 31011859 (S.D.N.Y. Sept. 9, 2002).
46.16 226 F. Supp. 2d 1238 (D. Idaho 2002).
46.17 308 F.3d 776 (7th Cir. 2002).
46.18 *Id.* at 781-82.
46.19 776 N.E.2d 1251 (Ind. App. 2002).
46.20 306 F.3d 1162 (1st Cir. 2002).
46.21 *Id.* at 1168-69.

[46.22] 306 F.3d 794 (1st Cir. 2002).
[46.23] *Id.* at 803.

Page 50, add following extract containing note 56 reference:

In *Thornton v. McClatchy Newspapers, Inc.*,[56.1] the court of appeals held that a former newspaper employee's inability to engage in continuous keyboarding or handwriting did not constitute a statutory disability. Even though it "diminished" the plaintiff's life, and even though "most lawyers or law office personnel would undoubtedly consider continuous keyboarding and handwriting to be activities of central importance to their lives, we cannot say that is so for 'most people's daily lives.'"[56.2]

[56.1] 292 F.3d 1045 (9th Cir. 2002).
[56.2] *Id.* at 1046.

[3] Substantial Limitation

Page 51, following note 62 reference, insert a paragraph break, and add:

Toyota also is discussed in § 3.02[A][2], as are lower court cases applying it.

Page 52, add at end of subsection:

In *Heisler v. Metropolitan Council*,[72.1] the court of appeals affirmed summary judgment for the employer, finding that the plaintiff's conclusory testimony was the only evidence that her depression interfered with the major life activity of sleeping and was therefore insufficient to meet the statutory requirement.[72.2]

The Eighth Circuit required a linkage between the specific limitation on major life activities used to qualify a person as statutorily disabled and an employer's obligation. A plaintiff with a back injury argued that, among other things, the impairment substantially limited the major life activity of procreation. The court of appeals interpreted the reasonable accommodation language of 42 U.S.C. § 12112(b)(5)(A) to require "employers to reasonably accommodate limitations, not disabilities."[72.3] "Where the reasonable accommodation requested is unrelated to the limitation, we do not believe an ADA action may lie. Put another way, there must be a causal connection between the major life activity that is limited and the accommodation sought."[72.4]

In *Hansen v. Seabee Corp.*,[72.5] the Iowa Supreme Court reversed judgment for an employee with a back injury. The evidence was limited to the plaintiff's testimony and the defendants' answers to various submissions. The evidence showed that the plaintiff's back limitations would not allow him to perform heavy lifting or bending jobs, such as concrete work or painting. There was no evidence that it restricted household chores or other daily activities outside the workplace. The Iowa Supreme Court held that the plaintiff was unable to show a substantial limitation on the major life activity of lifting because he admitted that he might be able to lift 25 pounds but could not lift 50 pounds. It construed federal precedent as standing for the proposition that a limitation on the amount of weight a person can lift does not substantially limit the major life activity of lifting. The evidence also was insufficient to support an inference that the plaintiff was substantially limited in the major life activity of working, because there was no evidence to support any conclusion about a broad class of jobs.

In *Coons v. Secretary of Treasury*,[72.6] the court of appeals affirmed summary judgment for the employer in a Rehabilitation Act case. It held that allegations that stress-related abdominal distress precluded extensive travel did not show substantial limitation on any major life activity. More broadly, it expressed doubt that travel was a major life activity.

Rohan v. Networks Presentations LLC[72.7] involved an actress who suffered from posttraumatic stress disorder, occasioned by abuse during her childhood. While on tour with a production company, she suffered a number of "episodes" that led to concerns about her well-being and her ability to continue in the production. The district court granted summary judgment to the employer, finding that the plaintiff was not qualified because she could not perform an essential function of her job, namely, interacting with others.[72.8] The court of appeals disagreed with the district court's analysis, finding instead that the plaintiff was not statutorily disabled.[72.9] It found that although the plaintiff had an impairment, the plaintiff had not demonstrated that her impairment substantially limited the only major life activity she had identified, which was interacting with others.[72.10] The court also expressed skepticism about whether interacting with others qualifies as a major life activity, but found it unnecessary to resolve that issue.[72.11] The most the evidence showed was that the plaintiff avoided making friends, even though she characterized some members of the cast as "friends," and that she avoided dealing with other individuals in the cast whose behavior she found immature and offensive. "The fact that she chose to avoid such individuals, however, does not distinguish her from the general population."[72.12] "Although Rohan appears to be almost completely incapable of interacting with others during her episodes, her episodes are sporadic and last, at most, 30 minutes. During the four months of her employment with Networks, Rohan appears to have experienced approximately 30 episodes. Intermittent manifestations of an illness are insufficient to establish a substantial limitation on a major life activity."[72.13]

In *French v. Hawaii Pizza Hut, Inc.*,[72.14] the Hawaii Supreme Court reversed summary judgment for the employer, finding sufficient factual disputes on the question whether a 25-pound lifting limitation qualified as a substantial limitation. It declined to follow the federal cases holding that a quantitative limitation does not qualify as substantial as a matter of law, and instead held that the factfinder must be allowed to determine the substantiality of the limitation "looking at the effect the impairment has on the life in the individual."[72.15] At the summary judgment stage, it was the defendants' burden to produce admissible evidence that the average person in the general population cannot lift more than 25 pounds. Thus, the plaintiff's failure to produce that evidence was not determinative.

In *Charbonneau v. Gorczyk*,[72.16] the Vermont Supreme Court affirmed the rejection of a Title 3 claim by an inmate objecting to a refusal to transfer him to a more desirable prison setting. The court found that the plaintiff's acknowledged physical impairment—angina—did not significantly limit the major life activity of working, based on evidence that the plaintiff satisfactorily performed a variety of laundry and janitorial jobs in the prison. "The fact that plaintiff could perform work while incarcerated demonstrates that his medical condition does not substantially limit his ability to work."[72.17]

In *Pegram v. Honeywell, Inc.*,[72.18] the court of appeals agreed with the district court that evidence that the plaintiff was able to perform his employment without a single absence of work as a result of his impairment—degenerative conditions in his back—undercut any conclusion that he was substantially limited in the major life activities of standing and sitting.[72.19]

In *Hill v. Steven Motors, Inc.*,[72.20] the court granted summary judgment to the employer, finding that the plaintiff had failed to show that her stroke substantially limited the major life activities of "remembering, thinking or learning, and moving." Occasional lapses in memory, occasionally losing her balance, and occasionally stubbing her toe were no different from experiences of the general population.

In *Wood v. Crown Redi-Mix, Inc.*,[72.21] the district court found that the plaintiff's back injury imposed only a "moderate" and not a substantial limitation on the major life activity of walking, and granted summary judgment to the employer.[72.22]

In *Fultz v. City of Salem*,[72.23] the court of appeals, affirming summary judgment for the employer, said that the "[p]laintiff has shown that his ability to perform some manual tasks is diminished," but "diminished is different from 'substantially limited,' at least as understood by Congress and the Supreme Court."[72.24] A few tasks, such as buttoning a shirt, are

> more difficult for him than they were before his injury, but the injury does not prevent or severely restrict Plaintiff from doing activities that are of central importance in most people's daily lives. For example, Plaintiff's doctor stated that he could do most of his activities, and Plaintiff admits that he can drive without difficulty. Under *Toyota* and *Thornton*, the evidence could not sustain a finding of substantial limitation in the major life activity of performing manual tasks."[72.25]

[72.1] 339 F.3d 622 (8th Cir. 2003).
[72.2] *Id.* at 628.
[72.3] *Id.* at 687.

[72.4] *Id.* (citing Felix v. New York City Transit Auth., 324 F.3d 102, 106-07 (2d Cir. 2003) (requested accommodation of not working in the subway was unrelated to limitation on major life activity of sleeping)).

[72.5] ___ N.W.2d ___, No. 02-2071, 2004 WL 2238636 (Iowa Oct. 6, 2004).

[72.6] 383 F.3d 879 (9th Cir. 2004).

[72.7] 375 F.3d 266 (4th Cir. 2004).

[72.8] *Id.* at 272 (characterizing district court's reasoning).

[72.9] *Id.* at 272-73.

[72.10] *Id.* at 274.

[72.11] *Id.* at 274 (characterizing interacting with others as an "amorphous" concept).

[72.12] *Id.* at 275.

[72.13] *Id.* at 276.

[72.14] 99 P.3d 1046 (Haw. 2004).

[72.15] *Id.* at ___ [*17].

[72.16] 838 A.2d 117 (Vt. 2003).

[72.17] *Id.* at 120.

[72.18] 361 F.3d 272 (5th Cir. 2004).

[72.19] *Id.* at 286.

[72.20] 228 F. Supp. 2d 1247 (D. Kan. 2002).

[72.21] 218 F. Supp. 2d 1094 (S.D. Iowa 2002).

[72.22] *Id.* at 1101-02.

[72.23] 51 Fed. Appx. 624 (9th Cir. 2002).

[72.24] *Id.*, quoting Thornton v. McClatchy Newspapers, Inc., 292 F.3d 1045, 1046 (9th Cir. 2002).

[72.25] 51 Fed. Appx. at 626.

[4] Disqualification from a Range of Jobs Rather than a Single Job

Page 52, add at beginning of subsection:

In *Toyota*,[72.26] the Supreme Court noted "conceptual difficulties" with the proposition that working constitutes a major life activity, and declined to decide in that case whether it does.[72.27] Assuming that working constitutes a major life activity, the Court reiterated its requirement in *Sutton*[72.28] that an ADA Title I plaintiff must establish substantial limitation with respect to a broad class of jobs rather than with respect to a single job.[72.29]

Most lower court case law treats working as a major life activity.

In *Rohan v. Networks Presentations LLC*,[72.30] the court of appeals found that a theater company's perception that an actress employee was disqualified, by her posttraumatic stress disorder, from working in a particular role, or even a perception that she was disqualified from a traveling production, did not represent disqualification from a sufficiently broad range of jobs to satisfy the "regarded as" definition of disability under the ADA.[72.31]

[72.26] Toyota Motor Mfg. Kentucky, Inc. v. Williams, 534 U.S. 184 (2002) (a person is not statutorily disabled unless impairment substantially limits an activity central to most people's daily lives outside the workplace). *Toyota* is analyzed more extensively in §§ 3.02[A][2] and [3].

[72.27] *Id.* at 198-99.

72.28 Sutton v. United Airlines, Inc., 527 U.S. 471 (1999) (whether a person is statutorily disabled must be assessed taking into account mitigating measures and appliances such as prostheses). Sutton is considered more fully in § 3.02[A][5].

72.29 534 U.S. at 200 (citing and quoting Sutton).

72.30 375 F.3d 266 (4th Cir. 2004).

72.31 *Id.* at 198-99.

[5] Effect of Mitigating Medicines or Appliances

Page 57, add before last paragraph of section:

In *Fraser v. Goodale*,[103.1] the court of appeals offered useful guidance in applying the mitigating measures doctrine:

> In sum, before determining whether a person's impairment is substantially limiting, we look at the nature, severity, duration, and impact of the impairment. 29 C.F.R. § 1630.2(j)(2)(i)-(iii). Under *Sutton*, we consider the mitigating measures the person uses, their effectiveness, their side effects and their burdens. This analysis requires a sensitive, fact-based analysis that knows no bright lines. We do not decide whether every diabetic is disabled, and we do not decide whether every severely obese person is not disabled. Instead, "[w]hether a person is disabled under the ADA is an individualized inquiry." *Thornton v. McClatchy Newspapers, Inc.*, 261 F.3d 789, 794 (9th Cir. 2001); *but see Albertson's*, 527 U.S. at 566, 119 S. Ct. 2162 (recognizing some impairments might constitute a per se disability).
>
> * * *
>
> Though we hold that eating is a major life activity, we do not thereby invite all those on a diet to bring claims of disability. Not every impediment to the copious and tasty diets our waistlines and hearts cannot endure is a substantial limitation of the major life activity of eating. We must carefully separate those who have simple dietary restrictions from those who are truly disabled. At the same time, we must permit those who are disabled because of severe dietary restrictions to enjoy the protections of the ADA. Based on the summary judgment record here, we must determine whether Fraser presented a genuine issue of material fact as to whether her diabetes and her rigorous treatment regimen substantially limit the major life activity of eating.
>
> * * *
>
> Unlike a person with ordinary dietary restrictions, Fraser must monitor much more than what and how much she eats. Unlike a person with ordinary dietary restrictions, she does not enjoy a forgiving margin of error. While the typical person on a heart-healthy diet will not find himself in

the emergency room if he eats too much at a meal or forgets his medication for a few hours, Fraser does not enjoy this luxury.

As in *Lawson*, even when taking insulin, her ability to "regulate h[er] blood sugar and metabolize food is difficult, erratic, and substantially limited." *Lawson*, 245 F.3d at 924. Even when followed with utmost skill and faithfulness, Fraser's treatment regimen does not completely save her from the havoc her diabetes wreaks on her ability to eat normally.

* * *

In short, Fraser presented evidence that the major life activity of eating is substantially limited because of her demanding and highly difficult treatment regimen.

In response, the Bank argues that *Lawson's* emphasis on the dire consequences of failing the treatment regimen runs counter to *Sutton's* command not to consider the plaintiff's hypothetical state. The Bank misreads *Lawson. Lawson* considered these consequences because diabetics like Lawson and Fraser suffer debilitating insulin reactions and significant limits on their major life activities despite their adherence to the treatment regimen. *Lawson*, 245 F.3d at 926. *Sutton* requires us to consider Fraser's actual state. 527 U.S. at 488, 119 S. Ct. 2139. *Sutton* does not require us to pretend that treatment measures are completely effective when there is evidence that they are not.

The Bank suggests that if Fraser carried a backpack with food and insulin shots, then she could control her blood sugar levels. The Bank contends that having to carry a backpack is not substantially limiting. This belittles Fraser's impairment. Even though she can (and does) carry a backpack, Fraser's perpetual, difficult, and multifaceted treatment regimen substantially limits the major life activity of eating. *Accord Lawson*, 245 F.3d at 924-25. Simply having the means to control an illness does not make controlling the illness easy.

Moreover, the backpack defense does not help here. If Fraser is not substantially limited in a major life activity because she could carry a backpack, then no diabetic is disabled, since all could carry backpacks. This goes too far because no employer would have to accommodate diabetics by letting them use the backpack. The injustice of this conclusion is best illustrated by the facts here: Fraser had food with her at her desk, but her employer refused to let her eat it. A backpack of food and insulin shots is nothing but a heavy accessory in light of an employer's refusal to accommodate. As Dr. Lockwood concluded:

> she's limited. . .by the requirements of—of the condition itself, just to maintain. So if she can't take a break to eat, can't take a break to get her shot, can't take a break to test herself, that's a potential problem.

> The Bank also asserts that, unlike Fraser, Lawson suffered a host of intermediate complications from his diabetes, such as proliferative diabetic retinopathy, impotence, proteinuria, and periodic episodes of limited joint mobility syndrome. *Lawson*, 245 F.3d at 919. Fraser, on the other hand, suffered from different ailments, such as adult respiratory distress syndrome, ulcers, chronic nausea, and diabetic gastroparesis. This difference is not critical to the Bank's summary judgment motion, as it does not demonstrate that Fraser's impairment is not substantially limiting. The Seventh Circuit likewise considered Lawson's intermediate complications irrelevant to the disability determination, as it did not detail whether Lawson's ailments are serious, and it did not even mention these ailments as being relevant to the disability issue. *Lawson*, 245 F.3d at 924. In fact, after listing only the evidence that is similar to Fraser's evidence, the court concluded that "*[t]his* evidence is sufficient for a jury to find that Mr. Lawson is substantially limited," implying that other evidence was not necessary. *Id.* (emphasis added).
>
> The Bank contends that Dr. Lockwood testified that as long as Fraser keeps regular habits and can keep her blood glucose normal, she would not have any substantial limitations. The Bank begs the question. The problem with a brittle diabetic is that it is very difficult to keep her blood glucose normal.[103.2]

The court found that a jury was entitled to decide if the plaintiff's diabetes met these tests, reversing summary judgment for the employer.[103.3]

One of the concerns about the *Sutton* mitigating measures doctrine is that, extended to its logical extreme, it would misclassify someone who, like an amputee, is disabled in any commonsense view of the word as outside statutory protection precisely because he has compensated well for his disability.[103.4]

[103.1] 342 F.3d 1032 (9th Cir. 2003).

[103.2] *Id.* at 1038-43.

[103.3] *Id.* at 1045.

[103.4] *See* Claudia Center & Andrew J. Imparato, *Redefining "Disability" Discrimination: A Proposal to Restore Civil Rights Protection for All Workers*, 14 Stan. L. & Pol'y Rev. 321, 288 ("even an amputee might no longer have a discrimination claim if he or she uses a prosthesis to perform major life activities about as well as others"); Rebecca Hanner White, Deference and Disability Discrimination, 99 Mich. L. Rev. 532, 535 (2000) ("Perhaps an amputee whose prosthetic limb enables her to walk or even run, may not be substantially limited in performing major life activities because of the mitigating effects. . . .).

[B] Having a Record of Impairment

Page 58, add following note 109 reference:

In *Hernandez v. Hughes Missile Systems Co.*,[109.1] the court of appeals held that a Title I plaintiff made out a prima facie case of being denied employment based on a record of disability supported by evidence that he was denied employment because of his record of past drug addiction.[109.2]

[109.1] 298 F.3d 1030 (9th Cir. 2002).
[109.2] *Id.* at 1034.

[C] "Regarded as Disabled"

Page 59, add following first paragraph:

The EEOC regulations addressing this category of disability define an individual who "is regarded as having such an impairment" as one who,

(1) Has a physical or mental impairment that does not substantially limit major life activities but is treated by a covered entity as constituting such limitation;

(2) Has a physical or mental impairment that substantially limits major life activities only as a result of the attitude of others toward such impairment; or

(3) Has none of the impairments defined in paragraph (h)(1) or (2) of this section but is treated by a covered entity as having a substantially limiting impairment.[118.1]

[118.1] 29 C.F.R. § 1630.2(l) (2001).

Page 59, add following note 121 reference:

The Third Circuit applied this definition in *Buskirk v. Apollo Medals*.[121.1] The plaintiff claimed qualification under the first definition because his back condition limited his ability to perform some work but his employer regarded the impairment as one substantially limiting major life activities. The court acknowledged that usually, "an employer's perception that an employee cannot perform a wide range of jobs suffices to make out a 'regarded as' claim."[121.2] The evidence showed that the employer perceived the plaintiff to be unable to perform any of its positions based on his medical condition and thus he established "regarded-as" disability.[121.3]

Because the court of appeals found that the employer provided the plaintiff with reasonable accommodations, it did not need to "answer the difficult question of whether [the employer] was obligated to do so." [121.4] The court reviewed other case law varying on the question whether a "regarded-as" plaintiff is entitled to reasonable accommodation:

> In Deane v. Pocono Medical Center, 142 F.3d 138, 148-49 n. 12 (3d Cir. 1998) (en banc), we examined, but did not decide, whether an employer is

required to provide reasonable accommodations to an employee it perceives as disabled and reviewed the primary arguments on each side of the debate. On the side of requiring the provision of reasonable accommodations, we noted that the plain language of the ADA does not differentiate between "regarded as" plaintiffs and plaintiffs who are actually disabled, id., and cited School Board of Nassau County v. Arline, 480 U.S. 273, 288-89, 107 S. Ct. 1123, 94 L. Ed. 2d 307 (1987), where the Supreme Court held that employers have an obligation to provide reasonable accommodations to employees who are regarded as disabled under the Rehabilitation Act, 29 U.S.C. § 701 et seq. In Arline, the Supreme Court stated that by protecting "regarded as" employees from discrimination under the Rehabilitation Act, Congress acknowledges that "society's accumulated myths and fears about disability and disease are as handicapping as are the physical limitations that flow from actual impairment." Id. at 284, 107 S. Ct. 1123. Finally, in Deane we recognized the plaintiff's argument that "failure to mandate reasonable accommodations for 'regarded as' plaintiffs would undermine the role the ADA plays in ferreting out disability discrimination in employment." 142 F.3d at 148 n. 12.

On the other side of the debate, we "acknowledge[d] the considerable force" of the argument that mandating reasonable accommodations would both permit healthy employees to demand changes in their working conditions through the threat of litigation and "create a windfall for legitimate 'regarded as' disabled employees who, after disabusing their employers of their misperceptions, would nonetheless be entitled to accommodations that their similarly situated co-workers are not, for admittedly non-disabling conditions." Id. at 149 n. 12; see also Taylor v. Pathmark Stores, Inc., 177 F.3d 180, 196 (3d Cir. 1999) (noting that "it seems odd to give an impaired but not disabled person a windfall because of her employer's erroneous perception of disability, when other impaired but not disabled people are not entitled to accommodation") (citing Deane, 142 F.3d at 149 n. 12). We did not decide the issue in either Deane or Taylor.[121.5]

Thus far, the Fifth, Sixth, and Eighth Circuits have held that "regarded as" employees are not entitled to reasonable accommodations. See Weber v. Strippit, Inc., 186 F.3d 907, 916-17 (8th Cir. 1999), cert. denied, 528 U.S. 1078, 120 S. Ct. 794, 145 L. Ed. 2d 670 (2000); Workman v. Frito-Lay, Inc., 165 F.3d 460, 467 (6th Cir. 1999); Newberry v. E. Tex. State Univ., 161 F.3d 276, 280 (5th Cir. 1998). The First Circuit has held that "regarded as" employees are entitled to reasonable accommodations. Katz v. City Metal Co., 87 F.3d 26 (1st Cir. 1996).[121.6]

[121.1] 307 F.3d 160 (3d Cir. 2002).
[121.2] *Id.* at 167.
[121.3] *Id.* at 167-68.
[121.4] *Id.* at 168.
[121.5] *Id.* at 168 n. 2.
[121.6] *Id.* at 168-69.

[1] Perceived Impairments

Page 59, add at end of first sentence:

In *Williams v. Motorola, Inc.,*[121.7] the court of appeals held that a "regarded as" Title I plaintiff need not prove an actual disability to litigate a claim, although it found in the facts before it a failure to make out a prima facie case of "regarded-as" disability discrimination.[121.8]

[121.7] 303 F.3d 1284 (11th Cir. 2002).
[121.8] *Id.* at 1290.

[2] Perceived Limitations

Page 64, add following carryover paragraph:

In *Mack v. Great Dane Trailers,*[145.1] the court of appeals reversed judgment on a jury verdict for the employee and held that he failed to establish "regarded-as" disability. While the evidence showed that the employer believed that the plaintiff was substantially limited in the major life activity of lifting at work, the court of appeals, applying *Toyota,* found that the perceived work limitation was insufficient to satisfy the statute:

> Furthermore, while Toyota did not address a claim that the employee was regarded as disabled, its analysis still controls in this case. Under the ADA, the concepts of "substantially limits" and "major life activity" are the same whether the employee is proceeding under a claim that she is actually disabled or regarded as disabled. The statute defines disability to include "being regarded as having such an impairment," 42 U.S.C. § 12102(2)(C)—the referenced impairment being that described in the definition of actual impairment. See 42 U.S.C. § 12102(2)(A). So if the condition that is the subject of the employer's belief is not substantially limiting, and the employer does not believe that it is, then there is no violation of the ADA under the "regarded as" prong of the statute. See Sutton, 527 U.S. at 489; see also EEOC v. United Parcel Serv., Inc., 306 F.3d 794, 2002 WL 31096703, at *7 (applying Toyota's analysis to "regarded as" claim); Gordon v. E.L. Hamm & Assocs., Inc., 100 F.3d 907, 913 (11th Cir. 1996) ("As with real impairments, . . . a perceived impairment must be substantially limiting and significant."). [145.2]

In *Waldrip v. General Electric Co.,* [145.3] the court of appeals rejected the plaintiff's argument that the employer regarded the impairment as substantially limiting, based on the employer's routinely permitting the plaintiff to take sick leave and evidence that its concern was based on the plaintiff's operating heavy machinery after taking pain medication rather than on limitations resulting from the impairment itself. [145.4]

In *EEOC v. JB Hunt Transport, Inc.*, [145.5] the court of appeals affirmed the district court and disagreed with the EEOC that the defendant, by disqualifying road truck drivers who took one or more of 836 medications, violated Title I of the ADA because it discriminated against persons "regarded as" disabled. The court held that regarded-as disability can be established only when an employer perceives a condition as significantly restricting the subject's ability to perform a class of jobs or a broad range of jobs in various classes. The over the road ("OTR") truck driver jobs in question were neither a class of jobs nor a broad range of jobs but rather specific jobs with specific requirements. "Such a position requires specific abilities, especially the ability to stay alert over long hours under difficult conditions. A Hunt OTR driver's alertness cannot flag. He or she must be able to stay alert and withstand the mesmerizing affect [sic] of driving an 18 wheel vehicle for hours at a stretch, sometimes at night, with continuous vibration over long distances. Given these demanding requirements, the fact that one may not be able to perform the specific job of a Hunt OTR driver does not mean that one could not successfully engage in other types of truck driving, let alone in other kinds of safety-sensitive work." [145.6]

In *McGeshick v. Principi*,[145.7] the court of appeals affirmed summary judgment for the Veterans Administration on a Rehabilitation Act claim. The court found that the evidence showed that the VA perceived the plaintiff as disqualified from performing specific tasks associated with the housekeeping job for which he applied but that this did not satisfy the requirement that a perceived-disability claimant show that the employer perceived him as disqualified from a wide range of jobs.[145.8]

In *City of New Bedford v. Massachusetts Commission Against Discrimination*,[145.9] the Massachusetts Supreme Judicial Court, applying federal case law, found that a police officer could not establish that he was perceived as disabled under the state disability discrimination law because the evidence showed only that his employing police department perceived him as disqualified from a particular position on a SWAT team and that such disqualification did not show "substantial limitation" in one or more major life activities. [145.10]

[145.1] 508 F.3d 776 (7th Cir. 2002).
[145.2] *Id.* at 781-82.
[145.3] 325 F.3d 652 (5th Cir. 2003).
[145.4] *Id.* at 657.
[145.5] 321 F.3d 69 (2d Cir. 2003).
[145.6] *Id.* at 75.
[145.7] 357 F.3d 1146 (10th Cir. 2004).
[145.8] *Id.* at 1150.
[145.9] 799 N.E.2d 578 (Mass. 2003).
[145.10] *Id.* at 590-91.

Page 69, add at end of subsection:

In *Schuler v. Supervalu, Inc.*,[173.1] the plaintiff was conditionally hired for a warehouse position at the defendant's warehouse, subject to an independent medical examination. During the medical examination, he disclosed that he had epilepsy, and the examining physician recommended him for employment subject to a restriction that he not drive forklifts or work around unprotected dangerous equipment or unprotected heights. The physician did not disclose his epilepsy. The employer withdrew the job offer. The court of appeals affirmed summary judgment for the employer, finding that the plaintiff, who denied actual disability, could not satisfy the "regarded as" category. Because the employer did not know of his epilepsy, it could not have held any perception regarding that impairment. The evidence did not show that the employer regarded Mr. Schuler as significantly restricted in his ability to perform a class of jobs or a broad range of jobs, but only disqualified from a specific warehouse job.[173.2]

Conversely, in *Ollie v. Titan Tire Corp.*,[173.3] the court of appeals affirmed judgment on a jury verdict for an employee with asthma. It found sufficient evidence to support a jury conclusion that the plaintiff was regarded as disabled. The employer believed that the plaintiff's medical restriction precluded him from any manufacturing or warehouse facility job in the Des Moines area because all such jobs would present an environment where dust and fumes would be present, thereby violating the medical restriction expressed by the plaintiff's physician.[173.4]

In *Jacques v. DiMarzio, Inc.*,[173.5] the court of appeals reversed judgment on a jury verdict awarding $190,000 in damages to a plaintiff who claimed that her employment was terminated in violation of the ADA. The plaintiff claimed that her bipolar disorder was a statutory disability; that she had been discriminated against in violation of 42 U.S.C. § 12102(2)(A) based on that disability; that she had been discriminated against in violation of 42 U.S.C. § 12102(2)(B) because of her record of an impairment; and that she had been discriminated against in violation of 42 U.S.C. § 12102(2)(C) because her employer regarded her as being disabled. The district court granted summary judgment for the employer on the actual disability and the record-of-disability claims, allowing only the regarded-as claim to go to the jury. The jury found that the employer terminated the plaintiff because it "'perceived' her as being disabled in the major life activity of 'interacting with others.'"[173.6] The trial court had given the following jury instruction:

> Relevant to this case, a person is considered "disabled" under the Disabilities Act if she is regarded or perceived as having a mental impairment that substantially limits a major life activity. The ability to interact with others is a major life activity. Jacques must prove that she was perceived as having relations with others that were characterized on a regular basis by severe problems, such as consistently high levels of hostility, social withdrawal, or failure to communicate when necessary, all due

> to her mental impairment. It is a perception case, in other words. Merely cantankerous persons are not deemed substantially limited in their major life activity of interacting with others. It has to be more than that.[173.7]

The court of appeals reiterated the general rule that a regarded-as ADA plaintiff must show that the "employer regarded the individual as disabled within the meaning of the ADA."[173.8]

The court of appeals' analysis of "interacting with others" as a major life activity is worth quoting:

> [In] the first case to address the issue, the First Circuit suggested that "the ability to get along with others" is never a major life activity under the ADA, observing that such an ability comes and goes, "triggered by vicissitudes of life which are normally stressful for ordinary people," and that "[t]o impose legally enforceable duties on an employer based on such an amorphous concept would be problematic." *Soileau v. Guilford of Maine, Inc.*, 105 F.3d 12, 16 (1st Cir. 1997).
>
> Two years later, the Ninth Circuit concluded otherwise, describing "interacting with others" as "an essential, regular function, like walking and breathing" that "easily falls within the definition of 'major life activity' " under the ADA. *McAlindin v. County of San Diego*, 192 F.3d 1226, 1234 (9th Cir. 1999), *cert. denied*, 530 U.S. 1243, 147 L. Ed. 2d 961, 120 S. Ct. 2689 (2000). But see *id.* at 1240 (Trott, J., dissenting) ("Not only is this 'disability' vague, but it's bizarre, ominous, and wholly outside of the group of serious disabilities Congress intended to cover with this statute."). All other circuits faced with the issue have (sometimes with exertion) avoided deciding whether "interacting with others" is a major life activity under the ADA.[8]
>
> [8] *See* Rohan v. Networks Presentations LLC, 375 F.3d 266, 274 (4th Cir. 2004) ("We decline to resolve this issue here because, assuming that interacting with others is a major life activity, [plaintiff] has not demonstrated that it is an activity in which she is substantially limited."); MX Group, Inc. v. City of Covington, 293 F.3d 326, 337 (6th Cir. 2002) (noting "that it has been held that 'interacting with others' is a major life activity" but declining to decide the issue); Heisler v. Metro. Council, 339 F.3d 622, 628 (8th Cir. 2003) (declining to hold that "interacting with others [is] a separate major life activity" because plaintiff failed to provide evidence that her mental impairment "substantially limited her ability to interact with others"); Steele v. Thiokol Corp., 241 F.3d 1248, 1254-55 (10th Cir. 2001) (declining to address whether interacting with others is a major life activity because plaintiff was not substantially limited in her ability to interact with others); *see also* Emerson v. Northern States Power Co., 256 F.3d 506, 511 (7th Cir. 2001) (describing "interacting with others" in apparent dicta as one of many "activities that feed into the major life activities of learning and working").
>
> The parties urge us to align ourselves with either the First Circuit's reasoning in *Soileau* or the Ninth Circuit's holding in *McAlindin.* We decline to subscribe to either analysis.

There is a difference between "get[ting] along with others" (the life activity considered in *Soileau*) and "interacting with others" (the life activity considered in *McAlindin*). We agree with the First Circuit's observation that "get[ting] along with others" is an unworkably subjective definition of a "major life activity" under the ADA—in much the same way that "perceiving" (as distinct from merely "seeing" or "hearing") would be an unworkably subjective "major life activity." See *Soileau*, 105 F.3d at 15. However, it is difficult to contradict the Ninth Circuit's characterization of "interacting with others" as "an essential, regular function" that "easily falls within the definition of 'major life activity.'" *McAlindin*, 192 F.3d at 1234. We also think that "interacting with others," as overarching as it may be, more objectively describes a life activity than does "getting along with others," which connotes proficiency or success and worsens the problem of subjectivity that concerned the First Circuit. Cf. *McAlindin*, 192 F.3d at 1235 ("trouble getting along with coworkers is not sufficient to show a substantial limitation" under the ADA). Although "interacting with others" is a more inclusive activity than (say) "seeing" or "standing," similarly overarching "major life activities" have been endorsed by all of the current members of the Supreme Court in one case or another. See, e.g., *Bragdon*, 524 U.S. at 638-39, 659, 665 (acknowledging "caring for one's self" as a valid "major life activity" under the ADA).

While we accept the Ninth Circuit's premise that "interacting with others" is a "major life activity" under the ADA, we conclude that the Ninth Circuit's test for determining when a limitation on this activity is "substantial" for ADA purposes is unworkable, unbounded, and useless as guidance to employers, employees, judges, and juries. According to the Ninth Circuit—whose opinion in *McAlindin* the district court's jury instructions in this case tracked—a plaintiff's impairment in "interacting with others" is "substantial" for purposes of the ADA when it is "characterized on a regular basis by severe problems, for example, consistently high levels of hostility, social withdrawal, or failure to communicate when necessary," *McAlindin*, 192 F.3d at 1235, so that a mere "cantankerous[ness]," is not enough. Id.

The Ninth Circuit's presumed demarcation—between persons who are "hostile" and those who are "cantankerous"—does not exist. The "cantankerous" are those "marked by ill humor, irritability, and determination to disagree." Webster's New International Dictionary 328 (3d ed. 1986). On the same hand, the most relevant definition of "hostile" is: "marked by antagonism or unfriendliness." Id. at 1094. It does not help much to require that the hostility be of a "consistently high level" or that the disability in interacting with others be otherwise "severe." Common personality traits such as hostility and argumentativeness are useful professional traits in many employment contexts. And traits associated with Jacques's impairment, such as apathy and poor judgment, see infra note 2, are (equally) useless indicia of whether a deficit in human relations is a "substantial" limitation. In a similar vein, the Ninth Circuit's phrase, "consistently high levels of . . . social withdrawal," fails to capture the appropriate standard.[9]

[9] "Social withdrawal" (even a high level of it) has an array of meanings, not all of which amount to a substantial limitation on a person's ability to interact with others. The range of personality includes people who are reclusive, or laconic, or acerbic. Some people choose to be alone. Others are isolated for other reasons. See, e.g., *United States v. Gementera,* 379 F.3d 596, 606 (9th Cir. 2004) (apparently using the term as a synonym for, or a consequence of, "stigmatization" by others).

The Ninth Circuit approach also frustrates the maintenance of a civil workplace environment. The more troublesome and nasty the employee, the greater the risk of litigation costs for an employer that disciplines or fires him. All things being equal, a "cantankerous" person or a curmudgeon would be more secure by becoming more unpleasant. And an employer faced with an employee who is (for example) an outspoken bigot or boor would have to choose between the risk of litigating that employee's ADA claim, or the risk of litigating the claims of others who experience an unchecked hostile work environment as a result of that employee's behavior.[10]

[10] Evidence in the record suggests that Jacques, on multiple occasions, used language in the workplace that was racist.[173.9]

We return to the distinction between "getting along with others" (a normative or evaluative concept) and "interacting with others" (which is essentially mechanical). We hold that a plaintiff is "substantially limited" in "interacting with others" when the mental or physical impairment severely limits the fundamental ability to communicate with others. This standard is satisfied when the impairment severely limits the plaintiff's ability to connect with others, i.e., to initiate contact with other people and respond to them, or to go among other people—at the most basic level of these activities. The standard is not satisfied by a plaintiff whose basic ability to communicate with others is not substantially limited but whose communication is inappropriate, ineffective, or unsuccessful. A plaintiff who otherwise can perform the functions of a job with (or without) reasonable accommodation could satisfy this standard by demonstrating isolation resulting from any of a number of severe conditions, including acute or profound cases of: autism, agoraphobia, depression or other conditions that we need not try to anticipate today.

Based on our conclusion regarding the proper standard to be applied, as discussed above, we conclude that the district court erred in the way it instructed the jury on the showing necessary to establish that Jacques was "regarded as" having a disability substantially limiting her in "interacting with others." See *Anderson v. Branen,* 17 F.3d 552, 556 (2d Cir. 1994) ("A jury instruction is erroneous if it misleads the jury as to the correct legal standard or does not adequately inform the jury on the law."). The next question is

> whether this error was "harmless." See *Girden,* 262 F.3d at 203 ("A new trial is required if, considering the instruction as a whole, the cited errors were not harmless, but in fact prejudiced the objecting party."). We think there is little doubt that DiMarzio was prejudiced by the erroneous jury instruction and that the error was not harmless. Indeed, the district court, in denying DiMarzio's summary judgment motion on Jacques's "regarded as" claim, stated that "DiMarzio perceived Jacques . . . as an 'extremely emotional' and 'irrational' individual." *Jacques,* 200 F. Supp. 2d at 161. This characterization falls far short of the correct standard for showing that Jacques was "regarded as" being "substantially limited" in "interacting with others." The judgment must be vacated and the case remanded for additional proceedings consistent with this opinion. See *Pahuta,* 170 F.3d at 129 ("[i]n the absence of a Rule 50(b) renewed motion . . . an 'appellate court is without power to direct the District Court to enter judgment contrary to the one it had permitted to stand'") (citations omitted). Nothing in this opinion inhibits the parties from entering a renewed motion in district court for summary judgment premised on the legal principles herein.

In *Williams v. Philadelphia Housing Authority Police Department,*[173.10] the court of appeals reversed summary judgment against a housing authority police officer, who was unable to carry a firearm as the result of a mental condition. The court of appeals held that the plaintiff did not establish an actual disability, because his testimony showed that he was not precluded from a broad range of jobs. However, the appeals court also held the district court erred by not considering whether the plaintiff's inability to carry a firearm foreclosed him from a class of jobs—those in law enforcement.[173.11] His regarded-as claim had more merit, the court of appeals found. The employer had perceived the plaintiff as being disqualified not only from jobs requiring the carrying of a firearm but also from jobs requiring him to be around people carrying firearms. This was a broader limitation.[173.12] Most significantly, the court of appeals, noting a circuit split, held that a regarded-as plaintiff is entitled to reasonable accommodation.[173.13]

In *Genthe v. Lincoln,*[173.14] the court of appeals affirmed judgment as a matter of law for the employer after a jury verdict for an employee with Marfan's Syndrome. It held that there was evidence that the supervisor had denied the plaintiff a promotion and regarded the plaintiff as "having some health conditions that impaired him."[173.15] However, this was insufficient evidence to support the jury's inference that the supervisor perceived the plaintiff as being substantially limited in a major life activity and of a causal connection between that perception and the adverse employment action.

In *Dyke v. O'Neal Steel, Inc.,*[173.16] the court of appeals affirmed summary judgment for the employer—finding, however, that even though a one-eyed plaintiff might not be actually disabled, the employer's action in denying his application for a permanent position based on his condition, without even giving him a vision test, would permit a reasonable jury to infer that the employer regarded him as having a substantially limiting impairment.[173.17]

Despite the fact that the plaintiff had been working at the position he desired on a temporary basis for two weeks without complaint, the court of appeals further affirmed the magistrate judge's conclusion that he could not show he was a qualified individual, because he could not demonstrate that he could pass the employer's eye test that required binocular vision. The only evidence cited by the court of appeals in support of its further conclusion that the eye tests related to an essential function of the position was a conclusory assertion by the employer's expert.[173.18]

In *Doebele v. Sprint/United Management Co.*,[173.19] the court of appeals, affirming in part summary judgment for the employer, held that an employee diagnosed with depression, bipolar disorder, and attention deficit disorder did not qualify as having a statutory disability, because she failed to present evidence that her impairments substantially limited any of the major life activities she identified.[173.20] It reversed, however, on the claim that the plaintiff was regarded as disabled, based on evidence that the plaintiff's supervisors regarded her as substantially limited from a broad class of jobs by her mental impairments.[173.21]

[173.1] 336 F.3d 702 (8th Cir. 2003).
[173.2] *Id.* at 705.
[173.3] 336 F.3d 680 (8th Cir. 2003).
[173.4] *Id.* at 686.
[173.5] 386 F.3d 192 (2d Cir. 2004).
[173.6] *Id.* at 200.
[173.7] *Id.*
[173.8] 386 F.3d at 201.
[173.9] *Id.* at 201-04.
[173.10] 380 F.3d 751 (3d Cir. 2004).
[173.11] *Id.* at 764.
[173.12] *Id.* at 767.
[173.13] *Id.* at 774-75.
[173.14] 383 F.3d 713 (8th Cir. 2004).
[173.15] *Id.* at 717.
[173.16] 327 F.3d 628 (7th Cir. 2003).
[173.17] *Id.* at 633.
[173.18] *Id.* at 634.
[173.19] 342 F.3d 1117 (10th Cir. 2003).
[173.20] *Id.* at 1130 (referring to activities of caring for herself, speaking, sleeping, learning, and interacting with others).
[173.21] *Id.* at 1133.

[3] Accommodating "Regarded as" Employees

Page 72, add at end of subsection:

In *Kaplan v. City of North Las Vegas*,[184.1] the court of appeals found that a "regarded as" ADA plaintiff is not entitled to reasonable accommodation. "If we were to conclude the 'regarded as' plaintiffs are entitled to reasonable accommodation, impaired employees would be better off under the statute if their employers treated them as disabled even if they were not. This would be a perverse and troubling result under a statute aimed at decreasing 'stereotypic assumptions not truly indicative of the individual ability of people with disabilities."[184.2] The court found that the plaintiff police officer was not qualified to perform the essential functions of his position without accommodation.[184.3]

[184.1] 323 F.3d 1226 (9th Cir. 2003).
[184.2] *Id.* at 1232.
[184.3] *Id.* at 1230-31.

Page 72, insert new subsections [D] and [D][1] and relabel former subsection [D] as [2].

[D] Status as "Employee"

Protection of persons who are not formally "employees" also is considered in §§ 4.02[B] and 9.04[B].

[1] Independent Contractors

In *Flannery v. Recording Industry Association of America*,[186.1] the plaintiff received a promise of continued use of his services as a consultant after his termination. After he filed ADA and ADEA claims, his services were not used, and he claimed retaliation. The court of appeals reversed the district court and held that even though independent contractors are not protected against employment discrimination by the ADA, "Mr. Flannery's consulting arrangement grew out of his employment relationship. . . . More importantly, the independent contracting arrangement was one part of his severance package."[186.2] Accordingly denial of any part of the severance package would constitute employment discrimination. Moreover, reasoned the court, employer withdrawal of part of an employee's severance package would "make other employees think twice before filing a discriminatory termination charge."[186.3]

[186.1] 354 F.3d 632 (7th Cir. 2004).
[186.2] *Id.* at 642.
[186.3] *Id.* at 643.

[2] Protection of Former Employees

§ 3.03 PHYSICAL DISABILITY

[B] AIDS/HIV

Page 76, add at end of subsection:

In *Blanks v. Southwestern Bell Communications, Inc.*,[203.1] the court of appeals affirmed summary judgment for an employer, finding that an HIV-positive plaintiff could not establish statutory disability because he was disqualified only from one job rather than a class of jobs, and because he and his wife had decided not to have any more children and thus he could show no substantial limitation on the major life activity of procreating.

In *Waddell v. Valley Forge Dental Associates, Inc.*,[203.2] the court of appeals determined that health risks associated with a dental hygienist's HIV-positive status could not be eliminated by reasonable accommodation and therefore that the plaintiff was not qualified for his position.[203.3]

203.1 310 F.3d 398 (5th Cir. 2002).
203.2 276 F.3d 1275 (11th Cir. 2001).
203.3 *Id.* at 1281.

[E] Asthma and Other Breathing Conditions

Page 78, add at end of subsection:

In *Liljedahl v. Ryder Student Transportation Services, Inc.*,[211.1] the court of appeals held that lung cancer, apparently cured by surgery, did not qualify as a disability.[211.2]

In *Albert v. Smith's Food & Drug Centers, Inc.*,[211.3] the court of appeals rejected a claim by the defendant that an asthmatic former employee failed to demonstrate that her asthma substantially limited her major life activity of breathing, based on evidence that she must avoid a wide variety of everyday situations, including crowds, nighttime or outdoor activities, cigarette smoke, and perfumes.[211.4]

211.1 341 F.3d 836 (8th Cir. 2003).
211.2 *Id.* at 842.
211.3 356 F.3d 1242 (10th Cir. 2004).
211.4 *Id.* at 1250.

[H] Cardiovascular Conditions

Page 81, add at end of subsection:

In *Charbonneau v. Gorczyk*,[223.1] the Vermont Supreme Court affirmed rejection of a Title 3 claim by an inmate objecting to a refusal to transfer him to a more desirable prison setting. The court found that the plaintiff's acknowledged physical impairment—angina—did not significantly limit the major life activity of working, based on evidence that the plaintiff satisfactorily performed a variety of laundry and janitorial jobs in the prison. "The fact that plaintiff could perform work while incarcerated demonstrates that his medical condition does not substantially limit his ability to work."[223.2]

223.1 838 A.2d 117 (Vt. 2003).
223.2 *Id.* at 120.

[M] Diabetes

Page 84, add at end of subsection:

In *Orr v. Wal-Mart Stores, Inc.*,[236.1] the court of appeals held that diabetes did not qualify as a statutory disability, refusing to consider an untimely argument that eating constitutes a major life activity.[236.2]

In *Fraser v. Goodale*,[236.3] the court of appeals, reversing summary judgment for the employer, found that brittle diabetes qualified as a statutory disability because it significantly restricted the major life activity of eating. The reversal allowed a jury to determine whether the condition did in fact impose such a limitation.[236.4]

[236.1] 297 F.3d 720 (8th Cir. 2002).
[236.2] *Id.* at 724-25.
[236.3] 342 F.3d 1032 (9th Cir. 2003).
[236.4] *Id.* at 1044.

[N] Digestive Conditions

Page 84, add at beginning of subsection:

In *Kammueller v. Loomis, Fargo & Co.*,[236.5] the court of appeals reversed summary judgment for the employer. An employee with kidney disease was required to spend 10 hours per week in dialysis and 4 to 5 additional hours in the hospital and traveling; this "rendered [him] incapable of doing activities of central importance to a person's life, such as cleansing one's own blood cells."[236.6] It found that these limitations qualified the plaintiff as disabled under the ADA, and therefore under the less stringent "materially limits" standard of the Minnesota disability discrimination statute.

In *Waldrip v. General Electric Co.*,[236.7] the court of appeals held that chronic pancreatitis is a physical impairment, interfering with the major life activity of eating. "By any measure, eating is of central importance to daily life and the life process."[236.8] The court found, however, that the plaintiff offered no evidence that *his* chronic pancreatitis substantially limited the major life activity of eating.

> A plaintiff cannot survive summary judgment by showing that an impairment like his own could substantially limit a major life activity of another person or in his own future. Rather, he must show that his impairment has actually and substantially limited the major life activity on which he relies.[236.9]
>
> * * *
>
> In short, neither the Supreme Court nor this court has recognized the concept of a per se disability under the ADA, no matter how serious

the impairment; the plaintiff still must adduce evidence of an impairment that has actually and substantially limited the major life activity on which he relies.

Waldrip does not begin to satisfy this exacting standard. He just asserts his conclusion that "pancreatitis is a serious condition that substantially limits his major life function of eating and digesting." Waldrip's doctor testified that, at most, he occasionally must miss a few days of work when his chronic pancreatitis flares up. This testimony does not demonstrate that Waldrip's chronic pancreatitis substantially limits his ability to eat; even if it did, such temporary effects do not amount to a substantial limit. *Burch*, 119 F.3d at 316. Based on this evidence, no reasonable jury could conclude that Waldrip's chronic pancreatitis "substantially limits" his ability to eat or, therefore, that he has a "disability" under § 12102(2)(A).[236.10]

[236.5] 383 F.3d 779 (8th Cir. 2004).
[236.6] *Id.* at 785.
[236.7] 325 F.3d 652 (5th Cir. 2003).
[236.8] *Id.* at 655 (applying standards of Toyota Motor Mfg. v. Williams, 534 U.S. 184, 197 (2002)).
[236.9] 325 F.3d at 656 (citing cases finding alcoholism, cancer, HIV, back injury, deformed leg, monocular vision, asbestosis, and permanent arm injury not to impose substantial limitation).
[236.10] *Id.* at 656-57.

[P] Drugs and Alcohol

Page 85, add at beginning of subsection:

In *Bailey v. Georgia-Pacific Corp.*,[240.1] the First Circuit concluded that alcoholism did not qualify as a statutory disability because the plaintiff was unable to show substantial limitation on major life activities other than working isolated overtime calls in one job.[240.2] It also concluded that the plaintiff failed to show "regarded-as" disability because the employer perceived him as being substantially limited only in his inability to meet the requirements of his particular job.[240.3]

[240.1] 306 F.3d 1162 (1st Cir. 2002).
[240.2] *Id.* at 1169.
[240.3] *Id.* at 1170.

[Q] Epilepsy

Page 87, add at end of subsection:

In *Brunke v. Goodyear Tire and Rubber Co.*,[245.1] the court of appeals held that the plaintiff's epilepsy did not qualify as a statutory disability because no evidence linked workplace behavior with the plaintiff's epilepsy and no evidence was presented that epilepsy substantially limited major life activities outside the workplace. The plaintiff had seizures at work in 1988 and 1989 but only suffered one seizure at work after his physician certified that his seizures were under control. The plaintiff had a number of confrontations and altercations with coworkers, but two staff physicians advised that there was no reason to believe that the misbehavior was caused by the plaintiff's epilepsy.[245.2]

[245.1] 344 F.3d 819 (8th Cir. 2003).
[245.2] *Id.* at 820-21.

[S] Foot and Leg Conditions

Page 88, add at end of section:

In *Rossbach v. City of Miami*,[249.1] the court of appeals held that three police officers who suffered from leg injuries, though classified as disabled by their police-department employer, did not qualify as disabled under the ADA. It held that "someone who walks, sits, stands or sleeps moderately below average is not disabled under the Act."[249.2] The court found that although the plaintiffs' conditions might have substantially limited their ability to work as police officers, that was too narrow a classification of "working" to qualify as a major life activity.[249.3]

[249.1] 371 F.3d 1354 (11th Cir. 2004).
[249.2] *Id.* at 1358.
[249.3] *Id.* at 1359-61.

[T] Hand and Arm Conditions

Page 88, add at beginning of subsection:

In *Gillen v. Fallon Ambulance Service, Inc.*,[249.1] the court of appeals rejected arguments that a one-handed individual was not statutorily disabled because she was able to lift as much as an ordinary person. It found that the plaintiff was significantly restricted in the major life activity of lifting.[249.2]

Fenney v. Dakota, Minnesota & Railroad Co.[249.3] involved a locomotive engineer who lost his thumb and middle finger and suffered damages to his arm in an accident on another railroad. Because of his injuries, the engineer requested that he be called for his assignments two and a half to three hours ahead of time, rather than the usual two hours, to give him extra time to bathe, dress, shave, prepare a meal, and drive himself to his assignment on time. He claims that the refusal of this accommodation violated the ADA. The district court granted summary judgment to the railroad, and the court of appeals reversed. The court of appeals rejected an interpretation of *Toyota* that would limit it to ADA cases in which the major life activity is manual tasks, and instead interpreted *Toyota* to apply no matter what the specific class of major life activity claimed.[249.4] A letter from the plaintiff's physician asserting that the lack of a right thumb makes it more difficult for him to do certain tasks like changing clothes in cold whether, and deposition testimony by the plaintiff that it takes him twice as long as an average person to perform "taking care of himself" tasks, represented sufficient evidence to establish a statutory disability under *Toyota*.[249.5]

The court of appeals also found that the plaintiff had established an adverse employment decision because the refusal of the accommodation necessitated his voluntary transfer to a conductor's position, which paid significantly less.[249.6]

In *Carruthers v. BSA Advertising, Inc.*,[249.7] the court of appeals held that an employee with bilateral hand strain and sprain failed to establish perceived disability because she offered no evidence that her employer perceived her limitations in performing manual tasks as having a permanent or long-term impact or as preventing or severely restricting her from performing activities of central importance to most persons' lives.[249.8]

249.1 283 F.3d 11 (1st Cir. 2002).

249.2 *Id.* at 24.

249.3 327 F.3d 707 (8th Cir. 2003).

249.4 *Id.* at 715 (noting that major life activity of working requires a different analysis under Sutton v. United Airlines, Inc., 527 U.S. 471, 491 (1999)).

249.5 327 F.3d at 715-16.

249.6 *Id.* at 717 (recognizing "constructive demotion," applying same standards as for constructive discharge).

249.7 357 F.3d 1213 (11th Cir. 2004).

249.8 *Id.* at 1217.

[AA] Multiple Sclerosis

Page 94, add at end of note 272:

; Gagliardo v. Connaught Labs., Inc., 311 F.3d 565 (3d Cir. 2002) (affirming award of $2 million in compensatory and $500,000 in punitive damages after jury trial for victim of multiple sclerosis who offered sufficient evidence to support finding of reckless indifference by employer to his ADA obligations).

Page 94, add at end of subsection:

In *Croy v. COBE Laboratories, Inc.*,[276.1] the court of appeals affirmed the district court's finding that a plaintiff with multiple sclerosis was not statutorily disabled because the evidence showed only that she was frequently forced to take unscheduled leave, was frequently unable to lift heavy objects, could not bear sustained exertion, and could not care for her children, complete household chores, or cook for her family. "We are sympathetic with appellant's impairment and presume that she often experiences the symptoms of multiple sclerosis to the extent that she is often temporarily unable to function as the average person would. However, she has failed to show that she is unable to work."[276.2] Of course, if she had shown that she was unable to work, she would have been unable to recover under the ADA because she would not have been qualified.

[276.1] 345 F.3d 1199 (10th Cir. 2003).
[276.2] *Id.* at 1204.

[MM] Vision

Page 101, add at end of subsection:

In *Shannon v. New York City Transit Authority*,[304.1] the court of appeals held that colorblindness disqualified the employee from performing essential qualifications for driving a bus, and therefore that a colorblind employee was not qualified for his position.[304.2]

In *Dyke v. O'Neal Steel, Inc.*,[304.3] a one-eyed plaintiff sued his employer after the employer denied his application for a transfer to another position, explicitly asserting his loss of an eye as the basis for the adverse employment decision. Remarkably, on appeal the plaintiff did not challenge the district judge's determination that he did not have a substantially limiting impairment.[304.4] The court of appeals found that the plaintiff had satisfied the "regarded as" prong of statutory disability:

> Dyke contends O'Neal mistakenly believed his lack of an eye substantially limited his ability to see, a major life activity under the ADA. See 29 C.F.R. § 1630.2(i). Judge Cosbey, without the benefit of the Supreme Court's decision in *Toyota*, held, "the fact that O'Neal requires all regular employees to have vision in both eyes raises an inference that O'Neal believes that a monocular individual is substantially limited in seeing." After *Toyota*, the Ninth Circuit, in *E.E.O.C. v. United Parcel Service, Inc.*, 306 F.3d 794 (9th Cir. 2002), addressed the issue of monocularity in connection with a "regarded as" discrimination claim. The Ninth Circuit held that a company's institution of vision standards alone was insufficient to show that it regarded those individuals who were unable to meet the standards as substantially limited in their overall ability to see in their everyday lives. *Id.* at 806. We agree with this assessment. While vision standards alone may not be sufficient evidence to support a finding of "regarded as" discrimination, Dyke was never given a vision test by O'Neal. Therefore, we must determine whether O'Neal perceived Dyke to be substantially limited in his ability to see because of his complete lack of a left eye. O'Neal asserts the only inference that can be drawn from the record is that O'Neal perceived Dyke to be unable to pass its vision test and, therefore, ineligible to work at its warehouse. However, there is evidence in the record which could support a reasonable inference that O'Neal believed Dyke's lack of an eye substantially limited his ability to see. As previously noted, O'Neal did not even administer the vision test to Dyke. O'Neal's human resources office in Birmingham did not inquire at any time as to the specifics of Dyke's

> condition. Harter's initial reaction upon seeing that Dyke had only one eye was that "it looked odd" and she "wanted to know what was wrong, or was there a problem." However, Harter did not inquire as to the specifics of Dyke's vision. A reasonable jury could infer that O'Neal regarded Dyke's monocular vision as a substantially limiting impairment.[304.5]

The court found, however, that the plaintiff was not qualified because he would not have been able to pass the vision test required of all employees. The district court estopped the plaintiff from claiming qualification because he had represented to the Social Security Administration that he was totally disabled, but the court of appeals did not base its conclusion on estoppel.[304.6]

[304.1] 332 F.3d 95 (2d Cir. 2003).

[304.2] *Id.* at 101 (noting that employee failed to identify any accommodation that would permit him to perform position).

[304.3] 327 F.3d 628 (7th Cir. 2003).

[304.4] *Id.* at 632.

[304.5] *Id.* at 632-33.

[304.6] *Id.* at 633.

Page 101, add new subsection:

[OO] Amputations[305.1]

The status of amputees under the ADA is worth particular consideration. Amputation is undeniably permanent, and most ordinary people would consider someone who has lost an arm or a leg undeniably "disabled," in comparison with claimants who have less visible physical impairments. But recent case law suggests that the status of amputees is a particularly fertile area in which to explore the requirement that qualification as "disabled" be determined after considering how the claimant functions with corrective measures, including prostheses.

In *Ordahl v. Forward Technology Industries, Inc.*,[305.2] the employer claimed that an employee whose left arm had been amputated did not qualify as "disabled" because it challenged whether his physical impairment substantially limited his major life activities. The employee presented evidence that "the activities of dressing, bathing, and carrying plates and glasses are substantially more difficult with his amputated hand/prosthesis than those activities were prior to the amputation. According to Ordahl, dressing himself takes twice as long as it would an unimpaired person."[305.3] The court rejected the employer's argument. It found "[t]hat Ordahl, through sheer force of will, learned accommodations, and careful planning, is able to perform a wide variety of activities despite his physical impairments does not mean that those activities are not substantially more difficult for him than they would be for an unimpaired individual. The Court therefore finds that Ordahl has successfully made out a prima facie case of discrimination under the ADA."[305.4]

In *Lowe v. Alabama Power Co.*,[305.5] the court of appeals reversed summary judgment for the employer and held that a double BK amputee was entitled to present evidence as to whether he could perform the essential functions of a mechanic's job. It concluded that the employer's physician erroneously concluded that all double amputees have similar limitations.[305.6]

In an unreported California Court of Appeals case, *Christensen v. City of Los Angeles*,[305.7] the court held that a BK amputee who is "able to engage in sports activities including running, softball, baseball and snow skiing, although the snow skiing has been with one ski with outriggers, not using his prosthesis," was not qualified, as a matter of law, to perform the essential functions of a police officer. It relied on testimony by an orthopedic physician that the plaintiff's disability would make it difficult for him to climb fences, 2 to 5 flights of stairs, ladders, and embankments, and to vault obstacles, because of the likelihood that his prosthesis would become unstable and might be dislodged. The physician emphasized the prosthetic instability that would result from rotational forces resulting from climbing fences, and atrophy in the residual limb, compared with the sound one.

The trial court found that Christensen was not statutorily disabled because he was able to participate in major life activities.[305.1]

[305.1] Sections 3.03[S] and 3.03[T] also refer to cases involving amputees. Section 3.07 considers other cases in which amputee ADA claimants confronted the dilemma of trying to prove qualification to perform the essential functions of jobs by emphasizing how fully functioning the amputee is, only to invite an argument that the amputee is not statutorily disabled because he or she is too well rehabilitated.

[305.2] 301 F. Supp. 2d 1022 (D. Minn. 2004).

[305.3] *Id.* at 1028.

[305.4] *Id.* at 1029.

[305.5] 244 F.3d 1305 (11th Cir. 2001).

[305.6] *Id.* at 1309.

[305.7] No. B149031, 2002 WL 1154578 (Cal. Ct. App. May 30, 2002).

§ 3.05 MENTAL DISABILITY

[C] Depression

Page 105, add at beginning of subsection:

In *Ogborn v. UFCW Local 881*,[332.1] the court of appeals found that the plaintiff's depression did not qualify as an actual disability or as a "regarded-as" disability because of no showing that the impairment resulted in substantial limitation of major life activities. The evidence simply showed that the condition prevented him from working for about eight weeks.[332.2]

[332.1] 305 F.3d 763 (7th Cir. 2002).

[332.2] *Id.* at 767-68.

[D] Learning Disabilities

Page 107, add at end of subsection:

In *Wong v. Regents of University of California*,[340.1] the court of appeals affirmed the district court's conclusion that a medical student, diagnosed relatively late in his medical school enrollment as having a learning disability, did not qualify as statutorily disabled, given his previous academic success. Even if he could not succeed in medical school, the plaintiff had "an enormous range of professional positions and occupations in which it is apparent that he could engage successfully."[340.2]

[340.1] 379 F.3d 1097 (9th Cir. 2004).
[340.2] *Id.* at 1102, 1108.

[E] Manic-Depressive

Page 108, add at end of subsection:

In *Doebele v. Sprint/United Management Co.*,[341.1] the court of appeals, affirming in part summary judgment for the employer, held that an employee diagnosed with depression, bipolar disorder, and attention deficit disorder did not qualify as having a statutory disability, because she failed to present evidence that her impairments substantially limited any of the major life activities she identified.[341.2] It reversed, however, on the claim that the plaintiff was regarded as disabled, based on evidence that the plaintiff's supervisors regarded her as substantially limited from a broad class of jobs by her mental impairments.[341.3]

[341.1] 342 F.3d 1117 (10th Cir. 2003).
[341.2] *Id.* at 1130 (referring to activities of caring for herself, speaking, sleeping, learning, and interacting with others).
[341.3] *Id.* at 1133.

[H] Panic Disorder

Page 109, add at end of subsection:

In *Felix v. New York City Transit Authority*,[344.1] a badly split panel of the United States Court of Appeals for the Second Circuit held that a subway clerk suffering from insomnia, a statutory disability, was not entitled to an accommodation for another impairment, post traumatic stress disorder, which did not constitute a statutory disability. The court reasoned as follows:

> A simple hypothetical of a car accident illustrates the point well. A passenger in a car is badly injured in an accident. The passenger loses the ability to walk, a major life activity[,] and thus has a "disability" that qualifies him

> for accommodation. The passenger also suffers some injury to his arms, which lower[s] his typing speed from one-hundred words per minute to forty words per minute, without seriously limiting his ability to perform the major life activity of working in general. Because his arm injuries do not substantially limit any major life activity, these injuries are not a disability. His employer terminates him from a position doing data entry and word processing because his productivity has decreased. The fact that the disability, the inability to walk, and the limitation of his typing stem from the same accident does not change the fact that he was not discriminated against "because of [his] disability." Similarly, Felix's inability to sleep (a significant limitation on a major life activity) is separate from her inability to work in the subway (not a significant limitation on the major life activity of working in general), even though both were caused by the subway firebombing and the resultant PTSD."[342.2]
>
> * * *
>
> Felix seeks a workplace accommodation for a mental condition which does not flow directly from her disability—the mental condition of insomnia that prevents her from sleeping. Felix did not argue to the NYCTA that she was unable to work in the subway because such work aggravated her insomnia; she told the NYCTA that she could not work in the subway because she was "terrified of being alone and closed in." Thus, in contrast to the cases upon which she relies, the impairment for which Felix seeks accommodation does not arise "because of the disability." If the requested accommodation addressed a limitation caused by Felix's insomnia, it would be covered by the ADA. Adverse effects of disabilities and adverse or side effects from the medical treatment of disabilities arise "because of the disability." However, other impairments not caused by the disability need not be accommodated.[344.3]

[344.1] 324 F.3d 102 (2d Cir. 2003).
[342.2] *Id.* at 105.
[344.3] *Id.* at 106.

Page 110, add new subsections following subsection [L]:

[M] Attention Deficit Disorder

In *Wright v. Comp USA, Inc.*,[354.1] the court of appeals held that an adult with attention deficit disorder did not suffer from a statutory disability because the evidence showed that he was not substantially limited in major life activities of reading, speaking, concentrating, hearing, and processing information, although there was some evidence that ADD affected various activities in his everyday life.[354.2]

In *Ristrom v. Asbestos Workers Local 34 Joint Apprentice Committee*,[354.3] the court of appeals affirmed summary judgment for the employer, finding that the plaintiff had failed to prove the substantial limitation element in his claim that his attention deficit disorder and depression substantially limited the major life activity of learning.[354.4]

[354.1] 352 F.3d 472 (1st Cir. 2003).
[354.2] *Id.* at 477.
[354.3] 370 F.3d 763 (8th Cir. 2004).
[354.4] *Id.* at 769.

[N] Tourette's Syndrome

In *Ray v. Kroger Co.*,[354.5] the court of appeals, affirming summary judgment for the employer, held that an employee of a grocery chain whose Tourette's Syndrome caused him to communicate ethnic slurs in front of customers was not qualified for his position as a grocery clerk and that his requested accommodation—giving out placards to offended customers explaining his condition—was unreasonable.

[354.5] 90 Fed. Appx. 3 (11th Cir. 2003).

§ 3.06 QUALIFIED INDIVIDUAL

Page 116, add following note 380 callout:

In *Peden v. City of Detroit*,[380.1] the Supreme Court of Michigan, reversing the intermediate court, reinstated summary judgment in favor of the defendant police department. The plaintiff, having suffered a heart attack in 1986, had worked for 10 years in restricted-duty positions with the police department. In 1995, the police department introduced new job requirements based on model standards developed by the Michigan Law Enforcement Officers Training Council. The new standards included requirements such as pursuing suspects on foot, engaging in vehicle pursuits, effecting forcible arrests, overcoming violent resistance, and qualifying with a firearm.[380.2] Because the plaintiff could not meet these requirements, the department placed him on involuntary disability retirement. He argued that the new job requirements were not essential to his former position because that position was essentially clerical. He also claimed that he could perform the requirements.[380.3] The Michigan Supreme Court held that the burden with respect to the essentiality of job functions is placed on the plaintiff. "[P]lacing the burden on the employer to show a certain job function is essential would place courts and jurors in the position of second guessing an employer's business judgment as to what the essential functions of a job are, without even requiring the plaintiff challenging the function to first come forward with evidence that the function is not essential."[380.4] It deflected the plaintiff's argument that he had never been called upon to perform any of the functions in controversy, on the ground that all Detroit police officers must be capable of performing police officer functions during times of riot or crises.[380.5] It found no triable issue of fact on the essentiality of the job functions,[380.6] which meant that the plaintiff could prevail only if he could show that he could perform those functions with or without reasonable accommodation.

The court allowed the police department to rely on the plaintiff's employment history as being limited in his work capability for more than 10 years:

> Plaintiff's medical records indicated, as would be expected, that plaintiff's heart condition continued to persist. Under such circumstances it would be pointless to require the department, before placing plaintiff on disability retirement, to have him undertake agility tests in order to determine whether he could perform the EFL tasks. Such tasks would essentially require plaintiff to perform those very tasks that, because of his heart condition, his medical records indicated he was to refrain from performing. When the department stated in 1995 that plaintiff was unable to perform the essential functions of a police officer position, it was relying on evidence that already had been conclusively established by plaintiff's own medical records and accepted as the truth by all parties.[380.7]

Whether a plaintiff is qualified can depend on an assessment of his or her capability to perform essential job functions after reasonable accommodation is taken into account. *Bartee v. Michelin North America, Inc.*,[380.8] provides a good example of how taking a reasonable accommodation into account may result in the conclusion that a disabled employee is qualified for a position when he would otherwise not be qualified without taking the reasonable accommodation into account. The plaintiff in *Bartee* had a hip problem that made it difficult for him to walk long distances. He requested accommodation of his disability in the form of a golf cart. The court of appeals, affirming in part a judgment in favor of the employee on his reasonable accommodation claim, found both that walking was not an essential function of the position from which the plaintiff had been excluded and that the use of the golf cart enabled the plaintiff to perform the essential functions of the position.[380.9]

[380.1] 680 N.W.2d 857 (Mich. 2004).
[380.2] *Id.* at 860.
[380.3] *Id.* at 861.
[380.4] *Id.* at 865-66.
[380.5] *Id.* at 869.
[380.6] *Id.* at 869-70.
[380.7] *Id.* at 872-73.
[380.8] 374 F.3d 906 (10th Cir. 2004).
[380.9] *Id.* at 915.

Page 117, add following third full paragraph:

In *Cameron v. Community Aid for Retarded Children, Inc.*,[389.1] the court of appeals affirmed summary judgment for the employer, finding that an assistant director of a community mental health facility was not qualified for her position because she demonstrated insufficient capacity to interact with the staff. Therefore, it was unnecessary to determine whether her anxiety disorder qualified as a disability or was the basis for the inability to interact.[389.2]

Rohan v. Networks Presentations LLC[389.3] involved an actress who suffered from posttraumatic stress disorder, occasioned by abuse during her childhood. While on tour with a production company, she suffered a number of "episodes" that led to concerns about her well-being and her ability to continue in the productions. The district court granted summary judgment to the employer, finding that the plaintiff was not qualified because she could not perform an essential function of her job, namely, interacting with others.[389.4] The court of appeals disagreed with the district court's analysis, finding instead that the plaintiff was not statutorily disabled.[389.5] The district court found that although the plaintiff had an impairment, the plaintiff had not demonstrated that her impairment substantially limited the only major life activity she identified, which was interacting with others.[389.6] The court also expressed skepticism about whether interacting with others qualifies as a major life activity, but found it unnecessary to resolve that issue.[389.7] The most the evidence showed was that the plaintiff avoided making friends, even though she characterized some members of the cast as "friends," and that she avoided dealing with other individuals in the cast whose behavior she found immature and offensive. "The fact that she chose to avoid such individuals, however, does not distinguish her from the general population."[389.8] "Although Rohan appears to be almost completely incapable of interacting with others during her episodes, her episodes are sporadic and last, at most, 30 minutes. During the four months of her employment with Networks, Rohan appears to have experienced approximately 30 episodes. Intermittent manifestations of an illness are insufficient to establish a substantial limitation on a major life activity."[389.9]

In *Brenneman v. Medcentral Health System*,[389.10] the court of appeals affirmed summary judgment for the employer, finding that an employee with diabetes failed to establish that he was qualified for his position. The evidence showed that the plaintiff had attendance problems and that he never referred to his diabetes as the reason for the absence triggering his termination. The court held that the plaintiff was not qualified to perform the essential functions of his pharmacy technician position because of his excessive absenteeism.

In *Hedrick v. Western Reserve Care System*,[389.11] the court of appeals affirmed summary judgment for the employer, finding that the plaintiff, by rejecting the employer's offer of a comparable position, albeit one with a lower salary, undercut her claim to be qualified.[389.12]

[389.1] 335 F.3d 60 (2d Cir. 2003).
[389.2] *Id.* at 64.
[389.3] 375 F.3d 266 (4th Cir. 2004).
[389.4] *Id.* at 272 (characterizing District Court's reasoning).
[389.5] *Id.* at 272-73.
[389.6] *Id.* at 274.
[389.7] *Id.* (characterizing interacting with others as an "amorphous" concept).
[389.8] *Id.* at 275.
[389.9] *Id.* at 276.
[389.10] 366 F.3d 412 (6th Cir. 2004).
[389.11] 355 F.3d 444 (6th Cir. 2004).
[389.12] *Id.* at 458.

Page 125, add new subsection:

[G] Evidentiary Strategies for Proving Qualification

Hoffman v. Caterpillar, Inc.[437.1] offers a useful and concrete illustration of evidentiary missteps in proving that a one-armed plaintiff could operate a high-speed document scanner at production levels required by the employer. The district court entered judgment on a jury verdict for the employer after the jury viewed a videotape of the plaintiff operating the machine in question. The court of appeals affirmed the judgment, among other things, rejecting the plaintiff's argument on appeal that the district court abused its discretion because it allowed the plaintiff only four hours of training and four-and- one-half days of practice on the high-speed scanner before taking an eight-hour videotaped test, instead of a two-week period of training, the denial of which had given rise to the ADA lawsuit. "At a pretrial conference . . . [the plaintiff] not only expressly agreed to these particular conditions, but also stated that if the District Court would allow an in-court demonstration in front of the jury, [the plaintiff] could operate the machine without any training, and that in any case, two weeks of training was unnecessary."[437.2] The court of appeals also found no abuse of discretion in the exclusion of an expert witness proffered by the plaintiff.[437.3]

The supplement to § 14.04 provides further analysis of evidentiary strategies for proving qualification and disability in the context of amputees.

[437.1] 368 F.3d 709 (7th Cir. 2004).
[437.2] *Id.* at 716 n.5.
[437.3] This part of the court's opinion is considered in this supplement to § 9.19[A].

§ 3.07 DISABLED BUT NOT TOO DISABLED

Page 127, add at end of section:

The combination of *Sutton*[452.1] and *Toyota*[452.2] creates the possibility that a person who would be considered disabled in any common sense application of the term is not legally "disabled" and therefore falls outside the protection of the ADA even though an employer denies him employment because of his impairment.

In a Title I case, the evidentiary positions of employer and employee are mirror images of each other. The employer wants to prove that the employee is not qualified to perform the specialized but essential functions of a job, while not being significantly impaired in a wide range of other activities. The employee wants to prove that he is substantially impaired in performing a wide range of major life activities, while remaining qualified to perform the narrow range of activities constituting the essential functions of the job desired by the employee. With respect to major life activities, counsel for both employer and employee must remember that substantial impairment may or may not exist in comparison with an average nondisabled person. For example, a disabled person does not prove substantial impairment with respect to the major life activity of running by citing that he could not run a marathon; an average nondisabled person could not run a marathon.

In *Croy v. COBE Laboratories, Inc.*,[452.3] the court of appeals affirmed the district court's finding that a plaintiff with multiple sclerosis was not statutorily disabled because the evidence showed only that she was frequently forced to take unscheduled leave, was frequently unable to lift heavy objects, could not bear sustained exertion, and could not care for her children, complete household chores, or cook for her family. "We are sympathetic with appellant's impairment and presume that she often experiences the symptoms of multiple sclerosis to the extent that she is often temporarily unable to function as the average person would. However, she has failed to show that she is unable to work."[452.4] Of course, if she had shown that she was unable to work, she would have been unable to recover under the ADA because she would not have been qualified.

Two extreme examples involve two recent trial-court determinations that amputees were not statutorily disabled.

In *Gillen v. Fallon Ambulance Service*,[452.5] for example, the district court found that a one-armed applicant for emergency medical service was not disabled because she could lift as much as a two-armed person. The court of appeals appropriately reversed.[452.6] In *Gillen*, the initial conclusion of no disability was the result of applying *Toyota*, and evaluating whether the plaintiff was substantially limited in the major life activity of lifting.

In *Christensen v. City of Los Angeles*,[452.7] the trial court found that a below-the-knee amputee was not statutorily disabled under the California statute because he was able to engage in sports activities, including running, softball, baseball, and snow skiing,[452.8] The police department refused to hire him because the absence of his leg was projected to prevent his meeting all of the physical requirements prescribed for a police officer. The trial court, evaluating his capabilities with his prosthesis under *Sutton*, nevertheless found that he was capable of performing major life activities, and was disqualified only from a single job—that of a police officer. Thus he was not disabled. The court of appeals affirmed summary judgment for the police department based on the rationale that the plaintiff could not demonstrate that he was qualified for the position in question, and did not have to address the correctness of the conclusion that he was not disabled.

At first exposure, these two trial court decisions seem preposterous as a matter of policy (though at least superficially consistent with *Sutton* and *Toyota*). But the limitations of *Sutton* and *Toyota* are aimed at a real problem. Congress presumably did not intend to extend ADA protection to someone who is normal in every way except, say, for an unusual allergy that coincides with chemicals used in a rare occupation. Such a person might well be excluded from that job because of the allergy, but would certainly not be excluded from the workforce.

The purpose of the ADA is to overcome exclusion from the labor force of a large group of people. From a policy perspective, it is also undesirable to have the legal intrusion that would result from extending ADA protection to narrow limitations a few of which virtually everyone has. Most people over 40 have some loss of visual acuity—easily correctable with glasses—but it is not desirable to turn all vision requirements in the workplace into a federal lawsuit.

Sullivan v. Neiman Marcus Group, Inc.[452.9] illustrates the conundrum. The plaintiff was terminated for violating employer policies by consuming alcohol on the job. He claimed an ADA violation based on his allegation that the employer terminated him, not because of his misconduct, but because of its concerns about his alcoholism. The district court granted summary to the employer. The court of appeals affirmed based on the absence in the summary judgment record that the plaintiff was disabled.[452.10] It agreed that alcoholism is an impairment under the ADA and went on to evaluate the plaintiff's claim that work was the major life activity substantially impaired by his alcoholism. It accepted that alcoholic ADA claimants face a conundrum. "This statutory provision[452.11] means that an employee who tries to use deficiencies in his job performance as evidence that alcoholism substantially impairs his ability to work is likely to establish the unhelpful proposition, for ADA coverage, that he cannot meet the legitimate requirements of the job."[452.12] Based on plaintiff's testimony that he satisfactorily performs his work not only at Neiman Marcus but also at a variety of other jobs, the court of appeals found that "there is simply no showing here that his alcoholism has substantially interfered with his ability to work."[452.13]

The soundest approach is to interpret *Toyota* and *Sutton*, especially *Toyota*, attentive to these broad statutory purposes and restraints. Plaintiffs should be able to define which major life activity is limited. The problem for Ms. Gillen was the trial court's preoccupation with the activity of lifting, to the apparent exclusion of all the other activities as to which a one-armed woman would be substantially limited. The problem in *Christensen* was taking life activities in the aggregate. Christensen exacerbated his legal position by admitting that with his prosthesis, he was not actually limited in performing any major life activities. The police evaluation of a below-the-knee amputee's limitations identified a number of specific activities such as squatting, climbing embankments, climbing fences, and jumping. Each of these activities reasonably qualifies as a major life activity outside of work, although the *Toyota* standard of "central importance" to most people's daily lives is potentially troubling because most people are sedentary and do not jump, climb fences, or climb embankments—although most do squat when they talk to children.

The supplement to § 14.04 provides further analysis of evidentiary strategies for proving qualification and disability in the context of amputation.

[452.1] Sutton v. United Airlines, Inc., 527 U.S. 471 (1999) (whether a person is statutorily disabled must be assessed taking into account mitigating measures and appliances such as prostheses). Sutton is analyzed more extensively in § 3.02[A][5].

[452.2] Toyota Motor Mfg. Kentucky, Inc. v. Williams, 534 U.S. 184 (2002) (a person is not statutorily disabled unless impairment substantially limits an activity central to most people's daily lives outside the workplace). Toyota is analyzed more extensively in §§ 3.02[A][2] and [3].

[452.3] 345 F.3d 1199 (10th Cir. 2003).

[452.4] *Id.* at 1204.

[452.5] 283 F.3d 11 (1st Cir. 2002).

[452.6] *Id.* at 22-25.

[452.7] 2002 WL 1154578 (Cal. App. May 30, 2002).

[452.8] He engaged in snow skiing with one ski and outriggers, not using his prosthesis.

[452.9] 358 F.3d 110 (1st Cir. 2004).

[452.10] *Id.* at 114.

[452.11] 42 U.S.C. § 12114 (c).

[452.12] 358 F.3d at 115-16.

[452.13] *Id.* at 117.

§ 3.10 ADMITTING DISABILITY IN OTHER FORUMS

Page 130, add following second paragraph terminating with note 461 reference:

In *Russell v. Cooley Dickinson Hospital, Inc.*,[461.1] the Massachusetts Supreme Judicial Court, interpreting state disability law the same as the ADA, held that a claim for workers' compensation benefits, accompanied by a representation that the plaintiff was "temporarily totally disabled," did not estop the plaintiff from establishing that she was a "qualified handicapped person" under state law. Applying the United States Supreme Court's reasoning in *Cleveland v. Policy Management Systems Corp.*,[461.2] the Massachusetts court said:

> A claim for disability benefits on the basis of total disability is evidence of the plaintiff's inability to perform the essential functions, but it is not

> dispositive if the plaintiff is able to raise a question of fact through other evidence of her ability (including her ability if provided "reasonable accommodation"), or through an explanation of how her disability claims and employment discrimination claims are consistent, sufficient to warrant a reasonable juror's conclusion that the plaintiff could perform the essential functions of the job.
>
> Here the plaintiff asserted that she wanted to return to work in some capacity in May, 1995, and had obtained a medical release stating conditions on which she could return to work "full time." She continued to receive workers' compensation benefits for which she had applied at the commencement of her leave in September, 1994, but filed no further application that would be inconsistent with her assertion that she could perform her job, at least under some conditions, as of May, 1995. Indeed, she communicated to Palmer that her condition had improved sufficiently as of May, 1995, such that she could return to at least some position. Having made full disclosure of her improved condition, the mere passive receipt of workers' compensation benefits beyond that date is not inconsistent with her claim that she could perform her job with reasonable accommodation. Viewing the evidence in the light most favorable to the plaintiff, the evidence was sufficient to raise a question as to her ability to perform the essential functions of an admitting assistant position, at least with a reasonable accommodation, and thereby survive an argument of estoppel.[461.3]

Nevertheless, the court affirmed judgment for the employer because it concluded that the plaintiff would be unable to prove failure to make reasonable accommodation.

[461.1] 772 N.E.2d 1054 (Mass. 2002).
[461.2] 526 U.S. 795 (1999).
[461.3] 772 N.E.2d at 1062.

Page 132, in third complete paragraph, discussing Devito, *quote should read:*

"the employee will sometimes be able to explain away . . ."

Page 132, add following note 483 callout:

In *Williams v. London Utility Commission*,[483.1] the court of appeals affirmed summary judgment for the employer. It found that the employee had failed to offer a sufficient explanation for the contradiction between his ADA claim that he was qualified and his claim for total disability benefits one day after his termination.[483.2]

In *Peden v. City of Detroit*,[483.3] the Supreme Court of Michigan, reversing the intermediate court, reinstated summary judgment in favor of the defendant police department. The plaintiff, having suffered a heart attack in 1986, had worked for 10 years in restricted-duty positions with the police department. In 1995, the police department introduced new job requirements based on model standards developed by the Michigan Law Enforcement Officers Training Council. The new standards included requirements such as pursuing suspects on foot, engaging in vehicle pursuits, effecting forcible arrests, overcoming violent resistance, and qualifying with a firearm.[483.4] Because the plaintiff could not meet these requirements, the department placed him on involuntary disability retirement.

The court allowed the police department to rely on the plaintiff's employment history as being limited in his work capability for more than 10 years:

> Plaintiff's medical records indicated, as would be expected, that plaintiff's heart condition continued to persist. Under such circumstances it would pointless to require the department, before placing plaintiff on disability retirement, to have him undertake agility tests in order to determine whether he could perform the EFL tasks. Such tasks would essentially require plaintiff to perform those very tasks that, because of his heart condition, his medical records indicated he was to refrain from performing. When the department stated in 1995 that plaintiff was unable to perform the essential functions of a police officer position, it was relying on evidence that already had been conclusively established by plaintiff's own medical records and accepted as the truth by all parties.[483.5]

Other aspects of the case are discussed at § 3.06 in the supplement.

[483.1] 375 F.3d 424 (6th Cir. 2004).
[483.2] *Id.* at 429.
[483.3] 680 N.W.2d 857 (Mich. 2004).
[484.4] *Id.* at 860.
[483.5] *Id.* at 872-73.

Page 133, add at end of section:

In *Justice v. Pike County Board of Education*,[486.1] the court of appeals, reversing the district court, held that accepting a teacher's disability pension based on a finding that the applicant could not perform the job of a teacher did not estop a subsequent ADA claim. The pension entitlement depended on whether she could perform a job without accommodation. The ADA claim depended upon whether a person can perform a job with accommodation; thus the inquiries were not exactly congruent.[486.2]

In *Murphey v. City of Minneapolis*,[486.3]the court of appeals reversed the district court for basing summary judgment against an ADA plaintiff on his prior claim for disability benefits. It held that a physician's opinion that the plaintiff was totally and permanently disabled did not constitute a sworn statement or representation by the plaintiff that he was permanently disabled and unable to work. Accordingly, the plaintiff's prior application for disability benefits was not inconsistent with the elements of an ADA claim, and therefore did not trigger any obligation to explain the nonexistent inconsistency.[486.4]

In *Rodal v. Anesthesia Group,*[486.5] the court of appeals reversed summary judgment for the employer. The plaintiff, an anesthesiologist and cancer patient, claimed that his employer's refusal to modify his schedule constituted a refusal to make reasonable accommodation in violation of the ADA. In a separate action pursued in state court for a financial settlement in conjunction with the plaintiff's disability leave, the plaintiff stated that he "became disabled and unable to perform substantially all of [his] duties due to illness."[486.6] The court of appeals held that the state court action did not involve any accommodation issues, and therefore the plaintiff's statement in state court could be reconciled with his position in the federal ADA action that he could perform the essential functions of his job with reasonable accommodation. Therefore, the employer was not entitled to summary judgment on a theory of judicial estoppel. "Instead, Dr. Rodal's statements, together with all other relevant evidence, will have to be weighed by the factfinder to determine whether the doctor has established a claim of disability discrimination."[486.7]

[486.1] 348 F.3d 554 (6th Cir. 2003).
[486.2] 348 F.3d at 565.
[486.3] 358 F.3d 1074 (8th Cir. 2004).
[486.4] 358 F.3d at 1079.
[486.5] 369 F.3d 113 (2d Cir. 2004).
[486.6] *Id.* at 119.
[486.7] *Id.* at 119-20.

CHAPTER 4
EMPLOYER OBLIGATIONS

§ 4.02 COVERAGE

[B] "Employee"

Page 142, add at end of subsection:

In *Wells v. Clackamas Gastroenterology Associates*,[13.1] the court of appeals held that physician-shareholders of a group medical practice were statutory employees under Title I of the ADA. It reached this conclusion in order to find that the group practice had a sufficient number of employees to qualify as a statutory employer.[13.2]

In *Lerohl v. Friends of Minnesota Sinfonia*,[13.3] the court of appeals found that concert musicians are independent contractors rather than statutory employees because they retained the discretion to perform elsewhere and to accept or reject playing in a particular concert series.[13.4] Thus, they were not common law employees despite the conductor's control over their musical performances.[13.5]

In *Levinger v. Mercy Medical Center*,[13.6] the court of appeals affirmed summary judgment and judgment on a jury verdict against a physician who claimed a hospital violated the ADA when it suspended his privileges after his license to practice medicine was suspended. The court of appeals held that Title I of the ADA does not protect independent contractors, but it went on to find that Title III of ADA allowed the physician to litigate whether the hospital's regarding him as disabled motivated its denial of hospital privileges; access to its facility; and the benefits of services, programs, and activities.[13.7]

[13.1] 271 F.3d 903 (9th Cir. 2001).
[13.2] *Id.* at 906.
[13.3] 322 F.3d 486 (8th Cir. 2003).
[13.4] *Id.* at 492.
[13.5] *Id.* at 492-93.
[13.6] 75 P.3d 1202, 2002 WL 1877968 (Idaho 2003).
[13.7] See also § 3.02[D].

[C] "Employer"

Page 144, add before last paragraph, following note 25 reference:

In *Satterfield v. Tennessee*,[25.1] the court of appeals rejected arguments that examining physicians were statutory "employers" with obligations under

Title I of the ADA, finding that ultimate decisions with respect to employment resided elsewhere.[25.2]

In *Trainor v. Apollo Medal Specialties, Inc.*,[25.3] the court of appeals reversed the district court and remanded for determination whether the employer defendant had the number of employees requisite for coverage by Title I. Among other things, the district court, in summary judgment proceedings, required the plaintiff to demonstrate the existence of an employment relationship between the employer and each of the necessary 15 employees for each working day of a specified number of weeks, subsequently holding that the plaintiff had failed to meet his burden of proof. "The court apparently believed Mr. Trainor bore this burden on summary judgment because he would be required to bear that burden at trial. In so doing the court erred."[25.4] The court of appeals held that summary judgment was not proper because a fact issue existed as to whether the employer's temporary workers were in fact statutory employees.[25.5]

The court of appeals also found that a shareholder in the closely held corporation constituting the employer could be an employee, counting toward the requisite 15 employees for statutory coverage, if the jury found the facts to be as alleged by the plaintiff.[25.6]

In *Bristol v. Board of County Commissioners of the County of Clear Creek*,[25.7] an en banc decision by the United States Court of Appeals for the Tenth Circuit, the court found that the Board of County Commissioners owed no duty to provide accommodation under the Americans with Disabilities Act to an employee of the county sheriff because, under state law, the board lacked the power to control the hiring, termination, or supervision of sheriffs' employees.[25.8]

[25.1] 295 F.3d 611 (6th Cir. 2002).
[25.2] *Id.* at 618.
[25.3] 318 F.3d 976 (10th Cir. 2002).
[25.4] *Id.* at 982.
[25.5] *Id.* at 982.
[25.6] *Id.* at 986-87 (extensively reviewing case law on shareholders as employees).
[25.7] 312 F.3d 1213 (10th Cir. 2002).
[25.8] *Id.* at 1215 (summarizing holding).

§ 4.03 PROHIBITED CONDUCT

[B] Resignation

Page 148, add at end of subsection:

Fenney v. Dakota, Minnesota & Railroad Co.[60.1] involved a locomotive engineer who lost his thumb and middle finger and suffered damages to his arm in an accident on another railroad. Because of his injuries, the engineer requested that he be called for his assignments two and a half to three hours ahead of time, rather than the usual two hours, to give him extra time to bathe, dress, shave, prepare a meal, and drive himself to his assignment on time. The court of appeals found sufficient evidence to establish a statutory disability under Toyota.[60.2]

The court of appeals also found that the plaintiff had established an adverse employment decision because the refusal of the accommodation necessitated his voluntary transfer to a conductor's position, which paid significantly less.[60.3]

[60.1] 327 F.3d 707 (8th Cir. 2003).

[60.2] *Id.* at 715-16.

[60.3] *Id.* at 717 (recognizing "constructive demotion," applying same standards as for constructive discharge).

[E] Associational Discrimination

Page 154, add at end of subsection:

In *Larimer v. International Business Machines Corp.*,[94.1] the court of appeals rejected an ADA associational claim by a former employee of IBM who claimed that he was dismissed because his daughters were born with conditions that might lead to future disability. In his opinion, Judge Posner suggested that associational discrimination prohibited by the ADA may take one of three forms: (1) when an adverse action is taken against an employee because someone else, such as a relative of the employee, imposes costs on the employer; (2) when the employer feels that the employee's association with a disabled person may cause the employee himself to become disabled, as by acquiring a disease; or (3) because the employer believes that the employee is distracted by his association with a disabled person.[94.2] The court of appeals panel for which Judge Posner wrote concluded that reliance on the *McDonnell Douglas* order of proof to establish some general form of associational discrimination could not lead to recovery under the ADA.[94.3]

[94.1] 370 F.3d 698 (7th Cir. 2004) (Posner, J.).

[94.2] *Id.* at 700.

[94.3] *Id.* at 702.

[H] Medical Examinations and Preemployment Inquiries

[1] ADA Prohibitions

Page 167, add after note 175 reference:

In *O'Neal v. City of New Albany*,[175.1] the court of appeals held that a post-offer medical examination need not be job-related.[175.2]

[175.1] 293 F.3d 998 (7th Cir. 2002).

[175.2] *Id.* at 1008.

[2] Medical Examinations

Page 171, add at end of subsection:

In *Conroy v. New York State Department of Correctional Services*,[195.1] the court of appeals held that an employer requirement that an employee present medical certification, including a general diagnosis entitling the employee to leave and supporting an evaluation for fitness to return to duty when an employee returns from sick leave, violated the ADA's prohibition on inquiries about disability.[195.2] It held that disputed facts relating to the employer's contention that its inquiry was job-related and consistent with business necessity precluded summary judgment.[195.3]

In *Fuzy v. S&B Engineers & Constructors, Ltd.*,[195.4] the plaintiff was rejected for a pipe fitter's job because of his inability to satisfy a 100-pound lifting requirement. The plaintiff conceded that he was not disabled but argued that he could sue under 42 U.S.C. § 12112(d) (prohibiting certain medical examinations and inquiries). He cited cases in other circuits allowing a nondisabled person to sue for violation of § 12112(d). The Fifth Circuit declined to reach that standing question because the employer presented summary judgment evidence that the 100-pound lifting requirement was job related, and the claimant failed to rebut that evidence.

[195.1] 333 F.3d 88 (2d Cir. 2003).
[195.2] *Id.* at 96.
[195.3] *Id.* (interpreting 42 U.S.C. § 12112(d)(4)(A)).
[195.4] 332 F.3d 301 (5th Cir. 2003).

[3] Other Preemployment Inquiries

Page 173, add after carryover paragraph:

In *Jones v. Georgia-Pacific Corp.*,[200.1] the South Carolina Supreme Court held that an employer was permitted to dismiss an employee who concealed disabilities on a questionnaire about worker's compensation at the onset of employment. The court held that a termination for fraud in filling out the form was permitted, notwithstanding the ADA's apparent prohibition on asking questions such as those asked on the worker's compensation form.

[200.1] 586 S.E.2d 111 (S.C. 2003).

Page 174, add at end of subsection:

In *Jones v. Georgia-Pacific Corp.*,[208.1] the South Carolina Supreme Court held that the prohibition in § 12112 (d)(2)(B) of the ADA disallowing inquiries into employee physical or mental conditions did not invalidate an employer's inquiry into preexisting conditions, in response to which the employee lied and was therefore denied workers' compensation benefits.

"The ADA does not trump the...determination of when fraud in the application process bars the applicant's attempt to collect workers compensation benefits."[208.2]

[208.1] 586 S.E.2d 111 (S.C. 2003).
[208.2] *Id.* at 114.

[I] Harassment

Page 174, add to beginning of note 210:

See Shaver v. Independent Stave Co., 350 F.3d 716, 719 (8th Cir. 2003) (joining other circuits and holding that hostile work environment claims are cognizable under ADA, but denying recovery on facts of particular case).

Page 174, add at bottom of page:

In *Gowesky v. Singing River Hospital Systems*,[217.1] the court of appeals affirmed summary judgment for an employer, finding that an emergency room physician successfully treated for hepatitis C had not met her burden of proving either disability-based workplace harassment or disability-based adverse employment action. The conversations about the plaintiff's fitness to return to work were reasonable and did not rise to the level of a hostile work environment. The failure to renew the plaintiff's contract was not motivated, the court found, by any perception of disability but rather by her repeated failures to return to work.[217.2]

[217.1] 321 F.3d 503 (5th Cir. 2003).
[217.2] *Id.* at 511.

[K] Retaliation for Asserting ADA Rights

Page 176, add at end of page:

In *Brown v. City of Tucson*,[224.1] the court of appeals analyzed § 503(b) of the ADA,[224.2] prohibiting "interference, coercion, or intimidation," as distinct from the retaliation provisions of § 503(a). The district court had applied the same framework of proof to the plaintiff's §§ 503(a) and (b) claims, which the court of appeals held to be error.[224.3] Reversing the district court's summary judgment for the employer, the court of appeals held that threatening the plaintiff with demotion or a forced retirement unless she stopped taking her medications for depression constituted a threat prohibited by § 503(b).[224.4]

[224.1] 336 F.3d 1181 (9th Cir. 2003).
[224.2] 42 U.S.C. § 12203(b).
[224.3] 336 F.3d at 1189.
[224.4] *Id.* at 1193.

Page 178, add at end of subsection:

In *Shellenberger v. Summit Bancorp, Inc.*,[236.1] the court of appeals reversed judgment as a matter of law for the employer on an ADA retaliation claim. The plaintiff had protested the existence of various fragrances in the workplace, claiming they triggered her chemical allergies. Among other things, she requested permission to "sniff" other employees sitting near her and, on one occasion, refused to let her supervisor come near her because of the fragrance she was wearing, insisting that the supervisor call her on the phone.

Over a period of some months, the employer accommodated the plaintiff's request to move her work station and to make various other changes to her environment. The plaintiff's physician requested accommodation, and subsequently involved the EEOC, after which the employer's cooperative spirit diminished.

The court of appeals found that the plaintiff offered sufficient evidence to survive judgment as a matter of law under either a "pretext" theory or a mixed motive theory.[236.2] As a threshold matter, the court of appeals noted that the plaintiff need not establish that she was disabled to recover for retaliation.[236.3] The court of appeals held that temporal proximity between the protected activity and the termination (10 days in Shellenberger's case) is itself sufficient to establish a causal link.[236.4] But it also found more than temporal proximity. One of the employer's decision makers in a final meeting with the plaintiff referred to her "taking the legal route," suggesting that she was not really motivated to work out an accommodation. That comment was sufficient to support an inference of intent to discriminate based on her protected conduct.[236.5] The employer claimed that the plaintiff was insubordinate during the meeting. The court of appeals held that a jury was entitled to decide whether retaliatory animus played a role in the employer's decision-making process and that it had a determinative effect on the outcome of that process, or that the employer's proffered reason was pretext.[236.6] at 190. In this branch of the court of appeals analysis the protected conduct was filing with the EEOC.

The plaintiff also alleged that her request for accommodation was protected conduct, and the court of appeals accepted that "Congress clearly did not intend to extend the reach of the ADA's umbrella to employees whose motivation for requesting an accommodation is something other than a good faith belief that an accommodation under the Act is necessary or appropriate. However, nothing on this record suggests that Shellenberger's request was motivated by anything other than good faith, and Summit has not argued to the contrary."[236.7] Accordingly, the court of appeals also reversed the district court's JMOL on this branch of her retaliation claim.

In *Treglia v. Manlius*,[236.8] the court of appeals reversed the district court and held that the temporal proximity between refusals of promotion and disciplinary actions and the plaintiff's assertion of ADA rights established a triable case of retaliation under the ADA. The district court had found that the plaintiff suffered no adverse employment action because he was "still on the police force." Among other things, the evidence showed that the police chief had said that the plaintiff would not receive a promotion to sergeant "now or ever," and that "if [the plaintiff] wants to play hardball, we can swing the bat back and play hardball too."[236.9] This evidence could show both prima facie retaliation and pretext.[236.10]

In *Freilich v. Upper Chesapeake Health, Inc.*,[236.11] the court of appeals found that a physician could not have believed in good faith that her protests over outsourcing and funding limitations constituted protected conduct under the ADA's anti-retaliation provisions. Although an ADA retaliation plaintiff need not establish that the conduct she opposed actually constituted an ADA violation, she "must allege the predicate for a reasonable, good faith belief that the behavior she is opposing violates the ADA."[236.12] Protests over failure to adhere to skin protocols, to transport patients in a timely manner, to address concerns regarding uncertified nurses, to diagnose a cervical fracture on a patient, to supervise dialysis of a patient, and to provide correct dialysis services for several patients were not infractions of the ADA but at most violations of state medical malpractice law.[236.13]

Candace Mitchell was terminated five days after she insisted on submitting certain applications to a selection committee, arguing that excluding the applications would violate state and federal disability discrimination law. The court of appeals affirmed the district court's conclusion that she failed to establish that her termination was linked to the protected conduct alleged.[236.14] The employer showed that it had presented a proposed budget three days before Ms. Mitchell was terminated, showing that immediate steps needed to be taken to cut costs. Moreover, there was no evidence to show that the person angered by Mitchell's insistence on submitting the applications to the selection committee was involved in the decision to terminate her. Further, there was no evidence that the three persons involved in deciding to reduce staff levels were even aware of the acrimonious incident before the termination decision was made.[236.15] The court of appeals found that the usual inference permitting causation to be found from proximity between protected conduct and an adverse employment decision had been rebutted by the evidence submitted by the employer: "[A]s we have said, there is no evidence that Ms. Piper played a part in the decision to terminate Ms. Mitchell or that those who made the decision knew of the dispute between her and Ms. Piper. A mere coincidence does not make out a case for the jury."[236.16]

In *Fogleman v. Mercy Hospital, Inc.*,[236.17] the court of appeals held that the ADA language making it unlawful for an employer "to coerce, intimidate, threaten, or interfere with any individual" exercising rights protected under the Act supported a claim by an employee that he was dismissed for assisting in his father's ADA claim.[236.18]

In *Wright v. Comp USA, Inc.*,[236.19] the court of appeals, reversing in part summary judgment for the employer, held that an employee, even though his attention deficit disorder did not amount to a statutory disability, nevertheless could litigate a retaliation claim based on evidence that he was dismissed shortly after requesting reasonable accommodation. "While this chronological proximity does not by itself establish causality...the record before us does not paint a picture of insubordination sufficient to undercut Wright's claim of causation.[236.20]

In *Shaver v. Independent Stave Co.*,[236.21] the court of appeals, reversing the district court, held that evidence that a former supervisor could not recommend a former disabled employee because he had "a get rich quick scheme involving suing companies" was sufficient evidence to permit a jury to find retaliatory motive.[236.22]

[236.1] 318 F.3d 183 (3d Cir. 2003).
[236.2] *Id.* at 187.
[236.3] *Id.* at 188.
[236.4] *Id.* at 189.
[236.5] *Id.* at 189.
[236.6] *Id.*
[236.7] *Id.* at 191.
[236.8] 313 F.3d 713 (2d Cir. 2002).
[236.9] *Id.* at 721-22.
[236.10] *Id.* at 722.
[236.11] 313 F.3d 205 (4th Cir. 2002).
[236.12] *Id.* at 216.
[236.13] *Id.* at 216-17.
[236.14] Mitchell v. Iowa Protection & Advocacy Servs., 325 F.3d 1011, 1013 (8th Cir. 2003).
[236.15] *Id.* at 1014.
[236.16] *Id.* at 1015.
[236.17] 283 F.3d 561 (3d Cir. 2002).
[236.18] *Id.* at 564 (quoting 42 U.S.C. § 12203(b)).
[236.19] 352 F.3d 472 (1st Cir. 2003).
[236.20] *Id.* at 478.
[236.21] 350 F.3d 716 (8th Cir. 2003).
[236.22] *Id.* at 723.

§ 4.04 EMPLOYER KNOWLEDGE OF DISABILITY

[A] Generally

Page 179, add at end of page:

In *Estades-Negroni v. Associates Corp.*,[241.1] the First Circuit stated that "[u]nder the ADA, requests for accommodation must be express and must be linked to a disability. An employer need not provide accommodations where it does not know an employee has a disability."[241.2]

[241.1] 345 F.3d 25 (1st Cir. 2003) (affirming summary judgment for employer).
[241.2] *Id.* at 33.

§ 4.05 REASONABLE ACCOMMODATION

Add as footnote to section heading:

* *See* Lauren W. Berns, Jr., *Wood v. Green*, 33 Stetson L. Rev. 823, 825 (2004) (citing this book as a "research reference").

[B] Individualized Assessment

[2] Specific Request for Accommodation

Page 189, add after first full paragraph:

In *Estades-Negroni v. Associates Corp.*,[289.1] the court of appeals held that requesting an accommodation before the employee even knew she had an impairment, and not subsequently linking the request to the impairment, vitiated any duty on the part of the employer to provide the accommodation.[289.2]

On further appeal,[289.3] the court of appeals affirmed summary judgment for the employee, finding that the employer denied a request for changes in job responsibilities at a time when it lacked knowledge that the plaintiff claimed a disability. Accordingly, the employer was not liable for refusing to grant reasonable accommodations.[289.4]

[289.1] 345 F.3d 25 (1st Cir. 2003).
[289.2] *Id.* at 34, reh'g granted, 362 F.3d 874 (1st Cir. 2004).
[289.3] Estades-Negroni v. Associates Corp., 377 F.3d 58 (1st Cir. 2004).
[289.4] *Id.* at 63.

[4] Interactive Process

Page 191, add following note 300 reference:

In *Shapiro v. Township of Lakewood*,[300.1] the court of appeals, reversing summary judgment for the employer, held that an employee's informal request for a transfer triggered the employer's duty to engage in an interactive process to explore reasonable accommodation, despite the employee's failure formally to apply for a vacant position.[300.2]

[300.1] 292 F.3d 356 (3d Cir. 2002).
[300.2] *Id.* at 361.

Page 194, add at end of page:

In *Allen v. Pacific Bell*,[313.1] the court of appeals explored the limits of the required interactive process. It held that the plaintiff's failure to participate in and cooperate with a collectively bargained accommodation search process terminated the employer's duty to explore further accommodation.[313.2]

[313.1] 348 F.3d 1113 (9th Cir. 2002).
[313.2] *Id.* at 115-16.

Page 197, add at end of subsection:

In *Stultz v. Reese Brothers, Inc.*,[327.1] the Pennsylvania intermediate court affirmed a judgment in favor of the plaintiff for $56,000 after a bench trial. The plaintiff proved that he had an eye disease, retinitis pigmentosa, and that he applied for employment as a telemarketer and provided the potential employer with a catalog of visual aid products. The employer, however, made no effort to ascertain whether anything in the catalog would be sufficient to accommodate the plaintiff's needs. Instead, it contacted the vendor for its software and was told that accommodation software would void the warranty for the telemarketing software used by the employer. The employer therefore determined that no reasonable accommodation could be made for the plaintiff and decided not to hire him.[327.2] The appellate court concluded that the employer had violated its duties under the ADA because it had made no effort to consult with the plaintiff to ascertain the precise job-related limitations imposed by his disability nor had it shared its preliminary findings with the plaintiff and consulted with him to identify alternative accommodations.[327.3] "Although appellant did not have an affirmative duty to prove that there was no reasonable accommodation available, it did have a duty to engage in a meaningful dialogue with appellee to determine if a reasonable accommodation could be made for him."[327.4]

[327.1] 835 A.2d 754 (Pa. Super. 2003).
[327.2] *Id.* at 759.
[327.3] *Id.* at 763.
[327.4] *Id.*

[D] No Duty to Modify Essential Functions

Page 200, note 342, add before "See also":

See Calef v. Gillette Co., 322 F.3d 75, 86 n.8 (1st Cir. 2003) (citing third edition of this book for proposition that employer has no obligation to afford reasonable accommodation by modifying essential functions).

Page 200, add footnote reference 342.1 at end of last sentence on page and add footnote:

[342.1] Calef v. Gillette Co., 322 F.3d 75, 86 (1st Cir. 2003) (citing third edition of this book for proposition that employer has no duty to modify essential functions and that essential functions concept overlaps with undue hardship defense).

Page 202, add after carryover paragraph:

In *Alexander v. Northland Inn*,[350.1] the court of appeals found that vacuuming was an essential function of a "working supervisor's" job in a hotel housekeeping activity. The employer's written job description for a housekeeping supervisor included as an essential function to "provide assistance in other job classifications as determined necessary by immediate supervisor." All of the other supervisors testified that that function included vacuuming.[350.2] The court further found that the employer was not obligated to eliminate vacuuming as a reasonable accommodation.[350.3] The facts of the case suggested that the plaintiff was unsympathetic, "suddenly" discovering her inability to vacuum, and suggesting the accommodation very late in the evolving controversy between her and the employer.

[350.1] 321 F.3d 723 (8th Cir. 2003).
[350.2] *Id.* at 727.
[350.3] *Id.* at 727-28.

Page 205, add after first full paragraph:

In *Davidson v. America Online, Inc.*,[376.1] the court of appeals, reversing summary judgment for the employer, held that a triable issue of fact existed as to whether being able to handle voice telephone calls was an essential function of a nonvoice phone position sought by a deaf applicant for employment in a call center.[376.2]

[376.1] 337 F.3d 1179 (10th Cir. 2002).
[376.2] *Id.* at 1190.

§ 4.06 PARTICULAR MODIFICATIONS OF DUTIES FOR DISABLED APPLICANTS OR EMPLOYEES

[B] Particular Needs

[9] Home Offices

Page 213, add at end of subsection:

In *Rauen v. U.S. Tobacco Manufacturing Ltd. Partnership*,[429.1] the plaintiff experienced a variety of difficulties at work because of treatment for and the consequences of surgery for rectal and breast cancer. Her physician represented that it would be beneficial for her to work from a home office. Despite extensive discussions about how she would perform her work from home, the employer ultimately refused the request. The court reasoned as follows in affirming summary judgment for the employer:

> Rauen's situation does not present the type of "very extraordinary case" where a home office would be reasonable. The central components of Rauen's job require her to be at the office. Even she admits that her primary job responsibilities involve monitoring contractors' work, answering contractors' questions as they arise, and ensuring that the contractors' work does not interfere with the manufacturing process. It is difficult to understand how these sorts of tasks could be performed from home. Rauen asserts that she would be at work when it was necessary, but she also made clear that she would determine when it was necessary for her to be there. Further, in the type of project and production work that Rauen's job involves, problems requiring immediate resolution would undoubtedly arise on the spur of the moment. Every description of Rauen's duties that either party has presented in the record shows that hers is the kind of job that requires teamwork, interaction, and coordination of the type that requires being in the work place.
>
> Thus, her situation does not present the exceptional case where a work-at-home accommodation would be reasonable.
>
> Tipping the scales even further against the reasonableness of Rauen's home office accommodation request is the fact that Rauen can perform all essential elements of her job without any accommodation. As noted above, we do not answer the question today of whether any accommodation could ever be reasonable for an employee who can perform all essential job functions without accommodation. But Rauen's ability to perform the essential functions of the job without accommodation surely weighs against the reasonableness of an accommodation. In other words, while it might not be impossible for a person that can perform all essential functions to show that an accommodation is reasonable, it is surely more difficult. Therefore, given that Rauen can perform the essential functions of her job without accommodation and given that she seeks a home office, which we have held is almost never reasonable, we find that the scales of the reasonable accommodation balance weigh against Rauen.[429.2]

In *Mason v. Avaya Communications, Inc.*,[429.3] the court of appeals affirmed summary judgment for the employer, finding that physical attendance at the employer's workplace was an essential function of a service dispatcher's position because of the need for supervision and teamwork with other employ[429.4] Accordingly, working from home was not reasonable accommodation.[429.5]

[429.1] 319 F.3d 891 (7th Cir. 2003).

[429.2] *Id.* at 897.

[429.3] 357 F.3d 1114 (10th Cir. 2004).

[429.4] *Id.* at 1120-21.

[429.5] *Id.* at 1122 (noting that federal court does not sit as "super personnel department that second guesses employers' business judgments").

[11] Leave and Leave Extensions

Page 217, add at end of first full paragraph:

In *Wood v. Green*,[443.1] the court of appeals reversed a judgment on jury verdict for an ADA plaintiff/employee. The district court reasoned that an apparent request for an indefinite leave was impliedly limited by the context of a 14-year history of relatively short-term leaves, at the conclusion of which an employee with periodic cluster headaches was able to return to work.[443.2] The court of appeals disagreed and held that a request for an indefinite leave of absence was not a reasonable accommodation.[443.3]

In *Byrne v. Avon Products, Inc.*,[443.4] the court of appeals distinguished between a brief leave to accommodate a flareup of arthritis or lupus, which might be a reasonable accommodation, from not working for a long period of time. "But Byrne did not want a few days off or a part time position; his only proposed accommodation is not working for an extended time, which as far as the ADA is concerned confesses that he was not a 'qualified individual' in late 1998. The rather common sense idea is that if one is not able to be at work, one cannot be a qualified individual."[443.5] The court held that "inability to work for a multi-month period removes a person from the class protected by the ADA."[443.6] The court did, however, vacate summary judgment for the employer on a FMLA claim.

In *Byrne v. Avon Products, Inc.*,[443.7] the court held that the ADA did not require leave for an extended period of time because requesting that accommodation "confessed that the plaintiff was not a qualified individual."[443.8]

443.1 323 F.3d 1309 (11th Cir. 2003).
443.2 *Id.* at 1312.
443.3 *Id.* at 1314.
443.4 328 F.3d 379 (7th Cir. 2003).
443.5 *Id.* at 381 [internal quotations and citations omitted].
443.6 *Id.* at 381.
443.7 328 F.3d 379 (7th Cir. 2003).
443.8 328 F.3d at 381 (distinguishing time off for intermittent condition such as arthritis or lupus).

[13] Modification of Specific Job Duties

Page 219, add at end of subsection:

In *Burchett v. Target Corp.*,[457.1] the court of appeals affirmed summary judgment for the employer, finding that the evidence showed declining performance by the plaintiff even after the employer repeatedly restructured her work assignment. She thus failed to show that she was qualified to perform the essential functions of her position:

> Not only did Burchett admit in her deposition that she could perform the functions of her position with the accommodations Target was providing,

> the record also shows that her doctor thought she could perform her job and in fact was expanding her hours and recommending that she return to full time in September. There is no dispute that Target made accommodations after being told that Burchett suffered from depression. It restructured her work load and reduced her work hours in accordance with her doctor's orders. "[R]eassignment is an accommodation of last resort," which does not become necessary unless it is the only accommodation that will enable an employee to continue working for the employer. We conclude that Burchett failed to make an evidentiary showing that Target was obligated to transfer her. She did not show that "accommodation within [her] current position would pose an undue hardship" so Target was not required to consider a transfer. She thus has not established a genuine issue of material fact concerning her claim that Target failed to provide reasonable accommodation for her disability.[457.2]

[457.1] 340 F.3d 510 (8th Cir. 2003).
[457.2] *Id.* at 518 (internal citations omitted).

[22] Relations with Supervisors and Co-workers

Page 227, add at end of subsection:

In *Rocafort v. IBM Corp.*,[498.1] the court of appeals affirmed summary judgment for the employer, finding that IBM reasonably accommodated a psychiatrist's request that it accommodate the plaintiff's panic and anxiety disorder by reassuring him and avoiding situations that would subject him to stress. It rejected the plaintiff's argument that subjecting the plaintiff to a routine investigation after a letter prohibited by IBM rules was found on his computer violated the reasonable accommodation required by the ADA.[498.2]

[498.1] 334 F.3d 115 (1st Cir. 2003).
[498.2] *Id.* at 120.

[23] Schedule

Page 228, add at end of subsection:

In *Rodal v. Anesthesia Group*,[502.1] the court of appeals, reversing summary judgment for the employer, held that the factfinder was entitled to decide whether an anesthesiologist cancer patient's request for a work schedule that did not require him to work evenings or weekends was unreasonable and, alternatively, whether granting the requested work schedule would impose undue hardship on the employer. The issues of unreasonableness and undue hardship were questions of fact, not questions of law.[502.2]

In *Davis v. Microsoft Corp.*,[502.3] the Washington Supreme Court held that neither the ADA nor the Washington disability discrimination statute required an employer to modify its requirement that employees within the plaintiff's class be available for work outside the regular schedule. The evidence showed that availability to work an irregular schedule was an essential function of the job.[502.4]

In *Russell v. TG Missouri Corp.*,[502.5] the court of appeals affirmed summary judgment for the employer, finding that the employer legitimately dismissed the plaintiff for walking off the job in the middle of an overtime shift on Saturday. A letter from the plaintiff's physician said that her bipolar disorder prevented her working more than eight hours per day, but did not put the employer on notice that she could not work more than 40 hours per week. Accordingly, the employer was not obligated to accommodate her disability by exempting her from Saturday work.[502.6]

In *Conneen v. MBNA America Bank*,[502.7] an employee who suffered from severe depression had received permission to report for work at 8:30 a.m. rather than the usual starting time of 8:00 a.m., to accommodate her condition. A new supervisor, who was unaware of the accommodation or the disability, asked the plaintiff to begin work at 8:00 a.m., and the plaintiff agreed, not requesting any accommodation. After she was counseled on tardiness, she once again answered in the negative the question whether there was any reason she could not report to work on time at 8:00 a.m. When she was threatened with termination, she raised the medical condition, and obtained a physician's letter requesting that she be allowed to report for work at 9:00 a.m. The employer accommodated the 9:00 a.m. time for a period, but cautioned the plaintiff that she would have to revert to an 8:00 a.m. reporting time on a specified date. Almost immediately, the plaintiff arrived late. Before terminating her, the employer offered a brief leave of absence and a transfer to other positions with different work schedules. The plaintiff rejected those alternatives and promised that she would report for work on time each day. After a month of punctuality, she began to be late again. Finally, the employer terminated the plaintiff.

The court of appeals rejected the argument that the 8:00 a.m. reporting time was an essential job function.[502.8] The employer's essentiality argument was that bank officers such as the plaintiff must set good examples for other employees. The court of appeals noted that the employer had not suggested that the plaintiff failed to perform her job satisfactorily when she arrived, or that the employer's business was injured by the extra hour it gave her to report. Thus, a jury was entitled to determine whether the 8:00 a.m. start time was an essential function. However, summary judgment was appropriate anyway because the evidence showed that the employer clearly engaged in the interactive process required under the ADA.[502.9] While recognizing that employees may be reluctant to discuss psychiatric disabilities, it held that the plaintiff failed to meet her obligation in participating in the interactive process by proffering only "excuses of heavy traffic, giving a parent a ride, or cleaning up after a pet when asked to explain tardiness."[502.10]

[502.1] 369 F.3d 113 (2d Cir. 2004).
[502.2] *Id.* at 121-22.
[502.3] 70 P.3d 126 (Wash. 2003).
[502.4] *Id.* at 133.
[502.5] 340 F.3d 735 (8th Cir. 2003).
[502.6] *Id.* at 742.
[502.7] 334 F.3d 318 (3d Cir. 2003).
[502.8] *Id.* at 328.
[502.9] *Id.* at 329.
[502.10] *Id.* at 332.

Page 236, add new subsection:

[28] Mobility Assistance

In *Bartee v. Michelin North America, Inc.*,[549.1] the court of appeals affirmed judgment for the plaintiff, finding that the employer had violated its duty to provide reasonable accommodation for the plaintiff's hip condition, which made walking difficult. The plaintiff had requested a regular-sized golf cart. Without offering any reason for declining the plaintiff's request, the defendant merely offered a three-wheeled cart that the plaintiff had already identified as being too small for him.[549.2]

[549.1] 374 F.3d 906 (10th Cir. 2004).
[549.2] *Id.* at 916.

§ 4.09 LAST CHANCE AGREEMENTS

Page 240, add at end of section:

In *Longen v. Waterous Co.*,[570.1] the court of appeals affirmed summary judgment for the employer, holding that a last chance agreement for an employee who had substance abuse problems did not violate the ADA even though it subjected the covered employee to more stringent disciplinary rules than employees not suffering from that disability.[570.2]

[570.1] 347 F.3d 685 (8th Cir. 2003).
[570.2] *Id.* at 689.

§ 4.10 DEFENSES

[B] Undue Hardship

Page 242, add as footnote to subsection heading:

* *See* Christopher R. Yukins, *Making Federal Information Technology Accessible: A Case Study in Social Policy and Procurement*, 33 Pub. Cont. L.J. 667, 700 n.121 (2004) (citing third edition of this book on analysis of undue hardship defense).

[C] Health or Safety Direct-Threat Defense

Page 249, add at end of second full paragraph:

On remand, the court of appeals reversed summary judgment for the employer and held that the employer had failed to consider the severity, imminence, and potential likelihood of harm and therefore had not met its burden of establishing the health or safety defense.[626.1]

[626.1] 336 F.3d at 1030-31.

§ 4.11 ADOPTION OF METHODS OF PROOF FROM THE CIVIL RIGHTS ACT OF 1964

[B] Causation

[4] Establishing Inference of Discrimination

[b] Establishing a Prima Facie Case

Page 274, add at end of subsection:

In *Desert Palace, Inc. v. Costa*,[761.1] the Supreme Court disagreed with precedent from the First, Fourth, Eighth, and Eleventh Circuits, and held that direct evidence is not necessary to establish a mixed motive case under Title[761.2] The Court approved the following mixed motive instruction given by the district court:

> "You have heard evidence that the defendant's treatment of the plaintiff was motivated by the plaintiff's sex and also by other lawful reasons. If you find that the plaintiff's sex was a motivating factor in the defendant's treatment of the plaintiff, the plaintiff is entitled to your verdict, even if you find that the defendant's conduct was also motivated by a lawful reason."
>
> "However, if you find that the defendant's treatment of the plaintiff was motivated by both gender and lawful reasons, you must decide whether the plaintiff is entitled to damages. The plaintiff is entitled to damages unless the defendant proves by a preponderance of the evidence that the defendant would have treated plaintiff similarly even if the plaintiff's gender had played no role in the employment decision."[761.3]

The Court characterized the case as the first opportunity to consider the effects of the 1991 Civil Rights Act on jury instructions in mixed motive cases. The Court found no indication that Congress meant to impose a heightened evidentiary standard by its use of the word "demonstrates" in 42 U.S.C.

§ 2000e (m). The Court also noted that in the law of evidence generally, circumstantial evidence not only usually is sufficient, but "may also be more certain, satisfying and persuasive than direct evidence."[761.4]

[761.1] 539 U.S. 90 (2003).
[761.2] *Id.* at 92-94.
[761.3] *Id.* at 96-97.
[761.4] *Id.* at 100.

Page 274, add new subsection:

[i] Proof by Temporal Proximity

In *Shellenberger v. Summit Bancorp, Inc.*,[761.5] the court of appeals reversed judgment as a matter of law for the employer on an ADA retaliation claim. The plaintiff had protested the existence of various fragrances in the workplace, claiming they triggered her chemical allergies. The court of appeals found that the plaintiff offered sufficient evidence to survive judgment as a matter of law under either a "pretext" theory or a mixed motive theory.[761.6] The court of appeals held that temporal proximity between the protected activity and the termination (10 days in Shellenberger's case) is itself sufficient to establish a causal link.[761.7] But it also found more than temporal proximity. One of the employer's decision makers in a final meeting with the plaintiff referred to her "taking the legal route," suggesting that she was not really motivated to work out an accommodation. That comment was sufficient to support an inference of intent to discriminate based on her protected conduct.[761.8] The employer claimed that the plaintiff was insubordinate during the meeting. The court of appeals held that a jury was entitled to decide whether retaliatory animus played a role in the employer's decision-making process and that it had a determinative effect on the outcome of that process, or that the employer's proffered reason was pretext.[761.9] In this branch of the court of appeals analysis the protected conduct was filing with the EEOC.

In *Treglia v. Manlius*,[761.10] the court of appeals reversed the district court and held that the temporal proximity between refusals of promotion and disciplinary actions and the plaintiff's assertion of ADA rights established a triable case of retaliation under the ADA. The district court had found that the plaintiff suffered no adverse employment action because he was "still on the police force." Among other things, the evidence showed that the police chief had said that the plaintiff would not receive a promotion to sergeant "now or ever" and that "if [the plaintiff] wants to play hardball, we can swing the bat back and play hardball too."[761.11] This evidence could show both prima facie retaliation and pretext.[761.12]

In *Buie v. Quad/Graphics, Inc.*,[761.13] the court of appeals affirmed summary judgment for the employer in an ADA and FMLA claim brought by an employee with AIDS. In determining the motion for summary judgment, the trial court had disregarded a portion of the plaintiff's affidavit asserting that he was subjected to disciplinary suspension almost immediately after he told the employer for the first time that he had AIDS, on the ground that self-serving affidavits are insufficient to defeat summary judgment. The court of appeals held that the trial court abused its discretion by refusing to consider that part of the affidavit because the affidavit met the criteria for evidence on summary judgment: It was based on personal knowledge and alleged specific facts relevant to whether his rights under the ADA were violated. But the court concluded that admission of the affidavit would have allowed a reasonable jury to find for the plaintiff. Accepting that suspicious timing is a type of circumstantial evidence under the direct method of proving discriminatory intent, it is not sufficient to support a conclusion of causation. Other evidence will show that the plaintiff was on the brink of dismissal before the employer knew he had AIDS.

In *Bones v. Honeywell International, Inc.*,[761.14] the court of appeals affirmed summary judgment for the employer on an ADA claim by an employee with tendonitis. The court held that the employee failed as a matter of law to establish that her termination was based on her alleged disability. Rather, the evidence showed that the employer had made a number of efforts to accommodate the plaintiff's tendonitis over a ten-month period and that "ten months is too long a time lapse, standing alone, to support an inference of a causal connection between Bones' alleged disability and her termination."[761.15]

[761.5] 318 F.3d 183 (3d Cir. 2003).
[761.6] *Id.* at 187.
[761.7] *Id.* at 189.
[761.8] *Id.*
[761.9] *Id.* at 190.
[761.10] 313 F.3d 713 (2d Cir. 2002).
[761.11] *Id.* at 721-22.
[761.12] *Id.* at 722.
[761.13] 366 F.3d 496 (7th Cir. 2004).
[761.14] 366 F.3d 869 (10th Cir. 2004).
[761.15] *Id.* at 879.

[c] Proffer of Nondiscriminatory Reasons and Pretext

Page 276, add at end of subsection:

In *Cleveland v. Home Shopping Network, Inc.*,[779.1] the court of appeals reversed the district court's grant of judgment as a matter of law, in favor of the employer after a jury verdict in favor of an ADA plaintiff. The court of appeals found that there was sufficient evidence of shifting explanations by the employer for the termination of the plaintiff to permit the jury to infer that the employer's stated reason for the dismissal was pretext.[779.2] It further held that an inference that the employer was lying about the reason for the dismissal would also support an inference that it was trying to cover up a discriminatory purpose. "Dishonesty can be affirmative evidence of guilt."[779.3]

In *Kincaid v. City of Omaha*,[779.4] the court of appeals affirmed summary judgment in favor of the defendant. It found that the plaintiff had failed to rebut two proffered nondiscriminatory explanations for the employer's decision to promote someone other than the plaintiff. First, the plaintiff failed to show that the employer's elimination of the plaintiff from consideration was not based on its standard policy of permitting injured employees to return to work only when they presented a physician's statement. The employer also explained why the person selected instead of the plaintiff to fill the job had superior qualifications. The court of appeals acknowledged, however, that an ADA plaintiff can support an inference of pretext by showing that someone selected for a position was less qualified than the plaintiff.[779.5]

In *Raytheon Co. v. Hernandez*,[779.6] the Supreme Court held that the ADA does not confer preferential rehire rights on disabled employees lawfully terminated for violating workplace conduct rules.[779.7] The plaintiff had been terminated for violating his employer's workplace conduct rules, occasioned by alcohol and cocaine abuse. After his dismissal, he sought treatment and apparently was drug and alcohol free when he applied for reemployment. The employer refused to rehire him based, it insisted, on a policy against rehiring employees who were terminated for workplace misconduct. The evidence was ambiguous as to whether the decision maker also had information about the plaintiff's drug and alcohol abuse. The Supreme Court held that the employer, by identifying the facially neutral rehire policy, satisfied its burden under *McDonnell Douglas and Burdine*[779.8] to articulate a nondiscriminatory reason sufficient to defeat a prima facie case of discrimination. By focusing on the disparate impact of the rehire policy, the court of appeals "ignored the fact that petitioner's no rehire policy is a quintessential legitimate, nondiscriminatory reason for refusing to rehire an employee who was terminated for violating workplace conduct rules. If petitioner did indeed apply a neutral, generally applicable, no-rehire policy in rejecting respondent's application, petitioner's decision not to rehire respondent can, in no way, be said to have been motivated by respondent's disability."[779.9] Because the court of appeals "strayed . . . by considering not only discriminatory intent but also discriminatory impact," the Supreme Court vacated its judgment and remanded the case for further proceedings under mixed motive and pretext analysis.

On remand, in *Hernandez v. Hughes Missile Systems, Co.*,[779.10] the court of appeals reversed summary judgment in favor of the employer finding that there was a genuine issue of material fact as to whether Raytheon failed to rehire Hernandez because of his "status as an alcoholic" rather than in reliance on a uniform no-rehire policy.[779.11]

[779.1] 369 F.3d 1189 (11th Cir. 2004).
[779.2] *Id.* at 1194.
[779.3] *Id.* at 1194-95 (internal quotations omitted).
[779.4] 378 F.3d 799 (8th Cir. 2004).
[779.5] *Id.* at 805.

[779.6] 540 U.S. 44 (2003).
[779.7] *Id.* at 46 (characterizing issue).
[779.8] Texas Dep't of Cmty. Affairs v. Burdine, 450 U.S. 428 (1981).
[779.9] 124 S. Ct. at 54-55.
[779.10] 362 F.3d 564 (9th Cir. 2004).
[779.11] *Id.* at 568.

Page 279, add new subsection:

[e] Temporal Proximity as Proof

In *Brown v. City of Tucson*,[782.1] an investigation of the plaintiff's handling of an assault case began on the very day that the plaintiff filed a complaint about what she perceived as harassment based on her disability. This fact provided sufficient evidence from which a retaliatory motive could be inferred.[782.2] The plaintiff, however, failed to show that the legitimate nondiscriminatory reason proffered by the employer was pretext.[782.3]

[782.1] 336 F.3d 1181 (9th Cir. 2002).
[782.2] *Id.* at 1187.
[782.3] *Id.* at 1188.

[5] Causation: Conduct or Disability?

Page 282, add at end of subsection:

In *Calef v. Gillette Co.*,[799.1] the court of appeals affirmed summary judgment for employer, finding that the ADA plaintiff failed to show that his hyperactivity syndrome constituted a statutory disability because there was no evidence of its impact on his daily activities. The court also found that the plaintiff was not qualified to perform the functions of his job, after reviewing a long list of workplace incidents in which the plaintiff threatened other employees and had been disruptive. "Put simply, the ADA does not require that an employee whose unacceptable behavior threatens the safety of others be retained, even if the behavior stems from a mental disability. Such an employee is not qualified."[799.2]

[799.1] 322 F.3d 75 (1st Cir. 2003).
[799.2] *Id.* at 87.

§ 4.13 DRUG ABUSE

Page 290, add at end of section:

In *Raytheon Co. v. Hernandez*,[845.1] the Supreme Court held the ADA does not confer preferential rehire rights on disabled employees lawfully terminated for violating workplace conduct rules.[845.2] The plaintiff had been terminated for violating his employer's workplace conduct rules, occasioned by alcohol and cocaine abuse. After his dismissal, he sought treatment and apparently was drug and alcohol free when he applied for reemployment. The employer refused to rehire him based, it insisted, on a policy against rehiring employees who were terminated for workplace misconduct. The evidence was ambiguous as to whether the decision maker also had information about the plaintiff's drug and alcohol abuse. The Supreme Court held that the employer, by identifying the facially neutral rehire policy, satisfied its burden under *McDonnell Douglas* and *Burdine*[845.3] to articulate a nondiscriminatory reason sufficient to defeat a prima facie case of discrimination. By focusing on the disparate impact of the rehire policy, the court of appeals "ignored the fact that petitioner's no rehire policy is a quintessential legitimate, nondiscriminatory reason for refusing to rehire an employee who was terminated for violating workplace conduct rules. If petitioner did indeed apply a neutral, generally applicable, no-rehire policy in rejecting respondent's application, petitioner's decision not to rehire respondent can, in no way, be said to have been motivated by respondent's disability.[845.4] Because the court of appeals "strayed...by considering not only discriminatory intent but also discriminatory impact," the Supreme Court vacated its judgment and remanded the case for further proceedings under mixed motive and pretext analysis.

On remand, in *Hernandez v. Hughes Missile Systems, Co.*,[845.5] the court of appeals reversed summary judgment in favor of the employer finding that there was a genuine issue of material fact as to whether Raytheon failed to rehire Hernandez because of his "status as an alcoholic" rather than in reliance on a uniform no re-hire policy.[845.6]

845.1 540 U.S. 44 (2003).

845.2 *Id.* at 46 (characterizing issue).

845.3 Texas Dep't of Cmty Affairs v. Burdine, 450 U.S. 428 (1981).

845.4 124 S. Ct. at 54-55.

845.5 362 F.3d 564 (9th Cir. 2004).

845.6 *Id.* at 568.

CHAPTER 5
GOVERNMENT OBLIGATIONS UNDER TITLE II

§ 5.02 COVERAGE OF FEDERAL ENTITIES

Page 315, add at end of section:

In *Office of the Architect of the Capital v. Office of Compliance*,[18.1] the court of appeals affirmed a decision by the Board of Directors of the Office of Compliance finding that an asthmatic employee of the Architect of the Capital must be transferred to a subway operator position as a reasonable accommodation. It rejected arguments that the remedy required a promotion or that it required the Architect to create a new position.[18.2]

[18.1] 361 F.3d 633 (Fed. Cir. 2004).
[18.2] *Id.* at 643. *See also* § 9.14.

§ 5.07 GENERAL GOVERNMENT PROGRAMS

[B] State Courts

Page 325, add following sentence with note 91 reference, and start a new paragraph with "Doe v. State rejected . . .":

In *Pacheco v. Bedford*,[91.1] the Rhode Island Supreme Court rejected a claim that the ADA entitled a mentally disabled child-custody litigant to court-appointed counsel. It found that the trial judge had not abused his discretion in refusing to appoint counsel after the claimant failed to present evidence that he had followed up on suggestions that he contact a local law school clinic or make any other effort to seek free representation. He also found that the claimant appeared able to read well enough and speak well enough to represent himself.[91.2]

[91.1] 787 A.2d 1210 (R.I. 2002).
[91.2] *Id.* at 1213.

Page 326, add at end of existing subsection:

[1] Sentencing

In *State v. Jacobs*,[95.1] the Iowa Supreme Court rejected summarily an argument that the ADA required a trial court to consider a convicted criminal defendant's bipolar disorder as a mitigating factor in sentencing.[95.2]

[95.1] 644 N.W.2d 695 (Iowa 2001).
[95.2] *Id.* at 696.

Page 326, retitle subsection [C], create new subsection [1] directly following [C], and add new subsection [2] at the end of the subsection as follows:

[C] Admission to Professions

[1] Admission to State Bar

[2] Admission to Medical Profession

Powell v. National Board of Medical Examiners,[98.1] involved an ADA claim by a medical student who had failed the National License Examination three times and also was deficient in 4 out of 10 courses. The evidence showed that the medical school actively assisted the plaintiff in trying to overcome her deficiencies, providing free tutoring services, overlooking an honor code violation, expressing concern with her level of stress, and repeatedly allowing her the opportunity to complete the requirements of certain subjects.[98.2] The National Examination Board rejected the plaintiff's request for additional time to take the examination based on its conclusion that the plaintiff's documentation did not establish that she was disabled because the documentation did not provide objective evidence of difficulties experienced before entering medical school as would be expected if the disability were a significant functional impairment.[98.3] The court concluded that the plaintiff failed both to show that she had a statutory disability and that she was qualified to continue in medical school because her self-described disabilities in basic memory function, vision, and reading comprehension undercut meeting her burden to demonstrate that she was qualified.[98.4]The court also found that allowing the plaintiff to progress in medical school without meeting requirements imposed on all students to prove mastery of basic medical sciences to advance into later stages of medical school and becoming a treating physician would unreasonably alter the nature of the school's program.[98.5]

[98.1] 364 F.3d 79 (2d Cir. 2004).
[98.2] *Id.* at 83.
[98.3] *Id.*

98.4 *Id.* at 87.
98.5 *Id.* at 88.

[E] Prisons

Page 331, add at end of existing subsection:

[1] Parole

In *Thompson v. Davis*,[137.1] the Ninth Circuit held that parole constituted a public program or activity under Title II of the ADA, and that categorically denying parole to inmates based on their history of drug addiction qualified plaintiffs for prospective injunctive relief under Title II of the ADA.[137.2]

137.1 295 F.3d 890 (9th Cir. 2002).
137.2 *Id.* at 896-97 (rejecting argument that ADA does not apply to parole decisions because it does not extend to substantive decision making in criminal law context).

[F] Police Services

Page 334, add at end of subsection:

In *Anthony v. City of New York*,[151.1] the court of appeals, agreeing with the district court, held that breaking into an apartment and seizing and transporting to a psychiatric hospital an incoherent Down Syndrome subject did not violate Title II of the ADA. There was no evidence that the seizure and hospitalization were motivated by discrimination against individuals with disabilities. The evidence instead showed that even if the police officers perceived the subject as disabled, they arrested her because she seemed to need assistance.[151.2]

151.1 339 F.3d 129 (2d Cir. 2003).
151.2 339 F.3d at 141.

[I] Parking Spaces

Page 335, add at end of subsection:

In *Jones v. City of Monroe*,[167.1] the court of appeals affirmed denial of a preliminary injunction sought by a plaintiff with multiple sclerosis to compel a municipality to provide a free all-day parking space. The court of appeals stepped through the traditional requirements for preliminary injunctive relief, and concluded that the district court had permissibly concluded that the plaintiff failed to establish sufficient likelihood of success on the merits:

> When considering a motion for preliminary injunction, the district court should consider four factors: (1) whether the moving party has a strong

likelihood of success on the merits; (2) whether the moving party will suffer irreparable injury without the injunction; (3) whether the issuance of the injunction would cause substantial harm to others; and (4) whether the public interest would be served by issuance of the injunction. The four considerations applicable to preliminary injunction decisions are factors to be balanced, not prerequisites that must be met. Moreover, a district court is not required to make specific findings concerning each of the four factors used in determining a motion for preliminary injunction if fewer factors are dispositive of the issue.[167.2]

* * *

In the one-hour parking area specifically addressed by Jones, Monroe is offering the benefit of free short-term parking to individuals who wish to transact retail or other business in the downtown business district. The short-term, one-hour nature of the benefit is designed to help downtown businesses by making parking spaces in close proximity to them more readily available. Monroe quite logically has determined that downtown shopping and other downtown business activities are discouraged when patrons cannot easily obtain parking places close to their destination. All-day parking in the current one-hour spaces would thus have a negative impact on downtown businesses.

In specific locations a short distance away from the one-hour parking, Monroe has also provided the benefit of free long-term, all-day parking to all individuals who come downtown, for whatever reason. While the all-day parking is not provided for the specific benefit of individuals who work downtown, they are free to use it.

Access to the one-hour and all-day parking places is facially neutral. The one-hour limit applies to individuals with disabilities and those without disabilities. Similarly, both disabled and able-bodied persons may park in all-day parking. Both one-hour and all-day parking areas have spaces for disabled and nondisabled individuals. The parking limitations do not affect disabled and nondisabled individuals differently in any respect. Thus, the district court did not err in determining that Jones was not excluded from parking benefits offered by Monroe.[167.3]

Judge Cole dissented, arguing that, "for Jones to be able to benefit from Monroe's parking program, she needs to be able to have access to the locations which non-disabled individuals can access from these parking lots."[167.4]

[167.1] 341 F.3d 474 (6th Cir. 2003).
[167.2] *Id.* at 476 (footnotes and internal citations omitted).
[167.3] *Id.* at 478 (footnotes and internal citations omitted).
[167.4] *Id.* at 484 (Cole, J., dissenting).

§ 5.08 PHYSICAL ACCESSIBILITY

[A] Scope of Requirement

Page 336, add before last paragraph in subsection:

In *Barden v. City of Sacramento*,[171.1] the court of appeals held that city sidewalks constituted a "service, program, or activity of the city," and therefore that Title II of the ADA compelled the city to make curb cuts or other sloped areas for disabled access.[171.2]

[171.1] 292 F.3d 1073 (9th Cir. 2002).
[171.2] *Id.* at 1076 (reversing district court).

§ 5.09 SOCIAL BENEFIT PROGRAMS

[H] Community Mental Health Services

Page 347, add at end of subsection:

In *Frederick L. v. Department of Public Welfare*,[224.1] the court of appeals vacated a judgment for the Pennsylvania Department of Public Welfare in an ADA and Rehabilitation Act case brought by inmates with mental disabilities at Norristown State Hospital. The court of appeals held that a government entity may not defend its refusal to provide community-based mental health services based on short-term costs alone. The court of appeals remanded so that the district court could develop a fuller record as to the total net costs of providing community-based services and the impact of doing so on other services provided by the department and so that the defendant could furnish specific evidence of the department's commitment to make progress on deinstitutionalization. It found that the evidence on costs was insufficient to justify an immediate order for the department to make 60 community residential slots available per year.

In *Townsend v. Quasim*,[224.2] the court of appeals held that denying community-based in-home nursing services to medically needy Medicaid recipients while allowing such services for categorically needy recipients violated Title II of the ADA. Medically needy persons had to receive Medicaid-funded long-term living and medical assistance in a nursing home setting or not at all. The court of appeals noted that the plaintiff was challenging the location of services, not whether services would be provided.[224.3] Accordingly, it distinguished cases, holding in the Medicaid context that the ADA does not obligate the state to provide services. It allowed, however, the state to offer further evidence on remand that forcing the state to offer community-based long-term care services to disabled medically needy persons would fundamentally alter well-considered policy decisions.[224.4]

[224.1] 364 F.3d 487 (3d Cir. 2004).
[224.2] 328 F.3d 511 (9th Cir. 2003).
[224.3] *Id.* at 517.
[224.4] *Id.* at 518.

[L] Health Care

Page 350, add at end of last paragraph on page:

In *Lovell v. Chandler*,[240.1] the court of appeals easily concluded that the state of Hawaii, by explicitly excluding the disabled from an expansion of its Medicaid program, violated Title II of the ADA.[240.2]

In *Garner v. State Department of Health and Social Services*,[240.3] the Alaska Supreme Court considered an ADA challenge to state Medicaid regulations that denied aggressive dental treatment to a profoundly disabled claimant because he was over 21 years old. It summarized the relationship between states and the federal government in the Medicaid program as follows:

> Title XIX of the Social Security Act [citing 42 U.S.C. § 1396] established the Medicaid program, a cooperative federal-state partnership under which participating states provide federally-funded medical services to needy individuals. Although participation in the program by a state is voluntary, once a state decides to participate, it must comply with federal statutory and regulatory requirements. States electing to participate in the Medicaid program must fund a minimum of seven mandatory services [citing 42 U.S.C. § 1396a(a)(10); 42 U.S.C. § 1396d(a)]. States may elect to cover additional optional services and, once they do, those services become part of the state's Medicaid plan and are subject to the requirements of federal law. [citing 42 U.S.C. § 1396d(a); 42 C.F.R. § 440.240; *Meyers v. Reagan*, 776 F.2d 241, 243 (8th Cir.1985) (explaining that once a state decides to provide optional services, it must comply with the federal regulations that govern those services)].[240.4]

The record of state administrative proceedings suggested that the state Medicaid agency had unaccountably failed to consider a provision of its own regulations allowing exceptions to the limitation of dental coverage for patients older than 21. The court analyzed the state's obligation to provide reasonable accommodation in terms of the same interactive process used for reasonable accommodation in the employment context.[240.5] The court of appeals found that the claimant had made out a prima facie case of disability-based discrimination and ordered remand to the state agency for further fact finding on whether relying on the claimants' caregivers to infer when he was experiencing pain (the state regulations allowed treatment of persons over 21 to relieve acute pain) was reasonable accommodation or whether the only reasonable accommodation was that requested by the claimant: covering the treatment requested.[240.6]

In *Henrietta D v. Bloomberg*,[240.7] the court of appeals affirmed judgment for plaintiffs on a claim that the New York City Health Services Agency had violated Title II of the ADA by failing to deliver promised benefits and services to patients with HIV infection. The failure occurred because the agency was disorganized and often unresponsive, because case workers provided no response or untimely responses to requests, and because benefits often were terminated with inadequate or no notice.[240.8]

In *Fisher v. Oklahoma Healthcare Authority*,[240.9] the court of appeals reversed summary judgment and held that terminating coverage of medically necessary prescription drugs for disabled persons in community health facilities, while continuing those benefits for institutionalized persons, potentially violated Title II of the ADA. The court also held that the question of whether requiring continuation of such benefits would fundamentally alter the program required trial on the facts.[240.10]

In *Radaszewski v. Maram*,[240.11] the court of appeals reversed judgment on the pleadings for a state agency, finding that evaluation of the costs of providing at-home, private-duty nursing care could not adequately be assessed in a motion for judgment on the pleadings. Assessment of the cost was necessary to decide the state agency's fundamental-alteration defense.

240.1 303 F.3d 1039 (9th Cir. 2002).
240.2 *Id.* at 1053-54.
240.3 63 P.3d 264 (Alaska 2003).
240.4 *Id.* at 268 [footnotes omitted].
240.5 *Id.* at 270-71.
240.6 *Id.* at 271.
240.7 331 F.3d 261 (2d Cir. 2003).
240.8 *Id.* at 277 ("demonstration that a disability makes it difficult for plaintiff to access benefits that are available to both those with and without disabilities is sufficient to sustain a claim for a reasonable accommodation").
240.9 335 F.3d 1175 (10th Cir. 2003).
240.10 *Id.* at 1182.
240.11 383 F.3d 599 (7th Cir. 2004).

[M] Education

Page 357, add before last paragraph on page a new subsection heading:

[1] IDEA Exhaustion

Page 358, add following note 287 reference:

In *Polera v. Board of Education*,[287.1] the Second Circuit considered the circumstances under which an ADA plaintiff must exhaust administrative remedies under the IDEA. More narrowly, it considered, "whether the exhaustion requirement of the IDEA should apply to Polera's claims despite the fact the relief sought—damages—is not available under the IDEA."[287.2] The court explained how exhaustion of the administrative requirements could resolve the underlying dispute especially when the plans for a disabled student are vague. It rejected arguments that exhaustion would be futile because it would require recourse to the same individuals allegedly violating the IDEA and the ADA and because it would take substantial time.[287.3] Because the plaintiff failed to exhaust her IDEA remedies, the court of appeals held that the district court lacked subject matter jurisdiction over IDEA and ADA claims.[287.4]

[287.1] 288 F.3d 478 (2d Cir. 2002).
[287.2] *Id.* at 486-87.
[287.3] *Id.* at 490.
[287.4] *Id.* at 490.

§ 5.10 STATUTES, AGENCY RULES, AND COMMON-LAW DOCTRINES VIOLATING ADA

Page 361, add new subsection:

[A] State Constitutional Provisions

In *South Dakota Farm Bureau, Inc. v. Hazeltine*,[302.1] the district court held that an amendment to the South Dakota Constitution barring corporations and syndicates from engaging in farming in South Dakota violated the ADA. The challenged amendment exempted family farm corporations, but only when a family member resides on the farm or engages in "both daily or routine substantial physical exertion and administration."[302.2] The ADA claim was based on the argument that this language discriminated against disabled farmers, such as two of the plaintiffs whose corporations could not qualify for the exemption because their owners were physically unable to participate in the daily labor and management of the land.[302.3]

The court of appeals, affirming the injunction on other grounds, held that the district court had impermissibly revived the ADA claim after the plaintiffs dropped it from their complaint, finding the course of the trial insufficient to support implied consent for posttrial amendment of the pleadings. "Without notice, the defendants lacked an adequate opportunity to cure the surprise caused by the District Court's constructive amendment to the pleadings: they could not present evidence or cross examine witnesses concerning any issue, factual or legal, related to the claim."[302.4]

[302.1] 340 F.3d 583 (8th Cir. 2003).
[302.2] *Id.* at 589 (quoting language of amendment).
[302.3] *Id.* at 590.
[302.4] *Id.* at 591.

§ 5.12 LICENSING DECISIONS BY PUBLIC AGENCIES

Page 365, add at end of section:

In *Sheridan's Case*,[325.1] the New Hampshire Supreme Court rejected an argument that a mental disability obligated the court to impose a lesser sanction than a one-year suspension on a lawyer who failed to file appropriate incorporation papers and to keep his clients informed of the rejection of the initial filing. The evidence was inconclusive as to whether the alleged mental disability constituted an ADA disability.[325.2]

[325.1] 813 A.2d 449 (N.H. 2002).
[325.2] *Id.* at 454.

Page 366, retitle § 5.13 and create new subsection [A] directly following § 5.13 as follows:

§ 5.13 APPLICATION OF ZONING, FIRE, AND OTHER CODES

[A] Zoning Decisions

Page 367, add before first full paragraph:

In *Oconomowoc Residential Programs, Inc. v. City of Milwaukee*,[331.1] court of appeals found that the City of Milwaukee violated Title II of the ADA by refusing to grant a variance permitting a group home for mentally disabled persons to be placed near another group facility because the city failed to prove that the requested accommodation was unreasonable or that it created an undue hardship.[331.2]

[331.1] 300 F.3d 775 (7th Cir. 2002).
[331.2] *Id.* at 787.

Page 367, add new subsection:

[B] Application of Fire Codes to Community Facilities

Tsombanidis v. West Haven Fire Department,[336.1] involved an ADA Title II action by an operator and residents of a halfway house for recovering alcoholics and drug addicts. After receiving complaints from neighbors, the city concluded that the halfway house constituted an illegal boarding house in a residential zone in violation of the city zoning regulations. The fire department also cited the house for failure to have additional equipment appropriate for rooming houses. The court of appeals rejected the district court's finding of disparate impact from the zoning and fire code regulations because it failed to assess the differential impact, if any, of the two challenged legal regimes between the class of disabled persons and the class of nondisabled persons.[336.2] The court of appeals agreed with the district court that the plaintiffs did not establish a failure of reasonable accommodation violation of the ADA because they had not fully exhausted administrative procedures that might have resulted in accommodation, and to the extent they did, their requested accommodation was provided.[336.3] As to claims against the city, the court of appeals found that the evidence supported the district court's conclusion that the city was motivated by discriminatory animus against the disabled and that the city failed to provide reasonable accommodation. It thought the evidence that the plaintiffs operated much like a family, and the minimal burden associated with reclassifying the halfway home as a single family use, justified the reasonable accommodation finding.[336.4] (The adverse court of appeals findings with respect to disparate impact and reasonable accommodation were with respect to claims against the fire district.)

[336.1] 352 F.3d 565 (2d Cir. 2003).
[336.2] *Id.* at 575.
[336.3] *Id.* at 579.
[336.4] *Id.* at 580.

§ 5.14 FAMILY SERVICES AND PARENTAL RIGHTS

Page 368, add at end of section:

In *In the Interest of Jane Doe*,[344.1] the Hawaii Supreme Court overruled *In re Jane Doe*[344.2] and held that an ADA claim may not be used as a defense in a proceeding to terminate parental rights. The child's father was incarcerated, and her mother suffered from a mental health disorder that had resulted in her scratching her forearms, stabbing herself in the abdomen and neck, and hitting her head.[344.3] The record showed several instances of abuse or neglect of the child and a failure by the parents to show up at family court hearings.

The court reviewed case law holding that a parental-rights-termination proceeding is not a service, program, or activity under the ADA and therefore the ADA does not apply to such proceedings, case law finding that careful fact finding in termination proceedings satisfies ADA obligations, and case law providing that the ADA may be a defense to termination of parental rights.[344.4] It held that "allegations of an ADA violation are not a defense to a termination proceeding because any purported violation may be remedied only in a separate proceeding brought under the provisions of the ADA."[344.5] The court reasoned that, "there is nothing in the ADA that indicates that an appropriate remedy for an ADA violation is the reversal of a parental termination order."[344.6] It cited case law from Vermont and Wisconsin agreeing with its reasoning.[344.7] Justice Moon concurred in the affirmance of the termination of parental rights but dissented from the majority's "overly broad holding" that an alleged ADA violation could never be raised as a defense to termination of parental rights.[344.8]

In *Arneson v. Arneson*,[344.9] the South Dakota Supreme Court allowed a trial court to consider a father's physical limitations resulting from cerebral palsy in deciding a child custody dispute between the parents. It acknowledged that the father had a disability under the ADA but concluded that "a custody proceeding is not a 'service, program or activity' under the provisions of the ADA" and therefore ruled that the ADA was inapplicable to the custody litigation.[344.10]

[344.1] 60 P.3d 285 (Haw. 2002).
[344.2] 58 P.3d 78 (Haw. Ct. App. 2002).
[344.3] 60 P.3d at 288.
[344.4] *Id.* at 290-91.
[344.5] *Id.* at 291.
[344.6] *Id.* at 292.
[344.7] *Id.* at 291-92.
[344.8] *Id.* at 297 (Moon, C.J., concurring in part and dissenting in part).
[344.9] 670 N.W.2d 904 (S.D. 2003).
[344.10] *Id.* at 911.

§ 5.15 CIVIL COMMITMENT

Page 369, add at beginning of section:

In *Hargrave v. Vermont*,[344.1] the court of appeals, affirming the district court, held that Vermont's Durable Power of Attorney for Healthcare Act violates Title II of the ADA. The act allowed involuntary medication of mentally ill persons who have been civilly committed. The plaintiff claimed that the structure of the act allowed individuals to execute a durable power of attorney (DPOA) refusing certain kinds of treatment, including medication, and that such a power conferred by state law represented a service program or activity under Title II. By denying qualified individuals like herself the same range of discretion afforded to nondisabled individuals, the statute violated Title II. The state defended on the ground that the plaintiff fell within an exception to Title II because she posed a significant risk to the health or safety of others. Because the state statute only authorized courts to override DPOAs of individuals who were subject to standing orders of civil commitment, and the criterion for civil commitment was danger of harm to himself or others, the statute necessarily qualified under the health or safety exception.

The court of appeals found it "unclear" whether the direct-threat defense applies outside of the employment context.[344.2] However, the court found that even if it does, the state had not met its burden of demonstrating that each and every patient subject to the statute posed a direct threat sufficient to exclude him or her from the protection of the ADA. For one thing, a civil commitment order could be based on a finding that the individual posed a danger to *himself*; the direct-threat ADA defense requires the person to pose a risk of harm to *others*.[344.3] Moreover, the state does not make an individualized and objective determination of the risk posed by a particular patient at the time it overrides a DPOA; instead, it relies on a finding made in an earlier commitment determination. Accordingly, the court found that the statute excluded from the state's DPOA program qualified individuals who meet essential eligibility requirements for maintaining DPOAs.[344.4] It further found that because mentally ill persons were treated specially under the act, the act discriminated based on disability.[344.5] Finally, it held that an injunction prohibiting enforcement of the statutory provisions permitting involuntary medication did not constitute a fundamental alteration of Vermont's DPOA program.[344.6]

[344.1] 340 F.3d 27 (2d Cir. 2003).
[344.2] *Id.* at 36.
[344.3] *Id.*
[344.4] *Id.*
[344.5] 340 F.3d at 37.
[344.6] *Id.* at 38.

§ 5.20 RETALIATION FOR ASSERTING TITLE II RIGHTS

Page 373, add at end of section:

In *Shotz v. City of Plantation*,[383.1] the United States Court of Appeals for the Eleventh Circuit held that individual municipal officials can be liable for retaliation prohibited by Title II of the ADA. The officials in this case leaked a background investigation about the plaintiff. The case arose when a city council member requested that the plaintiff conduct an inspection of the recently completed municipal community center to determine its compliance with the ADA. The plaintiff wrote a letter to the requesting council member identifying a number of ADA violations. After the letter circulated within the municipal government, an assistant mayor caused a background investigation to be conducted on the plaintiff. The municipality hired a private investigator who, among other things, made a video surveillance tape. The results of the investigation, including past involvement in professional disciplinary and other civil proceedings, conflict with a neighbor, and a criminal report involving the plaintiff's spouse, were released to the media.

The pertinent statutory provision says, "No person shall discriminate against any individual because such individual has opposed any act or practice made unlawful by this chapter or because such individual made a charge, testified, assisted, or participated in any manner in an investigation, proceeding, or hearing under this chapter."[383.2] The court of appeals focused on the word "person" in this statutory language and concluded that it "plainly includes individuals."[383.3] Moreover, the definitional section of the statute defines "person" to include individuals.[383.4] However, the mere statutory imposition of a duty on individuals did not definitively resolve the matter. "That a statutory provision imposes such a duty on a class of actors . . . does not compel the further conclusion that individual members of that class are amenable to private suit or otherwise liable for a breach of that duty. For that, we must also examine the remedies created by the statute."[383.5] The remedies for a violation of § 12203 are those of Title VI of the Civil Rights Act of 1964.[383.6] Case law affords a private right of action to enforce Title VI, but "precludes liability against those who do not receive federal funding, including individuals."[383.7]

The court of appeals summed up the dilemma as follows: "Did Congress intend the rights- and duty-creating language in the ADA antiretaliation provision to, itself, countenance liability against individuals for its violation, or did Congress intend the remedies available for Title VI violations to control exclusively the type of relief available as well as the appropriate scope of liability?"[383.8] Noting precedent denying individual liability in private actions under Title II,[383.9] the court of appeals determined that the overall statutory scheme militated in favor of individual liability:

> Even were we to ignore the plain meaning and look only to the available Title VI remedies in determining the scope of liability, we still could not conclusively establish that Congress intended to preclude individual liability under § 12203. Though we do not decide the question, and ultimately remain unconvinced, this approach might make sense for a violation of § 12203 in the employment context. There, the aggrieved person is ultimately referred to the remedies provided by Title VII of the Civil Rights Act of 1964, *see* § 12203(c); 42 U.S.C. § 12117(a), which prohibits discrimination by the same entities as prohibited by Subchapter I of the ADA regulating employment, and, as is apparent from the statutory language, those remedies do not include suit against individuals.[19] Indeed, employment is the context for virtually every case the appellees cite for the proposition that individual liability is unavailable for claims of retaliation under the ADA.[20]
>
> In the public services context, however, allowing the remedial provisions to govern the scope of liability would deviate considerably from the intent and purpose of the statute. The ADA makes *any* public entity liable for prohibited acts of discrimination, regardless of funding source. *See* 42 U.S.C. § 12132. By contrast, Title VI remedies are available only against federal funds recipients. . . . Thus, were the scope of liability confined to that of Title VI, not only would individuals who violate the Act be free from private suit, but public entities that do not receive federal funding as well, a result Congress logically did not intend. Otherwise, both Subchapter II and § 12203 in the public services context would be rendered superfluous[,] as the Rehabilitation Act also prohibits disability

discrimination by public entities receiving federal funds. *Compare* 29 U.S.C. § 794(a), *with* 42 U.S.C. § 12132. Indeed, an integral purpose of Subchapter II "is to make applicable the prohibition against discrimination on the basis of disability, currently set out in regulations implementing section 504 of the Rehabilitation Act of 1973, to all programs, activities, and services provided or made available by state and local governments or instrumentalities or agencies thereto, regardless of whether or not such entities receive Federal financial assistance." H.R.Rep. No. 101-485, pt. 2, at 84 (1990), *reprinted in* 1990 U.S.C.C.A.N. 303, 366-67. Had Congress intended to restrict liability to federal funds recipients, it would have been far easier to amend the Rehabilitation Act to account for the minor differences between it and Subchapter II of the ADA than to insert an otherwise unnecessary subchapter in the ADA itself.

Furthermore, permitting individual liability here would not create the same difficulties as doing so would under Title VI. For instance, the ADA was not enacted under Spending Clause authority as Title VI was. *See* 42 U.S.C. § 12101(b)(4) ("It is the purpose of [the ADA] . . . to invoke the sweep of congressional authority, including the power to enforce the fourteenth amendment and to regulate commerce. . . ."); *Pace v. Bogalusa City Sch. Bd.*, 325 F.3d 609, 615 (5th Cir. 2003) ("The ADA . . . does not in any way condition the receipt of federal funds on compliance with the ADA or waiver of state sovereign immunity."). Thus, liability need not be restricted only to those who contract with the federal government.[21]

There would also be no incongruency with the allowed scope of government enforcement action, if individual liability were recognized, as there would be under Titles VI or IX. . . . "Because . . . fund termination procedures . . . are inapplicable to State and local government entities that do not receive Federal funds, the major enforcement sanction for the Federal government [for ADA violations] will be referral of cases by these Federal agencies to the Department of Justice." S.Rep. No. 101-116, at 57 (1989). If there is an unresolved complaint, "the designated agency shall refer the matter to the Attorney General with a recommendation for appropriate action." 28 C.F.R. § 35.174. Neither the statute nor the regulations indicate that such action may not be taken against individuals.

* * *

FN19. Compare 42 U.S.C. § 12112(a) (prohibiting disability discrimination by a "covered entity," which is defined in § 12111(2) as "an employer, employment agency, labor organization, or joint labor-management committee"), with 42 U.S.C. § 2000e-5(b) (Title VII) (identifying the same parties as liable to a charge alleging an unlawful employment practice).

FN20. *See Baird v. Rose*, 192 F.3d 462, 471-72 (4th Cir. 1999) (holding, inexplicably so, that, since "[t]he remedies available for a violation of the antiretaliation provision of the ADA *in the employment context* are [ultimately] set forth . . . under Title VII," and "Title VII does not provide a remedy against individual defendants," there is no individual liability *under Subchapter II of the ADA concerning public services) (emphasis added); Hiler*, 177 F.3d at 545-46 (addressing retaliation in the employment context under the "Rehabilitation Act, which incorporates by reference § 12203(a) of the ADA"); *Swaim*, 170 F.Supp.2d at 583 (same); *Santiago v. City of Vineland*, 107 F.Supp.2d 512, 551-52 (D.N.J.2000) (same); *Kautio v. Zurich Ins. Co.*, 12 Nat'l Disability L. Rep. (LRP Publ'ns) & 243 (D.Kan. Mar. 19, 1998) (same); *Stern*, 982 F.Supp. at 692-93 (same); *Cable v. Dep't of Developmental Servs.*, 973 F.Supp. 937, 943 (C.D.Cal.1997) (same). The decisions in *Key* and *Van Hulle v. Pac. Telesis Corp.*, 124 F.Supp.2d 642, 644-646 (N.D.Cal.2000), however, address retaliation in the public services and public accommodations context, respectively. *Key* we have already addressed, and we discuss *Van Hulle infra* note 22.

FN21. It is true that, in *Barnes*, Justice Scalia suggested that the contract-law analogy useful in analyzing the scope of Spending Clause legislation applied in equal measure to the question of whether the ADA permitted punitive damages[,] because Congress "unequivocally" incorporated the remedies of § 794a(a)(2) of the Rehabilitation Act, "which *is* Spending Clause legislation." 122 S.Ct. at 2103 n. 3. Yet, that case concerned the *type* of relief available, as opposed to the question *who* may be sued, a question that is confused in this case by the statutory language in § 12203.[383.10]

The court also noted that the Department of Justice interprets § 12203 as making individuals acting in their individual capacities amenable to private suit.[383.11] Because Congress expressly authorized the Attorney General to make rules with the force of law implementing the ADA, the court of appeals found the DOJ regulation entitled to deference.[383.12]

The district court had granted summary judgment to the city also because it found the public release of personal information insufficiently adverse to establish a prima facie case of retaliation. The court of appeals found:

> Gathering sensitive and highly personal information which is irrelevant to an assessment of either the position or credibility of a citizen who is attempting to galvanize local government into satisfying its obligations under the ADA, as a favor to a city council member no less (no good deed goes unpunished!), and then releasing that information to the public, for whatever reason, is hardly incidental to the normal government-citizen relationship.[383.13] . . . In this case, a reasonable citizen in Shotz's position would not only view the city's actions as adverse, but appalling as well, even if they were not motivated by retaliatory animus. Accordingly, we conclude that Shotz has shown adverse action sufficient to demonstrate a prima facie case of retaliation under the ADA.[383.14]

383.1 344 F.3d 1161 (11th Cir. 2003).

383.2 42 U.S.C. § 12203(a).

383.3 344 F.3d at 1168-69.

383.4 *Id.* at 1168, quoting 42 U.S.C. § 12111(7).

383.5 *Id.*

383.6 344 F.3d at 1173, citing 42 U.S.C. § 12133, incorporating by reference 29 U.S.C. § 794a, which in turn incorporates remedies, procedures, and rights set forth in Title VII and Title VI.

383.7 *Id.* at 1170.

383.8 *Id.* at 1171.

383.9 *Id.* at 1172-73, citing and discussing Key v. Grayson, 163 F. Supp. 2d 697, 703-04 (E.D. Mich. 2001) (no individual liability in public services context), and Hiler v. Brown, 177 F.3d 542, 545 (6th Cir. 1999) (same).

383.10 344 F.3d at 1173-75.

383.11 *Id.* at 1177, citing nondiscrimination on the basis of disability in state and local government, 28 C.F.R. pt. 35 (2003).

383.12 *Id.* at 1186.

383.13 *Id.* at 1182.

383.14 *Id.* at 1183.

§ 5.21 TENTH AMENDMENT

Page 374, add at end of note 386:

See Sharon Ahearn, *HIV-Positive Athletes*, 7 Sports Law. J. 279, 288 (2000) (citing this book).

§ 5.22 ELEVENTH AMENDMENT

Page 374, add after last paragraph:

Although the Eleventh Amendment may block suits by individuals against states, it does not prevent the federal government from suing states under the ADA. The Fifth Circuit made this clear in *United States v. Mississippi Department of Public Safety*.[391.1] The district court dismissed a lawsuit brought by the United States against the Mississippi Department of Public Safety for discrimination against an individual highway safety patrol trainee based on a disability. The district court concluded that the United States was empowered to sue only to remedy a pattern of intentional discrimination under § 707 of the Civil Rights Act[391.2] but not under § 706 of the Civil Rights Act[391.3] because that put the United States in the "shoes" of an individual who could not sue in his own capacity.

The court of appeals rejected this reasoning, beginning with the proposition that, "in ratifying the Constitution, the states consented to suits brought by other states or by the federal government."[391.4] Invalidation of congressional efforts to authorize suits by private individuals against states for money damages under the ADA in *Garrett* had no impact on the power of the United States to enforce the ADA in suits for money damages.[391.5] "The fact that Collins could not sue the MDPS for the alleged violation of the law in no way diminishes the United States' interest in the action or the authority of the United States to bring suit against the MDPS for the benefit of the public generally and for Collins' benefit specifically. Nor does this transform the United States into a mere proxy for Collins. Collins has no right to compel the United States to bring suit or to dictate its complaint or prayer for relief in any way. In short, the United States' interest in and control over this case is entirely real."[391.6] It reversed the district court.

[391.1] 321 F.3d 495 (5th Cir. 2003).
[391.2] 42 U.S.C. § 2000e-6(a) (2002).
[391.3] 42 U.S.C. § 2000e-5(f) (2002).
[391.4] 321 F.3d at 498, quoting Alden v. Maine, 527 U.S. 706, 755-56 (1999).
[391.5] *Id.* at 498, citing *Garrett*, 531 U.S. at 374 n. 9 and *Alden*, 527 U.S. at 755-56.
[391.6] *Id.* at 499.

Page 380, add after third full paragraph:

In *Tennessee v. Lane*,[436.1] the Supreme Court of the United States held that Title II of the ADA could be applied to state courts, given the fundamental right of access to the courts. The Court distinguished *Garrett* as involving employment discrimination under Title I and noted that Congress enacted Title II against a "backdrop of pervasive unequal treatment in the administration of state services and programs, including systematic deprivations of fundamental rights."[436.2] "Given the sheer volume of evidence demonstrating the nature and extent of unconstitutional discrimination against persons with disabilities in the provision of public services, the dissent's contention that the record is insufficient to justify Congress' exercise of its prophylactic power is puzzling, to say the least."[436.3] The Court found that Congress had not exceeded its power under Section 5 of the 14th Amendment:

> Whatever might be said about Title II's other applications, the question presented in this case is not whether Congress can validly subject the States to private suits for money damages for failing to provide reasonable access to hockey rinks, or even to voting booths, but whether Congress had the power under § 5 to enforce the constitutional right of access to the courts. Because we find that Title II unquestionably is valid § 5 legislation as it applies to the class of cases implicating the accessibility of judicial services, we need go no further.[436.4]

How far beyond access to courts the *Lane* precedent will be extended by the lower courts remains to be seen.

In *Klingler v. Director, Department of Revenue*,[436.5] a case decided days before the *Lane* opinion was released, the court of appeals reversed declaratory and injunctive relief against imposition of a $2 fee for disability parking placards. The court observed that the DOJ regulation implementing Title II of the ADA expressly prohibits public entities from placing a surcharge on a disabled person for measures required to afford nondiscriminatory treatment. It concluded that application of the regulation to the $2 fee was unconstitutional, noting that "this is one of those rare occasions where the appropriate resolution of the constitutional issue is reasonably straightforward and determinant and the resolution of the statutory issue as, by contrast, difficult and complex."[436.6] The court began with the proposition that extension of Title II of the ADA to the states was not a proper exercise of Congress's power under Section 5 of the Fourteenth Amendment.[436.7] The court found that imposition of the placard fees did not substantially affect interstate commerce and that any effect between payment of the $2 fee and interstate commerce was too attenuated to justify federal regulation.

Circuit Judge Arnold dissented, arguing that the majority "overlooks the fact that those disabled individuals who pay the fee are being required to pay for their access to interstate commerce while nondisabled individuals are not."[436.8]

In *Miller v. King*,[436.9] the court of appeals reversed in part the district court's dismissal of the prisoner's claims under the ADA. The plaintiff, a paraplegic inmate at Georgia State Prison, was serving a life sentence for murder. He claimed a violation of the ADA, among other things, because his small cell left him no room to maneuver his wheelchair, because bathing and toilet facilities were not wheelchair accessible, and because prison officials had failed to provide rudimentary medical devices required for his condition. The court of appeals, disagreeing with the district court, held that the Eleventh Amendment does not bar ADA suits under Title II for prospective injunctive relief against state officials in their official capacities.[436.10] It held that Title II of the ADA, as applied in a prison case, does not validly abrogate the state's sovereign immunity in a suit for monetary damages. The plaintiff had unsuccessfully argued that Congress had power under the Eighth Amendment to impose ADA requirements on prison systems.

In *Phiffer v. Columbia River Correctional Institute*,[436.11] the court of appeals, on remand from the Supreme Court, held that states are not entitled to Eleventh Amendment immunity under Title II of the ADA, under the *Lane* decision. Circuit Judge O'Scannlain concurred on the grounds that the panel was bound by Ninth Circuit precedent, while expressing doubt that the precedent broadly finding valid abrogation of Eleventh Amendment immunity under Title II survived the "more exacting analysis under *Lane*."

[436.1] 124 S. Ct. 1978 (2004).

[436.2] *Id.* at 1989-90.

[436.3] *Id.* at 1991.

[436.4] *Id.* 1992-93.

[436.5] 366 F.3d 614 (8th Cir. 2004).

[436.6] *Id.* at 616.

[436.7] *Id.* at 617 (*citing* Alsbrook v. City of Maumelle, 184 F.3d 999, 1010 (8th Cir. 1999) (en banc)).

436.8 366 F.3d at 620, 621 (Arnold, J., dissenting).
436.9 384 F.3d 1248 (11th Cir. 2004).
436.10 *Id.* at 1264 (citing *Ex parte Young*, 209 U.S. 123 (1908), and ADA cases from other circuits).
436.11 384 F.3d 791 (9th Cir. 2004).

Page 380, add at end of note 438:

Ex parte Young suits are considered further in § 5.22[A].

Page 380, add before last paragraph:

Municipalities ordinarily do not have the status of "states" under the Eleventh Amendment, but this may be changed by state law. In *Epps v. City of Pine Lawn*,[437.1] the court of appeals held that Missouri municipalities enjoy statutory sovereign immunity; it further held that the municipality had not waived sovereign immunity by buying insurance for tort claims not covered by the sovereign immunity.[437.2]

437.1 353 F.3d 588 (8th Cir. 2003).
437.2 *Id.* at 594-95.

Page 384, add at end of section:

In *Savage v. Glendale Union High School*,[448.1] the court of appeals held that an Arizona High School District was not an arm of the state entitled to Eleventh Amendment immunity, applying the following tests:

1. Whether a money judgment would be satisfied out of state funds;
2. Whether the entity performs central governmental functions;
3. Whether the entity may sue or be sued;
4. Whether the entity has the power to take property in its own name or only in the name of the state; and
5. The corporate status of the entity.[448.2]

Applying Arizona state law to determine the status of the school district, it held that monies other than state funds in the school district's accounts could be used to satisfy judgments and comingling of state and other funds was insufficient to satisfy the first test, that the school district did not perform a central governmental function because state law granted local school districts "enormous autonomy" in the management of public education,[448.3] and that the state's imposition of minimum standards was not enough to satisfy the central-function test, that school districts in Arizona are explicitly granted the power to sue or be sued in their own name,[448.4] and that school districts can hold property in their own name.[448.5] That state law characterized school districts as "political subdivisions" of the state was not enough to overcome the other factors.[448.6]

In *Kiman v. New Hampshire Department of Corrections*,[448.7] the First Circuit, reviewing case law from the Fifth and Tenth Circuits invalidating Title II, and from the Second and Sixth Circuits partially upholding Title II abrogation, held that Title II of the ADA validly abrogates state immunity.[448.8] In *Thomas v. Nakatani*,[448.9] the Ninth Circuit refused to reconsider its earlier decision in *Hason v. Medical Board of California*,[448.10] finding that Title II of the ADA validly abrogates state sovereign immunity. In *Lovell v. Chandler*,[448.11] the court of appeals held that Title II of the ADA validly abrogates Eleventh Amendment immunity for claims against a state and its instrumentalities, and also held that a state's acceptance of Rehabilitation Act funds waived the state's Eleventh Amendment immunity for Rehabilitation Act claims. It noted that *Garrett* expressly reserved the question whether Title II validly abrogates Eleventh Amendment immunity and adhered to its decision in *Hason v. Medical Board of California*[448.12] that Title II claims may be brought against states.[448.13]

The court also rejected the state's waiver argument, a part of its analysis considered more fully in supplement § 8.13.

In *Thompson v. State of Colorado*,[448.14] the Tenth Circuit concluded that Title II of the ADA did not validly abrogate state sovereign immunity. In *Wessel v. Glendening*,[448.15] the Fourth Circuit concluded that Title II of the ADA did not validly abrogate Eleventh Amendment immunity in an ADA suit by a state prisoner.

Because Title II requires more than the Constitution, it failed the congruent and proportionality requirement of Eleventh Amendment abrogation.[448.16]

In *Chisolm v. McManimon*,[448.17] the court of appeals determined that a county court did not qualify as an arm of the state and therefore was not entitled to Eleventh Amendment immunity in a Title II ADA case.[448.18]

In *Eason v. Clark County School District*,[448.19] the Ninth Circuit, reversing the district court, held that a school district was not a state instrumentality entitled to Eleventh Amendment immunity:

> "It has long been settled that the [Eleventh Amendment] reference to actions 'against one of the United States' encompasses not only actions in which a State is actually named as the defendant, but also certain actions against state agencies and state instrumentalities." Regents of the Univ. of Calif. v. Doe, 519 U.S. 425, 429, 117 S. Ct. 900, 137 L. Ed. 2d 55 (1997) (citations omitted) (holding that California state university enjoys Eleventh Amendment immunity). In contrast, the Eleventh Amendment does not extend to counties and municipal corporations. Lincoln County v. Luning, 133 U.S. 529, 10 S. Ct. 363, 33 L. Ed. 766 (1890) (holding that Nevada counties are not immune under the Eleventh Amendment); see also Lake Country Estates, Inc. v. Tahoe Regional Planning Agency, 440

U.S. 391, 401, 99 S. Ct. 1171, 59 L. Ed. 2d 401 (1979) ("But the Court has consistently refused to construe the [Eleventh] Amendment to afford protection to political subdivisions such as counties and municipalities, even though such entities exercise a 'slice of state power.' "). Cf. Moor v. County of Alameda, 411 U.S. 693, 717-719, 93 S. Ct. 1785, 36 L. Ed. 2d 596 (1973) (holding that California counties are not arms of the state or alter egos of the state for purposes of diversity jurisdiction), overruled in part by Monell v. Dept. of Social Services, 436 U.S. 658, 98 S. Ct. 2018, 56 L. Ed. 2d 611 (1978) (overruling holding of Monroe v. Pape, 365 U.S. 167, 81 S. Ct. 473, 5 L. Ed. 2d 492 (1961), that local governments are immune from suit under § 1983).

The central question in this case is whether the Clark County School District is an "arm of the state," entitled to Eleventh Amendment immunity. Mt. Healthy City School District Board of Education v. Doyle, 429 U.S. 274, 280, 97 S. Ct. 568, 50 L. Ed. 2d 471 (1977). The Supreme Court has mentioned in passing that the Eleventh Amendment does not afford "local school boards" immunity from suit, Missouri v. Jenkins, 495 U.S. 33, n. 20, 110 S. Ct. 1651, 109 L. Ed. 2d 31 (1990), and in Mt. Healthy, the Court held an Ohio school district subject to suit because it was "more like a county or city than . . . like an arm of the State." Id. at 280, 97 S. Ct. 568. Moreover, most courts have held that school districts are not entitled to Eleventh Amendment immunity.[2]

[2] See, e.g., Cuesta v. School Board of Miami-Dade County, 285 F.3d 962, 966 (11th Cir. 2002) (Florida); Cash v. Granville County Bd. of Educ., 242 F.3d 219 (4th Cir. 2001) (North Carolina); Duke v. Grady Municipal Schools, 127 F.3d 972 (10th Cir. 1997) (New Mexico); Ambus v. Granite Bd. of Educ., 995 F.2d 992 (10th Cir. 1993) (Utah); Stewart v. Baldwin County Bd. of Educ., 908 F.2d 1499, 1509-11 (11th Cir. 1990) (Alabama); Lester H. v. Gilhool, 916 F.2d 865, 870-71 (3d Cir. 1990) (Pennsylvania); Rosa R. v. Connelly, 889 F.2d 435, 437-38 (2d Cir. 1989) (Connecticut); Lopez v. Houston Independent School Dist., 817 F.2d 351, 353 (5th Cir. 1987) (citing Kingsville Independent School Dist. v. Cooper, 611 F.2d 1109, 1112 (5th Cir. 1980)), overruled on another ground by Walton v. Alexander, 44 F.3d 1297 (5th Cir. 1995); Fay v. South Colonie Central School Dist., 802 F.2d 21, 27 (2d Cir. 1986) (New York); Minton v. St. Bernard School Bd., 803 F.2d 129, 131-32 (5th Cir. 1986) (Louisiana); Gary A. v. New Trier High School Dist. No. 203, 796 F.2d 940, 945 (7th Cir. 1986) (Illinois); Stoddard v. School Dist. No. 1, Lincoln County, 590 F.2d 829 (10th Cir. 1979) (Wyoming); Unified School Dist. No. 480 v. Epperson, 583 F.2d 1118, 1121-23 (10th Cir. 1978) (Kansas); Adams v. Rankin County Bd. of Educ., 524 F.2d 928, 929 (5th Cir. 1975) (Mississippi). But see Belanger v. Madera Unified School Dist., 963 F.2d 248 (9th Cir. 1992) (California); De Levay v. Richmond County School Bd., 284 F.2d 340 (4th Cir. 1960) (Virginia).

In *Mitchell v. Los Angeles*, 861 F.2d 198 (9th Cir. 1989), we articulated five factors to determine whether an agency is an arm of the state: (1) "whether a money judgment would be satisfied out of state funds," (2) "whether the entity performs central governmental functions,"

(3) "whether the entity may sue or be sued," (4) "whether the entity has the power to take property in its own name or only the name of the state" and (5) "the corporate status of the entity." Id. at 201. We consider each of these factors in turn.

The first Mitchell factor—whether a money judgment will be satisfied out of state funds—is the most important. See e.g., Edelman v. Jordan, 415 U.S. 651, 663, 94 S. Ct. 1347, 39 L. Ed. 2d 662 (1974); Belanger v. Madera Unified School Dist., 963 F.2d 248, 251 (9th Cir. 1992); Durning v. Citibank, N.A., 950 F.2d 1419, 1424 (9th Cir. 1991); Jackson v. Hayakawa, 682 F.2d 1344 (9th Cir. 1982). The Supreme Court stressed in Regents of the University of California that "it is the entity's potential legal liability, rather than its ability or inability to require a third party to reimburse it, or to discharge the liability in the first instance, that is relevant." 519 U.S. at 431, 117 S. Ct. 900 (finding irrelevant the fact that the federal government would indemnify the State of California for any damages judgment against the University); see also Durning, 950 F.2d at 1424 n. 2 ("The relevant question is whether the state would have a legal liability to pay the judgment, not whether the defendant entity would have the practical ability to pay it."); Duke, 127 F.3d at 981 (concluding that the "factor relating to the liability of the state treasury points away from Eleventh Amendment immunity, for the simple reason that the state of New Mexico is not legally liable for a judgment against a school district[,]" even though New Mexico schools receive about 95% of their funds from the state). Thus, the relevant inquiry is whether Nevada will be legally required to satisfy any monetary judgment obtained against the District.

No statutory provision requires Nevada to satisfy its school districts' debts, but defendants cite Belanger, where we granted California school districts Eleventh Amendment immunity, and contend that, as in California, state funds will necessarily satisfy any monetary judgment against the school district. In Belanger, however, we recognized that "California has selected a different path from that of most states." 963 F.2d at 254. Belanger is thus distinguishable because Nevada does not share the unique structure of the California school system. In California:

> The state sets a revenue limit for each school district based on average attendance, subtracts property tax revenues from that limit, and allocates the balance to the school district from the state school fund. In short, the state determines the amount of money that school districts may spend per pupil and then provides the necessary state funds." Id. at 252 (citations omitted). By virtue of this revenue limit system, "state and local revenue is commingled in a single fund under state control, and local tax revenue lost to a judgment must be supplanted by the interchangeable state funds already in the district budget." Id. Thus, in California, "any use of the commingled funds is a use of state funds." Id.

In contrast, even though Nevada school districts receive state funding, local funds lost to satisfy a money judgment will not necessarily be replaced with state funds. The State of Nevada does not set a maximum limit on per pupil spending. Instead, it establishes a minimum amount to be spent per pupil—known as the basic support guarantee—and it uses state funds to guarantee that each district will have that minimum amount. This funding scheme is entitled "The Nevada Plan." See "The Nevada Plan for School Finance: An Overview" at 2, 4 (hereinafter "Nevada Plan Overview");[3] Nev. Rev. Stat. §§ 387.121 (defining generally The Nevada Plan); 387.122 ("Establishment of basic support guarantees"); 387.1233 ("Calculation of basic support"). The amount of money contributed by the state varies by school district—school districts are required to earmark certain locally generated revenue to the minimum budget, this locally generated revenue is subtracted from the state guaranteed basic support and the difference (if there is any) is provided by the state. Nevada Plan Overview at 3 and Appendix B; Nev. Rev. Stat. §§ 387.121; 387.1235 (Identifying local funds in The Nevada Plan); 373.010 et seq. (Local School Support Tax Law); 387.195 (describing local property tax); 387.030 (describing state distributive account). Moreover, school districts generate local revenue beyond the amount allocated to the guaranteed basic support. Nevada Plan Overview at Appendix B. This additional local revenue is considered to be "'outside' the Nevada Plan formula." Nevada Plan Overview at 3. When these local revenues exceed or fall short of estimates, state aid does not decrease or increase. Id. Because the state guarantees only a minimum amount of per pupil spending, not a maximum, and because school districts may generate funds in addition to those provided by the state, it is not necessarily true that an amount withdrawn from a school district's account in order to pay a judgment will be replaced with state money.

[3] Defendants object to the plaintiffs' introduction of this document, a report prepared by the Legislative Counsel Bureau, a Nevada state agency, for the first time on appeal. The case they cite, Sablan v. Dept. of Finance, 856 F.2d 1317 (9th Cir. 1988), is inapposite because it merely reiterates the familiar proposition that we will not entertain new arguments on appeal. Id. at 1327. By bringing the Nevada Plan Overview to our attention, plaintiffs do not attempt to craft a new legal argument. Rather, they seek to bolster their description of the Nevada school system by introducing a supporting administrative report. We fail to see how this is improper—defendants do not suggest that this document is an unofficial record or otherwise inaccurate. In any event, we do not use the Nevada Plan Overview to resolve any disputed issues of fact.

Defendants make much of the fact that the State of Nevada limits school districts' ability to raise local revenue. The local funds "inside" the Nevada Plan consist of 25 cents of the 75 cent property tax earmarked for school operations and a 2.25 percent sales tax known as the Local School Support Tax. Nevada Plan Overview at 3 and Appendix B; Nev. Rev. Stat. §§ 387.1235 ("Local funds available for public schools"); § 374.010 et seq. ("Local School Support Tax Law"). The local funds "outside" the Nevada Plan include the remaining 50 cents of the 75 cent property tax, a portion of the motor vehicle privilege tax, franchise taxes, interest income, tuition and rent. Nevada Plan Overview at 3. Defendants correctly point out that these local sources of revenue are predetermined by state law and that "school districts have very little discretion in tax revenues." Nevada Plan Overview at 6. That the State of Nevada controls how local revenue is generated, however, is not relevant for purposes of the first Mitchell factor. Defendants cannot demonstrate that the State of Nevada bears a legal obligation to satisfy any adverse judgment against the District. Nor can they demonstrate that any money withdrawn from the District's account to satisfy such a judgment will necessarily be replaced with state funds, as in California.

The second Mitchell factor, "whether the entity performs central governmental functions," also distinguishes Nevada from California. Mitchell, 861 F.2d at 201. On balance, Nevada does not "treat[] public schooling as a state-wide or central governmental function." Belanger, 963 F.2d at 253. The State of Nevada created the school system and agreed to provide for its support, Nev. Const. Art. 11, §§ 2 and 6, and the county school districts are "political subdivision[s] . . . whose purpose is to administer the state system of public education." Nev. Rev. Stat. § 386.010. Nonetheless, the legislature has expressly "reaffirm[ed] its intent that public education in the State of Nevada is essentially a matter for local control by local school districts." Nev. Rev. Stat. § 385.005 ("Declaration of legislative intent"). Defendants cannot point to any authority supporting the proposition that Nevada school districts are "treated as state agencies under [Nevada] law" or that "[Nevada] law is well settled that providing public education is a state function." Compare Belanger, 963 F.2d at 253 ("[T]hrough the state constitution, statutes, and supreme court decisions, California has made public schooling a state governmental function."). Rather, local school districts possess "such rights and powers as are necessary to maintain control of education of the children within their respective districts." Nev. Rev. Stat. § 385.005; see also Nev. Rev. Stat. § 386.350 (defining general powers of board of trustees of school district).

Third, each county school district has "the power to sue and may be sued." Nev. Rev. Stat. § 386.010(3). The third Mitchell factor thus weighs slightly against holding that the District is an arm of the state. Belanger, 963 F.2d at 254 (holding that third Mitchell factor "is entitled to less weight than the first two factors").

Fourth, the District is not required to take property only in the name of the State of Nevada. The board of trustees, which runs the school district and the schools within that district, Nev. Rev. Stat. § 386.350, holds, manages and controls school district property. Nev. Rev. Stat. §§ 393.010; 393.030. The board of trustees has custody of the schoolhouses, and it may insure "the schoolhouses, furniture and school apparatus." Nev. Rev. Stat. § 393.020. Further, the board may sell, rent or lease real property belonging to the school district when it is "necessary or for the best interests of the school district," Nev. Rev. Stat. § 393.220. This factor also distinguishes Nevada from California, where property held in the name of a school district was nonetheless treated as "state property rather than local government property." Belanger, 963 F.2d at 254.

Finally, even though the school district itself is not a corporation, each board of trustees is a corporation. Nev. Rev. Stat. § 386.110. Accordingly, this factor weighs against granting the District Eleventh Amendment immunity. Once again, Belanger is distinguishable. There, we held that California "school districts have the corporate status of agents of the state for purposes of school administration." Belanger, 963 F.2d at 254. As we have discussed in addressing the other four Mitchell factors, there is no basis in Nevada law to so conclude here.

In sum, after examining the nature of school districts in Nevada and inquiring into Nevada's treatment of school districts, we conclude that the Mitchell factors weigh against a finding that the District is an arm of the state, entitled to Eleventh Amendment immunity. Most importantly, Nevada is not legally required to satisfy any judgment against the District. It is also not true that state funds will necessarily satisfy any such adverse judgment. In addition, the District does not perform a "central governmental function." Instead, Nevada has delegated responsibility for the state system of education to local units. Moreover, the District may sue and be sued and its board of trustees holds its property. Finally, even though the district itself is not a corporation, the board of trustees is. Consequently, the District is more like a local or county agency than like a state agency. Mt. Healthy, 429 U.S. at 280-81, 97 S. Ct. 568.[448.20]

In *Estes v. Wyoming Department of Transportation*,[448.21] the court of appeals held that a state, by removing an ADA and contract claim filed in state court to federal court, waived its Eleventh Amendment immunity as to both claims.[448.22]

In *Douglas v. California Department of Youth Authority*,[448.23] the court of appeals held that California waived its sovereign immunity against Rehabilitation Act claims by accepting federal funds under that Act.[448.24]

In *Koslow v. Commonwealth of Pennsylvania*,[448.25] the court of appeals held that Pennsylvania waived its immunity to Rehabilitation Act claims by accepting federal funding for its Department of Corrections.[448.26]

In *Pace v. Bogalusa City School Board*,[448.27] the court of appeals held that attempted congressional abrogation of Eleventh Amendment immunity for Title II ADA claims was ineffective because Congress failed to identify a history and pattern of unconstitutional discrimination by states against the disabled.

In *Bruggeman ex rel. Bruggeman v. Blagojevich*,[448.28] the court of appeals, in a decision written by Circuit Judge Posner, allowed litigation under the Rehabilitation Act despite an assertion of state immunity, but rejected *Ex parte Young* litigation based on the ADA. The plaintiffs were developmentally disabled adults who challenged the state's failure to build intermediate care facilities in northern Illinois.

Judge Posner faulted the district court for dismissing on standing grounds:

> The district judge ruled that none of these provisions [of the federal Medicaid statute, the Rehabilitation Act, and the Americans with Disabilities Act] entitled the plaintiffs to what they were seeking and that therefore the plaintiffs had not been injured by a violation of the statute and so lacked standing to sue. This is a misunderstanding of standing. A plaintiff has standing to sue—that is, he can invoke the jurisdiction of the court—if he is tangibly, materially, injured by the conduct of the defendant that he claims is unlawful and if the relief he seeks would redress the injury in whole or in part and thus confer a material benefit on him. Of course if his claim has no merit, then he has not been injured by any wrongful conduct of the defendant; but if the consequence were that he lacked standing, then every decision in favor of a defendant would be a decision that the court lacked jurisdiction, entitling the plaintiff to start over in another court. The district court decided that the plaintiffs have no right to live in an ICF/DD that is near their parents' home and so the defendants' refusal to adopt a plan that would create vacancies in ICF/DDs near the parents' home did not invade a legal right of the plaintiffs and so did not cause them an injury for which they are entitled to redress. This was a ruling on the merits, having nothing to do with jurisdiction.
>
> Not that standing and the merits are always or in this case clearly distinct. The more extreme a plaintiff's claim, the more likely he is to have standing to prosecute it; the more moderate his claim, the less likely he is to have standing. If all that the plaintiffs were seeking was a plan entitling them to reimbursement for the expense of residing in an ICF/DD anywhere in Illinois, they would, we may assume, have a legally sound claim; but they would have no standing to maintain it because there are ample vacancies in the southern part of the state, and so the absence of a plan would not impair any right that they claimed under the Medicaid statute. But if they claim a right to a wider choice of ICF/DD vacancies than the defendants are willing to permit the planning agency to authorize, then they are likely to have standing, because the absence of the plan they seek is a denial of such an entitlement. Although their brief could be clearer on the point, it seems that they are indeed pressing this more extreme claim. The district court rejected the claim, but that was a rejection on the merits inaccurately described as a ruling that the plaintiffs lack standing.
>
> But notice that we said only that the plaintiffs are *likely* to have standing; the doubt implicit in such a formulation arises from the tenuousness of the relation between the relief sought in the lawsuit and an actual benefit to the plaintiffs if they prevail. They seek merely a plan, which might not lead to an increase in the ICF/DD capacity in their immediate geographical area. Even if it did, they might not benefit. An increase in supply would evoke an increase in demand, since the plaintiffs are not

> the only developmentally disabled adults in northern Illinois whose parents would like to place them in a nearby ICF/DD and this is not a class action. So the plan the plaintiffs seek might not actually increase the vacancy rate. Meanwhile, there are *some* vacancies in ICF/DDs located near the plaintiffs' homes and for all that appears the plaintiffs will find places in an existing such facility long before the plan they seek would enable them to find a place in a new facility. The potential benefit to them from the relief that they seek thus is speculative.
>
> But not so speculative as to negate standing, which is a matter of probabilities rather than certainties. *North Shore Gas Co. v. EPA*, 930 F.2d 1239, 1242 (7th Cir.1991). The suit seeks to remove a logjam that is preventing the creation of facilities desired by the plaintiffs, and if the likelihood of success is conjectural so is the argument for failure based on the possibility that any new facilities will be overwhelmed by other applicants.[448.29]

Reaching the merits, the court of appeals held that the Civil Rights Act provision that "a state shall not be immune under the Eleventh Amendment of the Constitution of the United States from suit in federal court for a violation of Section 504 of the Rehabilitation Act,"[448.30] combined with the state's acceptance of federal financial assistance, which waived its Eleventh Amendment immunity, allowed maintenance of the suit against the state under the Rehabilitation Act.[448.31]

In *Miranda B. v. Kitzhaber*,[448.32] the court of appeals held that Congress validly displaced state immunity under Title II of the ADA, and that the Supreme Court's *Garrett* decision did not require a different conclusion.[448.33]

The Sixth Circuit distinguished between Congress's power under the due process clause of the Fourteenth Amendment and the equal protection clause, holding that although Title II of the ADA generally is unenforceable against states premised on equal protection power, in the case before it, Congress had power to enforce the due process clause by imposing on the courts duties to remove obstacles under Title II of the ADA.[448.34]

[A] *Ex parte Young*

In *Bruggeman ex rel. Bruggeman v. Blagojevich*,[448.35] the court of appeals, in a decision written by Circuit Judge Posner, held that a suit against state officials in their official capacities could be maintained under the ADA by virtue of *Ex parte Young*.[448.36] It held that a 2000 Seventh Circuit decision, *Walker v. Snyder*,[448.37] rejecting *Ex parte Young* suits under Title II of the ADA, had been rejected by other circuits and supplanted by the reasoning of the Supreme Court in *Garrett*, finding no material difference between Title I and Title II regarding the application of *Ex parte Young*.[448.38]

In *McCarthy ex rel. Travis v. Hawkins*,[448.39] the court of appeals held that state officers, alleged to have violated the ADA by failing to provide adequate community-based living options to mentally retarded plaintiffs, were subject to suit under *Ex parte Young*.[448.40] Circuit Judge Garza dissented in part on the ground that an *Ex parte Young* suit is not permitted except when the federal statute allegedly violated is constitutional as applied against the state.[448.41]

In *Klingler v. Director, Department of Revenue*,[448.42] the Eighth Circuit held that *Ex parte Young* allowed ADA Title II claims for declaratory and injunctive relief against a state fee for placards allowing use of accessible parking, but denied monetary damages.[448.43]

In *Carten v. Kent State University*,[448.44] the court of appeals held that a Title II ADA claim for prospective injunctive relief qualified for an *Ex parte Young* exception to Eleventh Amendment immunity.[448.45]

In *Koslow v. Commonwealth of Pennsylvania*,[448.46] the court of appeals held that the Eleventh Amendment did not bar injunctive relief against a state official under Title II of the ADA, under the *Ex parte Young* doctrine.[448.47]

[448.1] 343 F.3d 1036 (9th Cir. 2003).
[448.2] *Id.* at 1041 (listing factors).
[448.3] *Id.* at 1044.
[448.4] *Id.* at 1049.
[448.5] *Id.* at 1050.
[448.6] *Id.* at 1051.
[448.7] 301 F.3d 13 (1st Cir. 2002).
[448.8] *Id.* at 20.
[448.9] 309 F.3d 1203 (9th Cir. 2002).
[448.10] 279 F.3d 1167 (9th Cir. 2002).
[448.11] 303 F.3d 1039 (9th Cir. 2002).
[448.12] 279 F.3d 1167 (9th Cir. 2002).
[448.13] 303 F.3d at 1050-51.
[448.14] 278 F.3d 1020 (10th Cir. 2001).
[448.15] 306 F.3d 203 (4th Cir. 2002).
[448.16] *Id.* at 214-15.
[448.17] 275 F.3d 315 (3d Cir. 2001).
[448.18] *Id.* at 322.
[448.19] 303 F.3d 1137 (9th Cir. 2002).
[448.20] *Id.* at 1140-44.
[448.21] 302 F.3d 1200 (10th Cir. 2002).
[448.22] *Id.* at 1206.
[448.23] 271 F.3d 812 (9th Cir. 2001).
[448.24] *Id.* at 819.
[448.25] 302 F.3d 161 (3d Cir. 2002).
[448.26] *Id.* at 167.
[448.27] 325 F.3d 609, 612 (5th Cir. 2003).
[448.28] 324 F.3d 906 (7th Cir. 2003).
[448.29] *Id.* at 909-10.
[448.30] *Id.* at 912 (citing 42 U.S.C. § 2000d-7(a)(1)).
[448.31] *Id.* at 912.
[448.32] 328 F.3d 1181 (9th Cir. 2003).
[448.33] *Id.* at 1184.
[448.34] Lane v. Tennessee, 315 F.3d 680, 683 (6th Cir. 2003). *Accord*, Angel v. Kentucky, 314 F.3d 262 (6th Cir. 2003), citing Popovich v. Cuyahoga County Court of Common Pleas, 276

F.3d 808, 811 (6th Cir. 2002) (Congress did not properly abrogate Eleventh Amendment immunity in equal protection claims brought under Title II of ADA but did properly do so in due process claims brought under same title).

[448.35] 324 F.3d 906 (7th Cir. 2003).

[448.36] *Id.* at 913 (citing Ex parte Young, 209 U.S. 123 (1908)).

[448.37] 213 F.3d 344 (7th Cir. 2000).

[448.38] 324 F.3d at 912-13. *See also* Carten v. Kent State Univ., 282 F.3d 391 (6th Cir. 2002); Miranda B v. Kitzhaber, 328 F.3d 1181 (9th Cir. 2003) "an official who violates Title II of the ADA does not represent 'the state' for purposes of the Eleventh Amendment, yet he or she nevertheless may be held responsible in an official capacity for violating Title II, which by its terms applies only to 'public entities' " (quoting Carten v. Kent State Univ., 282 F.3d 391, 396 (6th Cir. 2002), and citing Bruggeman v. Blagojevich, 324 F.3d 906 (7th Cir. 2003), and Randolph v. Rodgers, 253 F.3d 342, 348 (8th Cir. 2001), as agreeing.

[448.39] 381 F.3d 407 (5th Cir. 2004).

[448.40] *Id.* at 414 (citing cases reaching same conclusion from Second, Sixth, Seventh, Eighth, and Ninth Circuits).

[448.41] *Id.* at 417-18 (Garza, J., concurring in part and dissenting in part).

[448.42] 281 F.3d 776 (8th Cir. 2002).

[448.43] *Id.* at 777.

[448.44] 282 F.3d 391 (6th Cir. 2002).

[448.45] *Id.* at 396.

[448.46] 302 F.3d 161 (3d Cir. 2002).

[448.47] *Id.* at 179.

CHAPTER 6

REQUIREMENTS UNDER TITLE III FOR PUBLIC ACCOMMODATIONS AND SERVICES OPERATED BY PRIVATE ENTITIES

§ 6.01 INTRODUCTION

Page 389, add at end of first paragraph:

See Christopher M. Parent, *Casey Martin's Four-Year Struggle with the PGA Tour*, 9 Sports Law. J. 57, 62 n. 25 (2002) (citing this book on purpose of Title III).

§ 6.02 COVERAGE

[A] Scope

Page 394, add after carryover paragraph:

In *Disabled Rights Action Committee v. Las Vegas Events, Inc.*,[35.1] the court of appeals reversed dismissal of a complaint against the owners and operators of a rodeo event. The promoters and operators of a rodeo staged in facilities owned by a university had potential liability under the public accommodations provisions of the ADA.[35.2] The appeals court also held that the university owner was not an indispensable party under Fed. R. Civ. P. 19(a).[35.3] The university was not subject to Title III.

[35.1] 375 F.3d 861 (9th Cir. 2004).
[35.2] *Id.* at 873.
[35.3] *Id.* at 879.

[B] Case Law on Coverage

Page 396, add after first full paragraph:

In *Levinger v. Mercy Medical Center*,[45.1] the court of appeals affirmed summary judgment and judgment on a jury verdict against a physician who claimed a hospital violated the ADA when it suspended his privileges after his license to practice medicine was suspended. The court of appeals held that Title I of the ADA does not protect independent contractors, but it went on to find that Title III of ADA allowed the physician to litigate whether the hospital's regarding him as disabled motivated its denial of hospital privileges; access to its facility; and the benefits of services, programs, and activities.

[45.1] 75 P.3d 1202 (Idaho 2003).

Page 397, add at end of first paragraph, containing note 54 reference:

In *Rendon v. Valleycrest Productions, Ltd.*,[54.1] the court of appeals held that an automated touchtone hotline linked with a television competition was a place of public accommodation under Title III of the ADA. Plaintiffs complained that they could not participate in the competition either because they were deaf and could not hear the questions on the automated system or because they could not move their fingers rapidly enough to record their answers on their telephone keypads.[54.2]

[54.1] 294 F.3d 1279 (11th Cir. 2002).
[54.2] *Id.* at 1280-81.

Page 399, add at end of section:

In *Spector v. Norwegian Cruise Line, Ltd.*,[68.1] the court of appeals, reversing the district court in part, utilized the rule that domestic law applies to foreign vessels entering the United States only if there is an affirmative intention by Congress clearly expressed and held that Title III of the ADA does not apply to foreign-flag cruise vessels.[68.2] The court declined to give effect to opinions to the contrary expressed in DOJ and DOT technical assistance manuals and public comments, which it found were not entitled to *Chevron* deference because they lacked the force of law, unlike rules and adjudicatory decisions.[68.3]

[68.1] 356 F.3d 641 (5th Cir. 2004).
[68.2] *Id.* at 644.
[68.3] *Id.* at 650.

[D] Individual and Vicarious Liability

Page 399, add following first paragraph:

In *Emerson v. Thiel College*,[72.1] however, the United States Court of Appeals for the Third Circuit rejected the proposition that individuals may be liable under Title III of the ADA,[72.2] because the individual defendants did not "operate" the university that had obligations under Title III. It also concluded that individual defendants could not be liable under the Rehabilitation Act.[72.3] It reasoned that the college was the recipient of federal financial assistance, and not the individual defendants.[72.4]

In *Lentini v. California Center for the Arts*,[72.5] the court of appeals affirmed a judgment against individual supervisory personnel who excluded a quadriplegic Title III plaintiff's service animal. It held that persons having authority over operations qualify as "any person who ... operates a place of public accommodation" under 42 U.S.C. § 12182(a).[72.6]

[72.1] 296 F.3d 184 (3d Cir. 2002).
[72.2] *Id.* at 188-89.
[72.3] *Id.* at 190.
[72.4] *Id.*
[72.5] 370 F.3d 837 (9th Cir. 2004).
[72.6] *Id.* at 849.

§ 6.03 BASIC PROHIBITIONS AGAINST DISCRIMINATION

[B] Obligation to Modify Policies, Practices, and Procedures

Page 403, add at end of note 88:

See Julie L. Livergood, *Walking with Tradition v. Riding into Tomorrow:* Olinger v. United States Golf Association, 51 DePaul L. Rev. 125, 136 n. 77 (2001) (citing this book).

Page 405, add at end of subsection:

In *Dudley v. Hannaford Brothers Co.*,[94.1] the court of appeals, agreeing with the district court, held that a store selling alcoholic beverages was required by Title III of the ADA to modify its usual policy of not permitting the store manager to reconsider a clerk's refusal to sell alcoholic beverages when the clerk thought a patron was intoxicated. The facts of the case showed enforcement of the no-reconsideration policy even after a disabled plaintiff, whose symptoms made him appear intoxicated, demonstrated to the manager that he was disabled and not intoxicated.[94.2]

In *Lentini v. California Center for the Arts*,[94.3] the court of appeals affirmed judgment for a quadriplegic plaintiff who claimed that her service dog was excluded from a public facility for the arts. The court of appeals held that the defendant was obligated to make an exception to its written policies to admit service animals, and more particularly that "the center's policies, practices and procedures may not exclude a service animal who has made a noise on a previous occasion, even if such behavior is disruptive, if the noise was made and intended to serve as a means of communication for the benefit of the disabled owner or if the behavior would otherwise be acceptable to the center if engaged [in] by humans."[94.4] The court of appeals rejected the defendants' argument that such a requirement would require a fundamental alteration in the services offered by the defendant.[94.5]

In *Webster Bank v. Oakley*,[94.6] the Connecticut Supreme Court held that the public accommodations provisions of Title III of the ADA do not require alteration of standard foreclosure terms of mortgage loan agreements to accommodate the special circumstances of a borrower who is mentally disabled. It held that the ADA requires equal access to services such as mortgage loans, but does not regulate the content of such services.[94.7]

[94.1] 333 F.3d 299 (1st Cir. 2002).
[94.2] *Id.* at 310.
[94.3] 370 F.3d 837 (9th Cir. 2004).
[94.4] *Id.* at 842 (quoting district court).
[94.5] *Id.* at 845-46.
[94.6] 830 A.2d 139 (Conn. 2003).
[94.7] *Id.* at 161.

[D] Removal of Physical Barriers

[3] Places of Entertainment

Page 410, add at end of subsection:

In *Oregon Paralyzed Veterans v. Regal Cinemas, Inc.*,[128.1] the court of appeals, reversing the district court, upheld the validity of the Department of Justice's interpretation of its own regulation stating that movie theaters are obligated by Title III of the ADA to provide comparable lines of sight for wheelchair-bound and nonwheelchair-bound moviegoers.[128.2] It held that the DOJ interpretation was reasonable and entitled to deference.[128.3]

In *United States v. Hoyts Cinemas Corp.*,[128.4] the court of appeals, partially reversing summary judgment in favor of the government and against movie theater chains, nevertheless agreed that movie theaters must provide disabled patrons with nondiscriminatory viewing angles as well as unobstructed lines of sight.[128.5] Nevertheless, it found that the district court had not justified a finding that required stadium seating rather than slope seating. It found that the district judge's reliance on judicial notice to establish the preferences of movie theater patrons did not qualify under Fed. R. Evid. 201.[128.6]

In *Fortyune v. American Multi-Cinema, Inc.*,[128.7] the court of appeals affirmed summary judgment on behalf of a wheelchair-bound movie patron based on a movie theatre's refusal to remove a non-companion patron from the seat reserved for "companions" of disabled patrons. It found that the plaintiff, a quadriplegic, cannot and does not attend movies without his wife or another companion, and therefore the presence of his wife was a condition precedent to the plaintiff's enjoyment of the services and facilities provided by the theatre. The court held that the theatre was obligated to remove unqualified persons sitting in a companion seat when that seat was necessary to a disabled person's enjoyment of the services provided by the theatre.

It is not altogether clear from the court's discussion why it was necessary for the plaintiff's companion to sit next to him as opposed to sitting somewhere else in the theatre.

In *Chaffin v. Kansas State Fair Board*,[128.8] the court of appeals affirmed an injunction compelling the Kansas State Fair to provide better access for wheelchair patrons. The court rejected the argument that use of a special wheelchair section by wheelchair-bound patrons was sufficient on evidence that the view from the wheelchair section often was blocked by standing patrons, that users of this section could not get to restrooms unless many other wheelchair users were moved, and that users were climbed over, stepped on, and bumped into by other attendees.[128.9]

[128.1] 339 F.3d 1126 (9th Cir. 2003).
[128.2] *Id.* at 1129 (upholding part of ADAAG, 28 C.F.R. pt. 36, app. A, § 4.33.3).
[128.3] 339 F.3d at 1133.
[128.4] 380 F.3d 558 (1st Cir. 2004).
[128.5] *Id.* at 567.
[128.6] *Id.* at 570.
[128.7] 364 F.3d 1075 (9th Cir. 2004).
[128.8] 348 F.3d 850 (10th Cir. 2003).
[128.9] *Id.* at 854.

Page 413, add new subsection:

[7] DOJ Regulations

In *Oregon Paralyzed Veterans v. Regal Cinemas, Inc.*,[147.1] the court of appeals, reversing the district court, upheld the validity of the Department of Justice's interpretation of its own regulation stating that movie theatres are obligated by Title III of the ADA to provide comparable lines of sight for wheelchair-bound and nonwheelchair-bound moviegoers.[147.2] It held that the DOJ interpretation was reasonable and entitled to deference.[147.3]

[147.1] 339 F.3d 1126 (9th Cir. 2003).
[147.2] *Id.* at 1129 (upholding part of ADAAG, 28 C.F.R. pt. 36, app. A, § 4.33.3).
[147.3] 339 F.3d at 1133.

[F] Maintaining Facilities in Operable Condition

Page 417, add at end of subsection:

In *Foley v. City of Lafayette*,[187.1] the court of appeals affirmed summary judgment for a municipality, finding that a temporarily inoperative elevator necessary to reach a train platform did not constitute a violation of the ADA. The evidence showed that the municipality took reasonable efforts in the middle of severe winter weather conditions to repair an inoperative elevator.[187.2]

[187.1] 359 F.3d 925 (7th Cir. 2004).
[187.2] *Id.* at 930.

§ 6.09 INSURANCE

Page 433, add after third full paragraph in section:

The Sixth Circuit agreed, in *Kolling v. Blue Cross & Blue Shield of Michigan*,[266.1] with the lower court that "[a] benefit plan offered by an employer, like those healthcare benefit plans covering the appellants in the present case, is not goods offered by a place of public accommodation. The appellants did not obtain their healthcare coverage directly from Blue Cross Michigan nor did they buy their respective policies from an insurance office. Rather, they obtained their benefits through their employer. Thus, there is no nexus between the disparity in benefits and the services which Blue Cross Michigan offers to the public from its office. A public accommodation is limited to a physical place and cannot be applied to the contents of employer-furnished benefit plans."[266.2]

[266.1] 318 F.3d 715, 716 (6th Cir. 2003) (finding Parker v. Metropolitan Life Ins. Co., 121 F.3d 1006 (6th Cir. 1997), dispositive in requiring dismissal of plaintiff's claims for disparity benefits provided under employer healthcare plan for speech therapy).

[266.2] 318 F.3d at 716.

CHAPTER 7

TRANSPORTATION AND COMMUNICATIONS SYSTEM REQUIREMENTS UNDER TITLE IV

§ 7.05 DOT REGULATIONS

Page 463, add at end of section:

In *Keirnan v. Utah Transit Authority*,[86.1] the court of appeals agreed with the district court that a wheelchair-bound plaintiff had shown that the first three factors for a preliminary injunction favored the plaintiff, in her claim that a rule change by the state transit authority (excluding oversized wheelchairs such as the plaintiff's from paratransit services) violated Title II of the ADA:

> The first factor, that "[she] will suffer irreparable injury unless the injunction issues," has been demonstrated by Appellant in her briefs and at the hearing. She will lose the ability to attend religious services and medical appointments. She will also lose contact with friends and family. Appellant and other paratransit riders affected by the service change will be incapable of living their lives in the independent fashion to which they have become accustomed. Additionally, because Appellant is not alleging intentional discrimination or out-of-pocket expenses, damages might not be available should a court later find in her favor on the merits.
>
> The second factor, that "the threatened injury . . . outweighs whatever damage the proposed injunction may cause the opposing party," also supports Appellant's position. Surely Appellant will suffer a great deal more at the loss of her independence than UTA will suffer in continuing to provide service to Appellant and others as it has done for years. Additionally, while UTA stresses linkage concerns, UTA has offered no documented information regarding the severity of these concerns. Furthermore, this is UTA's sole offer of negative impact on it if a preliminary injunction were to issue.
>
> * * *
>
> "The third factor, which takes into account the public interest, also weighs in Appellant's favor. A preliminary injunction would simply maintain the status quo pending a final determination on the merits. Because UTA has been providing this service without any documented detriment to the

public, we fail to see how a temporary extension would harm the public interest in any capacity. Appellee is unable to point to anything adverse to the public interest should the preliminary injunction issue."[86.2]

The court of appeals agreed, however, with the district court that there was no reasonable expectation of success on the merits, even under the more lenient standard for probability of success when the first three requirements for injunctive relief tilt in the plaintiff's favor; "the mov[ant] need only show questions going to the merit so serious, substantial, difficult, and doubtful, as to make them a fair ground for litigation."[86.3] It held that the DOT regulation requiring that only common wheelchairs be transported was entitled to deference.[86.4]

[86.1] 339 F.3d 1217 (10th Cir. 2003).
[86.2] *Id.* at 1220-21 (internal citations omitted).
[86.3] *Id.* (internal quotations omitted).
[86.4] *Id.* at 1222-23 (quoting and citing 49 C.F.R. § 37.165(b)).

§ 7.08 BUS, VAN, AND OTHER NONRAIL TRANSPORTATION SYSTEMS

Page 468, add at end of section:

In *Anderson v. Rochester-Genesee Regional Transportation Authority*,[140.1] the court of appeals held that a regional transportation authority violated the ADA because its paratransit service required advance notice up to 14 days and otherwise imposed significant restrictions and waiting lists for access to the service. It held that the DOT regulations require paratransit service providers "to plan to meet 100% of the demand for next day ride requests."[140.2]

[140.1] 337 F.3d 201 (2d Cir. 2003).
[140.2] 337 F.3d at 212.

CHAPTER 8
REHABILITATION ACT OF 1973

§ 8.02 RELATIONSHIP BETWEEN REHABILITATION ACT AND ADA

[B] Statutory Differences

Page 486, add after second paragraph, containing note 46 reference:

Section 504 of the Rehabilitation Act applies, under precedent in some circuits, to employers with fewer than 15 employees. In *Schrader v. Fred A. Ray, M.D., P.C.*,[46.1] for example, the Tenth Circuit, reviewing conflicting case law from other courts, held that the 1992 amendments to the Rehabilitation Act were not intended to apply the ADA definition of employer to that Act. Accordingly, employers with fewer than 15 employees are subject to liability under Section 504 of the Rehabilitation Act.[46.2] The employer waived any argument that it was not the intended beneficiary of federal funds by failing to argue it in the lower court.[46.3]

[46.1] 296 F.3d 968 (10th Cir. 2002).
[46.2] *Id.* at 972-73.
[46.3] *Id.* at 975.

[C] Statutory Convergence

Page 490, add at end of subsection:

In *Dyrek v. Garbey*,[77.1] an air traffic controller sued the FAA under the Rehabilitation Act for disqualifying him from his controller position because of his diabetes. The court of appeals held that the standards under the ADA were appropriate in determining whether a violation of the Rehabilitation Act had occurred.[77.2] The court of appeals failed to find pretext in the FAA's application of its own rules which required specific evidence that a controller's diabetes was under control.[77.3]

[77.1] 334 F.3d 590 (7th Cir. 2003).
[77.2] *Id.* at 597 n.3.
[77.3] *Id.* at 599.

§ 8.12 SOLE-REASON REQUIREMENT

Page 507, add after carryover paragraph:

In *Soledad v. United States Department of Treasury*,[192.1] the court of appeals affirmed a district court's conclusion that it erroneously instructed a Rehabilitation Act jury that it could find for a plaintiff "because of" the plaintiff's disability, rather, "solely because of" the disability. It disagreed with the district court, however, and found that the plaintiff had adduced sufficient evidence to justify a reasonable jury in finding "solely because of" disability, and remanded. The court of appeals explicitly rejected the argument that 1992 amendments to the Rehabilitation Act changed the sole reasons standard.[192.2]

[192.1] 304 F.3d 500 (5th Cir. 2002).
[192.2] *Id.* at 505.

§ 8.13 CONSTITUTIONALITY OF CLAIMS AGAINST STATES AND THEIR INSTRUMENTALITIES

Page 511, add before first full paragraph:

In *Nieves-Marquez v. Puerto Rico*,[219.1] the court of appeals held that the Commonwealth of Puerto Rico waived its sovereign immunity against Rehabilitation Act liability by accepting federal funding.[219.2]

In *Doe v. Nebraska*,[219.3] the court of appeals rejected an argument by the State of Nebraska that the financial inducement offered by Congress to Nebraska's social services programs was so great that Nebraska was coerced into accepting the federal funding, and thus waiving its immunity to suit under Section 504 of the Rehabilitation Act.[219.4] The court held that Nebraska knowingly and validly waived its sovereign immunity under Section 504 of the Rehabilitation Act by accepting federal funds.[219.5]

[219.1] 353 F.3d 108 (1st Cir. 2003).
[219.2] *Id.* at 128-29.
[219.3] 345 F.3d 593 (8th Cir. 2003).
[219.4] *Id.* at 598 (characterizing argument).
[219.5] *Id.* at 604.

Page 511, add at end of section:

In *Barbour v. Washington Metropolitan Area Transit Authority*,[222.1] the court of appeals held that the statutory waiver language was sufficiently explicit and that the transit authority knowingly waived its Eleventh Amendment immunity by accepting funds. The court also rejected constitutional challenges to the statutory waiver.

In *Miranda B v. Kitzhaber*,[222.2] the court of appeals held that because the state voluntarily accepted federal funds under § 504, it had waived its immunity from a Rehabilitation Act suit under the Eleventh Amendment.[222.3] It also allowed *Ex Parte Young* liability for state officials. "Under *Ex Parte Young*, a suit against a state official in his or her official capacity is not a suit against the official but rather is a suit against the official's office." Such claims thus fall within the scope of the liability imposed by Title II of the ADA against "public entities."[222.4]

In *Douglas v. California Department of Youth Authority*,[222.5] the court of appeals held that California waived its sovereign immunity against Rehabilitation Act claims by accepting federal funds under that Act.[222.6]

In *Koslow v. Commonwealth of Pennsylvania*,[222.7] the court of appeals held that Pennsylvania waived its immunity to Rehabilitation Act claims by accepting federal funding for its Department of Corrections.[222.8]

In *Lovell v. Chandler*,[222.9] the court of appeals held that a state's acceptance of Rehabilitation Act funds waived the state's Eleventh Amendment immunity for Rehabilitation Act claims. It noted that *Garrett* expressly reserved the question whether Title II validly abrogates Eleventh Amendment immunity and adhered to its decision in *Hason v. Medical Board of California*,[222.10] that Title II claims may be brought against states.[222.11]

The court also rejected the state's waiver argument:

> The State also argues that its acceptance of federal RA funds did not constitute a valid waiver of its Eleventh Amendment immunity as to claims under § 504 of the RA. But our decision in Douglas v. California Department of Youth Authority, 271 F.3d 812 (9th Cir. 2001), forecloses that argument. In Douglas, decided after Garrett, we reaffirmed Clark's alternative holding that Congress validly conditioned a state's receipt of RA funding on its consent to waive its Eleventh Amendment immunity from suit under § 504 of the RA.[6] See id. at 820-21; see also Vinson v. Thomas, 288 F.3d 1145, 1151 (9th Cir. 2002). It is uncontested that the State accepted federal RA funds.
>
> [6] The amended Rehabilitation Act provides, "A State shall not be immune under the Eleventh Amendment of the Constitution of the United States from suit in Federal court for a violation of section 504 of the Rehabilitation Act of 1973." 42 U.S.C. § 2000d-7.
>
> Finally, we reject the State's argument that Congress exceeded its Spending Clause powers and the conditions set forth in South Dakota v. Dole, 483 U.S. 203, 107 S. Ct. 2793, 97 L. Ed. 2d 171 (1987), when it conditioned the receipt of RA funds on a waiver of sovereign immunity. The Act's tying arrangement does not violate Dole's "relatedness" requirement and is not unduly coercive. Congress has a strong interest in ensuring that federal funds are not used in a discriminatory manner and in holding states responsible when they violate funding conditions. The term "program or activity" in section 504, moreover, does not encompass all the activities of the State. Instead, it only covers all the activities of the department or the

agency receiving federal funds. See 29 U.S.C. § 794(b)(1)(A); Jim C. v. United States, 235 F.3d 1079, 1082 (8th Cir. 2000) (en banc). If a state does not wish to relinquish immunity, it could follow the "simple expedient of not yielding." Oklahoma v. U.S. Civil Serv. Comm'n, 330 U.S. 127, 143-44, 67 S. Ct. 544, 91 L. Ed. 794 (1947) (internal quotation marks omitted). There is no showing of the type of "extraordinary circumstances," California v. United States, 104 F.3d 1086, 1092 (9th Cir. 1997), required by our case law that would allow us to hold that Congress has exceeded constitutional boundaries.

We therefore agree with our sister circuit, see Jim C., 235 F.3d at 1081-82, that the Rehabilitation Act is a valid exercise of Congress's spending power. The Eleventh Amendment is thus not a bar to Lovell and Delmendo's § 504 claims against the State. See Vinson, 288 F.3d at 1151; Douglas, 271 F.3d at 820-21.[222.12]

[222.1] 374 F.3d 1161 (D.C. Cir. 2004).
[222.2] 328 F.3d 1181 (9th Cir. 2003).
[222.3] *Id.* at 1186.
[222.4] *Id.* at 1188.
[222.5] 271 F.3d 812 (9th Cir. 2001).
[222.6] *Id.* at 819.
[222.7] 302 F.3d 161 (3d Cir. 2002).
[222.8] *Id.* at 167.
[222.9] 303 F.3d 1039 (9th Cir. 2002).
[222.10] 279 F.3d 1167 (9th Cir. 2002).
[222.11] 303 F.3d at 1050-51.
[222.12] *Id.* at 1051.

CHAPTER 9
PROCEDURAL AND EVIDENTIARY ISSUES

§ 9.04 PARTIES TO ADA CLAIMS

[B] Independent Contractors as Plaintiffs Under Title I

Page 526, add note[54.1] reference at end of subsection and new note 54.1 text:

54.1 *See also* § 3.02[D].

[D] Standing

Page 527, add following first paragraph:

In *Access Now, Inc. v. Southwest Airlines Co.*,[61.1] the plaintiffs, an advocacy organization for the blind, unsuccessfully claimed that Southwest Airlines' Web site was a place of public accommodation. The district court dismissed, and the court of appeals declined to hear, the plaintiffs' new theory on appeal that the Web site was a connection to a travel service, which was a place of public accommodation. It dismissed the appeal.

In *Steir v. Girl Scouts*,[61.2] the court of appeals affirmed the district court's determination that a former Girl Scout lacked standing to seek injunctive relief under Title III of the ADA. Because there was evidence that the plaintiff intended to return to the Girl Scouts, "she thus faces no threat of future harm of discrimination from the defendants and therefore lack[s] standing to obtain injunctive relief."[61.3]

In *Tandy v. City of Wichita*,[61.4] the court of appeals held that disabled bus passengers had standing to seek prospective relief against a municipal bus system, based on a stated intention to continue to use the bus system in the future, combined with concrete past incidents in which her travels were delayed because of equipment malfunctions.[61.5] It also held that "testers"—persons intending to use the bus system only to determine its compliance with the ADA—also had standing.[61.6] It also held that several of the plaintiffs had standing to seek damages because of concrete allegations of past injury due to violations of the ADA.[61.7]

In *National Alliance for Mentally Ill v. Board of County Commissioners*,[61.8] the court of appeals held that one individual lacked standing to sue for denial of funding for mental health residential treatment facilities, because he had merely alleged that he "might" use such facilities. Two other individuals lacked standing to litigate on behalf of the first individual, and an association lacked standing based on its failure to provide any details about lost resources because of the defendants' violations of the ADA.[61.9]

In *Bird v. Lewis & Clark College*,[61.10] the court of appeals denied standing to seek an injunction requiring a college to change its overseas programs to a paraplegic plaintiff who had already graduated and did not allege that she planned to return as a student or participate in the overseas programs.[61.11] On the other hand, it held that the same plaintiff had standing to seek an injunction compelling a change of her grades.[61.12]

In *MX Group, Inc. v. City of Covington*,[61.13] the court of appeals, finding Second Circuit precedent persuasive, held that a drug treatment entity had standing to assert violation of Title II of the ADA on its own behalf when it was denied a license to operate.[61.14]

In *Discovery House v. Consolidated City of Indianapolis*,[61.15] the court of appeals held that Discovery House, a for-profit corporation that operates drug addiction rehabilitation programs, lacked standing to seek damages for lost profits due to delays in approving the siting of a drug rehab facility, delays that were obviated by a state court decision upholding Discovery House's zoning claim. The court of appeals readily accepted the proposition that organizations such as Discovery House have standing to seek injunctive relief against practices that violate the ADA, but distinguished its claim for profit-related damages, which would not obviate any ADA violation that already had been obviated by a state court decision. It also rejected Discovery House's claim under Section 1983 for an equal protection violation, finding that Discovery House was unable to adduce evidence of discriminatory intent, a necessary element of the constitutional claim since no fundamental right was involved.

61.1 385 F.3d 1324 (11th Cir. 2004).
61.2 383 F.3d 7 (1st Cir. 2004).
61.3 *Id.* at 15.
61.4 380 F.3d 1277 (10th Cir. 2004).
61.5 *Id.* at 1284.
61.6 *Id.* at 1287.
61.7 *Id.* at 1288.
61.8 376 F.3d 1292 (11th Cir. 2004).
61.9 *Id.* at 1275-96.
61.10 303 F.3d 1015 (9th Cir. 2002).
61.11 *Id.* at 1020.
61.12 *Id.*
61.13 293 F.3d 326 (6th Cir. 2002).
61.14 *Id.* at 333-34.
61.15 319 F.3d 277 (7th Cir. 2003).

Page 528, add at end of subsection:

In *Pickern v. Holiday Quality Foods, Inc.*,[71.1] the court of appeals reversed the district court and held that a wheelchair-bound Title III plaintiff need not engage in the futile gesture of seeking access to a place of public accommodation he knew to have architectural barriers before suing for an injunction to compel removal of those barriers.[71.2]

McInnis-Misenor v. Maine Medical Center[71.3] involved an ADA Title III lawsuit brought by a wheelchair-bound woman and her husband anticipating that she might become pregnant and would need wheelchair access to the defendant's medical center. When her first child was delivered at the medical center, she was unable to transfer to the most appropriate part of the hospital because it was wheelchair inaccessible. The court framed the issue in terms of whether Ms. McInnis was "about to be subjected to discrimination," under 42 U.S.C. § 12188(a)(1), a question it determined to be congruent "with the usual prudential analysis as to whether McInnis-Misenor's claims are too contingent and premature."[71.4] It extinguished cases in which an ADA plaintiff had not returned for services because of the existence of architectural barriers. Even though it found the legal issues simple and fairly well crystallized, it concluded that the case was not fit for review, because a judicial decision was not unavoidable, since the present case depended on a chain of contingencies.[71.5]

In *Bruggeman ex rel. Bruggeman v. Blagojevich*,[71.6] the court of appeals, in a decision written by Circuit Judge Posner, faulted the district court for dismissing on standing grounds:

> The district judge ruled that none of these provisions [of the federal Medicaid statute, the Rehabilitation Act, and the Americans with Disabilities Act] entitled the plaintiffs to what they were seeking and that therefore the plaintiffs had not been injured by a violation of the statute and so lacked standing to sue. This is a misunderstanding of standing. A plaintiff has standing to sue—that is, he can invoke the jurisdiction of the court—if he is tangibly, materially, injured by the conduct of the defendant that he claims is unlawful and if the relief he seeks would redress the injury in whole or in part and thus confer a material benefit on him. Of course if his claim has no merit, then he has not been injured by any wrongful conduct of the defendant; but if the consequence were that he lacked standing, then every decision in favor of a defendant would be a decision that the court lacked jurisdiction, entitling the plaintiff to start over in another court. The district court decided that the plaintiffs have no right to live in an ICF/DD that is near their parents' home and so the defendants' refusal to adopt a plan that would create vacancies in ICF/DDs near the parents' home did not invade a legal right of the plaintiffs and so did not cause them an injury for which they are entitled to redress. This was a ruling on the merits, having nothing to do with jurisdiction.

> Not that standing and the merits are always or in this case clearly distinct. The more extreme a plaintiff's claim, the more likely he is to have standing to prosecute it; the more moderate his claim, the less likely he is to have standing. If all that the plaintiffs were seeking was a plan entitling them to reimbursement for the expense of residing in an ICF/DD anywhere in Illinois, they would, we may assume, have a legally sound claim; but they would have no standing to maintain it because there are ample vacancies in the southern part of the state, and so the absence of a plan would not impair any right that they claimed under the Medicaid statute. But if they claim a right to a wider choice of ICF/DD vacancies than the defendants are willing to permit the planning agency to authorize, then they are likely to have standing, because the absence of the plan they seek is a denial of such an entitlement. Although their brief could be clearer on the point, it seems that they are indeed pressing this more extreme claim. The district court rejected the claim, but that was a rejection on the merits inaccurately described as a ruling that the plaintiffs lack standing.
>
> But notice that we said only that the plaintiffs are *likely* to have standing; the doubt implicit in such a formulation arises from the tenuousness of the relation between the relief sought in the lawsuit and an actual benefit to the plaintiffs if they prevail. They seek merely a plan, which might not lead to an increase in the ICF/DD capacity in their immediate geographical area. Even if it did, they might not benefit. An increase in supply would evoke an increase in demand, since the plaintiffs are not the only developmentally disabled adults in northern Illinois whose parents would like to place them in a nearby ICF/DD and this is not a class action. So the plan the plaintiffs seek might not actually increase the vacancy rate. Meanwhile, there are *some* vacancies in ICF/DDs located near the plaintiffs' homes and for all that appears the plaintiffs will find places in an existing such facility long before the plan they seek would enable them to find a place in a new facility. The potential benefit to them from the relief that they seek thus is speculative.
>
> But not so speculative as to negate standing, which is a matter of probabilities rather than certainties. *North Shore Gas Co. v. EPA*, 930 F.2d 1239, 1242 (7th Cir.1991). The suit seeks to remove a logjam that is preventing the creation of facilities desired by the plaintiffs, and if the likelihood of success is conjectural so is the argument for failure based on the possibility that any new facilities will be overwhelmed by other applicants.[71.7]

Reaching the merits, the court of appeals held that the Civil Rights Act provision that "a state shall not be immune under the Eleventh Amendment of the Constitution of the United States from suit in federal court for a violation of Section 504 of the Rehabilitation Act,"[71.8] combined with the state's acceptance of federal financial assistance, which waived its Eleventh Amendment immunity, allowed maintenance of the suit under the Rehabilitation Act against the state.[71.9]

71.1 293 F.3d 1133 (9th Cir. 2002).
71.2 *Id.* at 1136.
71.3 319 F.3d 63 (1st Cir. 2003).
71.4 *Id.* at 69.
71.5 *Id.* at 72.
71.6 324 F.3d 906 (7th Cir. 2003).
71.7 *Id.* at 909-10.
71.8 *Id.* at 912 (citing 42 U.S.C. § 2000d-7 (a)(1)).
71.9 *Id.* at 912.

[E] Litigation by Public Agencies

Page 529, add after first full paragraph:

In *EEOC v. WH Braum, Inc.*,[77.1] the court of appeals, reversing the district court, held that the EEOC was entitled to seek monetary relief on behalf of an ADA claimant whose earlier individual suit had been dismissed. The court rejected the district court's reasoning that state limitations barred the individual from refiling her federal claim and that her inability to do so foreclosed the EEOC from seeking monetary relief on her behalf.[77.2]

77.1 347 F.3d 1192 (10th Cir. 2003).
77.2 *Id.* at 1198.

[F] Class Actions and Other Representative Litigation

Page 531, add at end of section:

Scrutiny of class certification is especially important in consent decree litigation. In *Molski v. Gleich*,[91.1] a panel of the Ninth Circuit withdrew its earlier opinion[91.2] and reversed class certification supporting a consent decree that compelled ARCO to undertake certain accessibility enhancements at its locations where mobility-impaired individuals had been denied access, to pay monetary damages to the named plaintiff, to pay class counsel fees, and to make donations to eight disability rights organizations. Settlement negotiations had occurred after Molski filed an individual lawsuit and notified ARCO that he intended to amend the complaint to include class allegations.[91.3] After agreement on basic terms of the settlement had been reached, Molski filed an amended complaint, presenting class allegations and a motion for approval of the proposed consent decree and certification of the class. The district court ordered that notice be issued to the putative class members by posting notices near the cash window of each gas station or mini market owned or operated by ARCO; publication of a notice in the *Los Angeles Times*, the *San Diego Union Tribune*, the *Sacramento Bee*, and the *San Francisco Chronicle/Examiner*; and mailing the notice to more than 80 disability rights organizations in California.[91.4] After the notices appeared, three dozen objectors filed, many objecting to the release of state statutory damages and others objecting to the adequacy of the injunctive relief provided in the proposed decree.

Preliminarily, the court of appeals rejected an apparent effort by the district court to reinstate the right of class members to bring lawsuits for actual damages. "[A] District Court cannot unilaterally modify the provisions of a consent decree through its order of proving the proposed decree. The settlement must stand or fall in its entirety."[91.5] The court rejected the argument that the district court potentially violated due process by certifying a mandatory class (no opt out) because money damages were the prevalent form of relief rather than injunctive relief. Recognizing that Federal Rule 23 (b) disfavors mandatory classes when monetary damages are at the center of the case, it concluded that injunctive relief was the predominant form of relief sought by the class and, "particularly in light of the fact that claims of physical injury were preserved, the injunctive relief appeared to be the primary goal in the litigation and the settlement agreement. Thus, we hold that the District Court did not abuse its discretion in certifying a Rule 23 (b)(2) class."[91.6] On the other hand, it found that the district court erred by failing to afford notice and right to opt out as to the claims for treble damages.[91.7]

Furthermore, the court of appeals found that the class notice was inadequate, both in its language, which failed to make it sufficiently clear that class members would release substantial damages, and as to the methods used. "Because the class members have the right to opt out, they also had the right to the best notice practicable. Yet, the District Court failed to do so. Notice could have been given through individual mailing to disabled drivers, using the names maintained by the Department of Motor Vehicles."[91.8] Because no individualized efforts were undertaken, the court of appeals invalidated the class notice, holding that it "failed to comport with the requirements of due process."[91.9]

Further, the court of appeals found that the terms of the proposal were not fundamentally fair, adequate, and reasonable. It released almost all of the absent class members' claims with little or no compensation, emphasizing that the cy pres award (the requirement for tax deductible contributions to disability advocacy organizations) was inappropriate.[91.10] Finally, it found inadequate representation, supported in significant part because the named plaintiff, class counsel, and the defendant settled so quickly on terms that allowed the defendants to escape with little penalty.[91.11]

Circuit Judge Graber specially concurred,[91.12] disagreeing with several of the reasons given by the majority but believing that the Ninth Circuit decision in *Brown v. Ticor Title Insurance Co.*[91.13] compelled the Molski panel to reject the consent decree. He argued that the majority was incorrect, and reasoning that the consent decree released almost all of the class members' claims for actual damages,[91.14] further disagreed with the majority's conclusion of inadequate representation.[91.15] But Judge Graber found that statutory treble damages were significant enough to require that each class member have an opportunity to opt out, as a matter of due process.[91.16]

91.1 318 F.3d 937 (9th Cir. 2003).

91.2 Molski v. Gleich, 307 F.3d 1155 (9th Cir. 2002).

91.3 318 F.3d at 942.

91.4 *Id.* at 943.

91.5 *Id.* at 946, quoting Hanlon v. Chrysler Corp., 150 F.3d 1011, 1026 (9th Cir. 1998), and Evans v. Jeff D., 475 U.S. 717, 726 (1986)).

91.6 318 F.3d at 950.

91.7 *Id.* at 951.

91.8 *Id.* at 952.

91.9 *Id.* at 952.

91.10 *Id.* at 955.

91.11 *Id.* at 956.

91.12 982 F.2d 386 (9th Cir. 1992).

91.13 318 F.3d at 956 (Graber, J., concurring).

91.14 *Id.* at 959.

91.15 *Id.* at 959 (Graber, J., concurring).

91.16 *Id.*

[H] Individual Liability Under Title II

Page 534, change subheading to read, "Individual Liability Under Title II," and add at beginning of subsection:

In *Shotz v. City of Plantation*,[121.1] the United States Court of Appeals for the Eleventh Circuit held that individual municipal officials can be liable for retaliation prohibited by Title II of the ADA. The officials in this case leaked a background investigation about the plaintiff. The case arose when a city council member requested that the plaintiff conduct an inspection of the recently completed municipal community center to determine its compliance with the ADA. The plaintiff wrote a letter to the requesting council member identifying a number of ADA violations. After the letter circulated within the municipal government, an assistant mayor caused a background investigation to be conducted on the plaintiff. The municipality hired a private investigator who, among other things, made a video surveillance tape. The results of the investigation, including past involvement in professional disciplinary and other civil proceedings, conflict with a neighbor, and a criminal report involving the plaintiff's spouse were released to the media.

The pertinent statutory provision says, "No person shall discriminate against any individual because such individual has opposed any act or practice made unlawful by this chapter or because such individual made a charge, testified, assisted, or participated in any manner in an investigation, proceeding, or hearing under this chapter."[121.2] The court of appeals focused on the word "person" in this statutory language and concluded that it "plainly includes individuals."[121.3] Moreover, the definitional section of the statute defines "person" to include individuals.[121.4] However, the mere statutory imposition of a duty on individuals did not definitively resolve the matter. "That a statutory provision imposes such a duty on a class of actors . . . does not compel the further conclusion that individual members of that class are amenable to private suit or otherwise liable for a breach of that duty. For that, we must also examine the remedies created by the statute."[121.5] The remedies for a violation of § 12203 are those of Title VI of the Civil Rights Act of 1964.[121.6] Case law affords a private right of action to enforce Title VI, but "precludes liability against those who do not receive federal funding, including individuals."[121.7]

The court of appeals summed up the dilemma as follows: "Did Congress intend the rights- and duty-creating language in the ADA antiretaliation provision to, itself, countenance liability against individuals for its violation, or did Congress intend the remedies available for Title VI violations to control exclusively the type of relief available as well as the appropriate scope of liability?"[121.8] Noting precedent denying individual liability in private actions under Title II,[121.9] the court of appeals determined that the overall statutory scheme militated in favor of individual liability:

> Even were we to ignore the plain meaning and look only to the available Title VI remedies in determining the scope of liability, we still could not conclusively establish that Congress intended to preclude individual liability under § 12203. Though we do not decide the question, and ultimately remain unconvinced, this approach might make sense for a violation of § 12203 in the employment context. There, the aggrieved person is ultimately referred to the remedies provided by Title VII of the Civil Rights Act of 1964, see § 12203(c); 42 U.S.C. § 12117(a), which prohibits discrimination by the same entities as prohibited by Subchapter I of the ADA regulating employment, and, as is apparent from the statutory language, those remedies do not include suit against individuals.[19] Indeed, employment is the context for virtually every case the appellees cite for the proposition that individual liability is unavailable for claims of retaliation under the ADA.[20]
>
> In the public services context, however, allowing the remedial provisions to govern the scope of liability would deviate considerably from the intent and purpose of the statute. The ADA makes *any* public entity liable for prohibited acts of discrimination, regardless of funding source. *See* 42 U.S.C. § 12132. By contrast, Title VI remedies are available only against federal funds recipients. . . . Thus, were the scope of liability confined to that of Title VI, not only would individuals who violate the Act be free from private suit, but public entities that do not receive federal funding as well, a result Congress logically did not intend. Otherwise, both Subchapter II and § 12203 in the public services context would be rendered superfluous[,] as the Rehabilitation Act also prohibits disability discrimination by public entities receiving federal funds. *Compare* 29 U.S.C. § 794(a), *with* 42 U.S.C. § 12132. Indeed, an integral purpose of Subchapter II "is to make applicable the prohibition against discrimination on the basis of disability, currently set out in regulations implementing section 504 of the Rehabilitation Act of 1973, to all programs, activities, and services provided or made available by state and local governments or instrumentalities or agencies thereto, regardless of whether or not such entities receive Federal financial assistance."

H.R.Rep. No. 101-485, pt. 2, at 84 (1990), *reprinted in* 1990 U.S.C.C.A.N. 303, 366-67. Had Congress intended to restrict liability to federal funds recipients, it would have been far easier to amend the Rehabilitation Act to account for the minor differences between it and Subchapter II of the ADA than to insert an otherwise unnecessary subchapter in the ADA itself.

Furthermore, permitting individual liability here would not create the same difficulties as doing so would under Title VI. For instance, the ADA was not enacted under Spending Clause authority as Title VI was. *See* 42 U.S.C. § 12101(b)(4) ("It is the purpose of [the ADA]... to invoke the sweep of congressional authority, including the power to enforce the fourteenth amendment and to regulate commerce...."); *Pace v. Bogalusa City Sch. Bd.*, 325 F.3d 609, 615 (5th Cir.2003) ("The ADA... does not in any way condition the receipt of federal funds on compliance with the ADA or waiver of state sovereign immunity."). Thus, liability need not be restricted only to those who contract with the federal government.[21]

There would also be no incongruency with the allowed scope of government enforcement action, if individual liability were recognized, as there would be under Titles VI or IX.... "Because... fund termination procedures... are inapplicable to State and local government entities that do not receive Federal funds, the major enforcement sanction for the Federal government [for ADA violations] will be referral of cases by these Federal agencies to the Department of Justice." S.Rep. No. 101-116, at 57 (1989). If there is an unresolved complaint, "the designated agency shall refer the matter to the Attorney General with a recommendation for appropriate action." 28 C.F.R. § 35.174. Neither the statute nor the regulations indicate that such action may not be taken against individuals.

* * *

FN19. Compare 42 U.S.C. § 12112(a) (prohibiting disability discrimination by a "covered entity," which is defined in § 12111(2) as "an employer, employment agency, labor organization, or joint labor-management committee"), with 42 U.S.C. § 2000e-5(b) (Title VII) (identifying the same parties as liable to a charge alleging an unlawful employment practice).

FN20. *See Baird v. Rose*, 192 F.3d 462, 471-72 (4th Cir.1999) (holding, inexplicably so, that, since "[t]he remedies available for a violation of the antiretaliation provision of the ADA *in the employment context* are [ultimately] set forth... under Title VII," and "Title VII does not provide a remedy against individual defendants," there is no individual liability *under Subchapter II of the ADA concerning public services*) (emphasis added); *Hiler*, 177 F.3d at 545-46 (addressing retaliation in the employment context under the "Rehabilitation Act, which incorporates by reference § 12203(a) of the ADA"); *Swaim*, 170 F.Supp.2d at 583 (same); *Santiago v. City of Vineland*, 107 F.Supp.2d 512, 551-52 (D.N.J.2000) (same); *Kautio v. Zurich Ins. Co.*, 12 Nat'l Disability L. Rep. (LRP Publ'ns) & 243 (D.Kan. Mar. 19, 1998) (same); *Stern*, 982 F.Supp. at 692-93 (same); *Cable v. Dep't of Developmental Servs.*, 973 F.Supp. 937, 943 (C.D.Cal.1997) (same). The decisions in *Key* and *Van Hulle v. Pac. Telesis Corp.*, 124 F.Supp.2d 642, 644-646 (N.D.Cal.2000), however, address retaliation in the public services and public accommodations context, respectively. *Key* we have already addressed, and we discuss Van *Hulle infra* note 22.

> FN21. It is true that, in *Barnes*, Justice Scalia suggested that the contract-law analogy useful in analyzing the scope of Spending Clause legislation applied in equal measure to the question of whether the ADA permitted punitive damages[,] because Congress "unequivocally" incorporated the remedies of § 794a(a)(2) of the Rehabilitation Act, "which *is* Spending Clause legislation." 122 S.Ct. at 2103 n. 3. Yet, that case concerned the *type* of relief available, as opposed to the question *who* may be sued, a question that is confused in this case by the statutory language in § 12203.[121.10]

The court also noted that the Department of Justice interprets § 12203 as making individuals acting in their individual capacities amenable to private[121.11] Because Congress expressly authorized the Attorney General to make rules with the force of law implementing the ADA, the court of appeals found the DOJ regulation entitled to deference.[121.12]

In *Miller v. King*,[121.13] the court of appeals held that Title II of the ADA not impose liability for money damages against individuals, distinguishing 42 U.S.C. § 12132 (applicable to public entities) and 42 U.S.C. § 12203(a) (applicable to "persons"). Section 12203(a) imposes liability for retaliation claims.

[121.1] 344 F.3d 1161 (11th Cir. 2003).

[121.2] 42 U.S.C. § 12203(a).

[121.3] 344 F.3d at 1168-69.

[121.4] *Id.* at 1168, quoting 42 U.S.C. § 12111(7).

[121.5] *Id.*

[121.6] 344 F.3d at 1173, citing 42 U.S.C. § 12133, incorporating by reference 29 U.S.C. § 794a, which in turn incorporates remedies, procedures, and rights set forth in Title VII and Title VI.

[121.7] *Id.* at 1170.

[121.8] *Id.* at 1171.

[121.9] *Id.* at 1172-73, citing and discussing Key v. Grayson, 163 F. Supp. 2d 697, 703-04 (E.D. Mich. 2001) (no individual liability in public services context), and Hiler v. Brown, 177 F.3d 542, 545 (6th Cir. 1999) (same).

[121.10] 344 F.3d at 1173-75.

[121.11] *Id.* at 1177, citing nondiscrimination on the basis of disability in state and local government, 28 C.F.R. pt. 35 (2003).

[121.12] *Id.* at 1186.

[121.13] 384 F.3d 1248 (11th Cir. 2004).

§ 9.05 RIPENESS AND MOOTNESS

Page 546, add at end of section:

In *Dudley v. Hannaford Brothers Co.*,[183.1] the court of appeals held that section 12188(a)(1) does not authorize a private right of action for a single act of past discrimination that is unlikely to recur.[183.2] However, the court rejected the defendants' argument that a plaintiff whose disability made him appear intoxicated, and who was refused the sale of alcoholic beverages, must not repeatedly try to buy the beverages. Because the lawsuit challenged a policy forbidding reconsideration of a refusal to sell alcoholic beverages, the policy would likely make further efforts by the plaintiff futile.[183.3]

183.1 333 F.3d 299 (1st Cir. 2002).
183.2 *Id.* at 304.
183.3 *Id.* at 306 (also considering likelihood that plaintiff would frequent the same store in a small town).

§ 9.06 PLEADING

Page 547, add after third paragraph:

In *Swierkiewics v. Sorema N.A.*,[187.1] the Supreme Court resolved a circuit split and held that a Title VII plaintiff need not plead facts making out a prima facie case under *McDonnell Douglas v. Green*.[187.2] Rather, the Court held that a plaintiff need only meet the literal requirements of Fed. R. Civ. P. 8(a)(2) and that a "complaint must include only a short and plain statement of the claim showing that the pleader is entitled to relief." Such a statement must simply "give the defendant fair notice of what the plaintiff's claim is and the grounds upon which it rests."[187.3]

> Applying the relevant standard, petitioner's complaint easily satisfies the requirements of Rule 8(a) because it gives respondent fair notice of the basis for petitioner's claims. Petitioner alleged that he had been terminated on account of his national origin in violation of Title VII and on account of his age in violation of the ADEA. His complaint detailed the events leading to his termination, provided relevant dates, and included the ages and nationalities of at least some of the relevant persons involved with his termination. These allegations give respondent fair notice of what petitioner's claims are and the grounds upon which they rest. In addition, they state claims upon which relief could be granted under Title VII and the ADEA.[187.4]

187.1 534 U.S. 506 (2002).
187.2 411 U.S. 792 (1973).
187.3 534 U.S. at 512.
187.4 *Id.* at 514 (internal citations omitted).

Page 550, add following carryover paragraph:

In *Zivkovic v. Southern California Edison Co.*,[205.1] the court of appeals rejected the argument that making reasonable accommodation is an affirmative defense that must be pleaded by the defendant.[205.2] Rather, proving reasonable accommodation negates an element an ADA Title I plaintiff must prove.

In *Heisler v. Metropolitan Council*,[205.3] the court of appeals reversed the district court's grant of summary judgment on an ADA retaliation claim, finding that the district court lacked the power to grant summary judgment on issues not raised or discussed by the parties, and that the defendant's generalized motion for summary judgment on "all claims" did not meet the requirements of Federal Rule 56(c) that it particularize its contention that insufficient facts existed to support the plaintiff's claim.[205.4] Significantly for questions of initial pleading, the court of appeals rejected the argument that the plaintiff had never pursued a retaliation claim, finding a count in her complaint explicitly captioned retaliation/ ADA.[205.5]

In *Steir v. Girl Scouts*,[205.6] the court of appeals affirmed judgment for the defendants. The plaintiff, who suffered from cerebral palsy, claimed a violation of the ADA because of activities in which she could not participate, and a subsequent refusal to allow her to transfer to another troop because of her disability. The district court found that the plaintiff lacked standing to seek injunctive relief under Title III of the ADA and denied a motion to amend the plaintiff's complaint after the close of discovery to add a claim for money damages under the Rehabilitation Act. The court of appeals found that adding the Rehabilitation Act claim would prejudice the defendant because it would add questions of money damages to the case and require reopening discovery. The plaintiff had unsuccessfully argued that the defendants' answer to an interrogatory regarding receipt of federal financial assistance warranted amendment. The court of appeals noted that plaintiff's counsel did not timely pursue efforts to resolve the ambiguity in the answer. Though noting that the defendants' evasive response was subject to criticism, "the failure of Marika's counsel to inquire into the memoranda of understanding that were mentioned in the answer to the interrogatory is inexplicable." It held that it would have been well within the discretion of the district court to allow amendment, but it was not an abuse of discretion to deny it.

[205.1] 302 F.3d 1080 (9th Cir. 2002).
[205.2] *Id.* at 1088.
[205.3] 339 F.3d 622 (8th Cir. 2003).
[205.4] *Id.* at 631.
[205.5] *Id.*
[205.6] 383 F.3d 7 (1st Cir. 2004).

§ 9.07 PERSONAL JURISDICTION AND SERVICE OF PROCESS

Page 550, add new subsection before first paragraph:

[A] Venue

In re Horseshoe Entertainment[206.1] involved a writ of mandamus issued to the district court compelling it to transfer an ADA case. The employer filed a motion for transfer under 28 U.S.C. § 1404(a), and later answered the complaint, arguing that the workplace, the plaintiff's residence, all the relevant witnesses, and all the relevant conduct occurred within the Shreveport division of the Western District of Louisiana. The lawsuit was filed in the United States District Court for the Middle District of Louisiana.[206.2] The court of appeals first held that refusal of a change of venue is reviewable on a petition for mandamus.[206.3] The court of appeals noted the special venue provisions in 42

U.S.C. § 2000e-5(f)(3), and found that the § 1404(a) "might have been brought" language was satisfied by the explicit authorization of venue for districts where the unlawful practices were alleged to have been committed, where the employment records are maintained, and where the aggrieved person worked, these factors clearly authorized transfer.[206.4] The district court apparently conceded that transfer might increase convenience, but denied transfer because the possibility of delay, location of counsel, and plaintiff's choice of forum.[206.5]

The court of appeals held that location of counsel is irrelevant and an improper consideration in transfer-of-venue questions.[206.6] It also held that the district court had offered no basis for its conclusion that delay or prejudice might result from transfer.[206.7]

206.1 337 F.3d 429, vacating 305 F.3d 354 (5th Cir. 2003).
206.2 *Id.* at 430-31 (background facts and employer allegations).
206.3 *Id.* at 432.
206.4 *Id.* at 433.
206.5 *Id.*
206.6 337 F.3d at 434.
206.7 *Id.*

§ 9.08 EXHAUSTION OF ADMINISTRATIVE REMEDIES

[A] Exhausting EEOC Procedures

[1] Generally

Page 553, add at end of subsection:

In *Zerilli-Edelglass v. New York City Transit Authority*,[221.1] the court of appeals held that a letter to the EEOC inquiring about "how to proceed" with a retaliation claim did not qualify as a formal EEOC complaint filed within the 300-day limitation period.[221.2]

In *Ebbert v. DaimlerChrysler Corp.*,[221.3] the court of appeals saved an ADA plaintiff from losing her ADA lawsuit because of EEOC inefficiency and error. The following passage from the court of appeals opinion is better than any summary in explaining what happened:

> On April 28, 1997, Ebbert filed a charge of disability discrimination with the EEOC. On February 24, 1998, she informed the EEOC that she had moved and gave her new mailing address. On March 17, 1999 she received, at her new address, a letter from EEOC Supervisory Investigator, Howard Gurmankin, informing her that the EEOC was going to dismiss her case and that "the Dismissal and Notice of Rights" which the EEOC would be sending to her would "allow" her to file a private suit if she wished. Ebbert telephoned in response and was told that the follow-up letter was in the mail. A "right to sue" letter may have been sent to Ebbert's former address instead of her current address but it is not

> clear.[2] In any event, Ebbert denies ever receiving the letter and there is no undisputed evidence that she did. After waiting a month, Ebbert telephoned the EEOC again and was told that the earlier letter had been premature and the EEOC had decided to reopen her case. Then after further investigation, the EEOC again decided to dismiss her case. The case log shows that Investigator Karin Porter told Ebbert on September 21, 1999 that the charge would be dismissed.[3] On November 4, 1999 the EEOC issued Ebbert a second notice letter but mailed the letter to her former address. Ebbert again denies having received this second letter and there is again no direct or undisputed proof that she did. On August 14, 2000 Ebbert sent a letter to Porter requesting a status update and shortly thereafter Porter informed her by telephone that her case was closed and that the letter had been sent some time ago. Ebbert recounted the phone conversation in her letter to Porter of August 23, 2000. On October 16, 2000 the EEOC sent Ebbert a third notice, this time to the correct address, and Ebbert instituted this lawsuit on January 16, 2001.
>
> ---
>
> [2] According to Gurmankin's November 20, 2001 affidavit, there was no copy of the letter in the EEOC files and the EEOC Case Log indicates that the letter was not sent (but without any explanation of how that was determined).
>
> [3] Again, this is according to Gurmankin's November 20, 2001 affidavit.

The court of appeals held that failure to exhaust is an affirmative defense; therefore the employer had the burden of proof, which in turn "clearly requires proof of the lawful start date for the limitations period."[221.5] The court found that the EEOC lacked power to construe the statutory requirement of notice as requiring a writing,[221.6] and instead applied a common law of construing limitation periods[221.7] and held that oral notice could be sufficient to commence the running of the limitations period in Title VII.[221.8] But even though, "in this case, oral notice was just as complete as written notice . . . , there is no proof that Ebbert knew when the 90-day statute of limitations period would start as a result of her phone conversations with the EEOC. More specifically, no evidence shows that Ebbert was told or otherwise knew that the 90 days would start running from the date of the conversation. DaimlerChrysler had the burden of proving the oral notice was as comprehensive as the written provision and, in particular, that it included an explanation of the 'start date.' "[221.9] Accordingly, it reversed grant of summary judgment for the defendant on exhaustion grounds.

[a] Disclosure of Disability

Doe v. U.S. Postal Service[221.10] involved an ADA and Rehabilitation Act claim based on alleged disclosure of the plaintiff's HIV-positive status by his employer. The court of appeals, reversing the district court, found that the plaintiff produced enough evidence to survive summary judgment on his federal Privacy Act claim and also found that he disclosed the information about his condition only in response to an "inquiry, under the ADA and the Rehabilitation Act."[221.11] The fact that the plaintiff could have avoided disclosing his condition by foregoing his entitlement to FMLA leave did not make his disclosure voluntary.[221.12]

221.1 333 F.3d 74 (2d Cir. 2003).

221.2 *Id.* at 80 (noting also that plaintiff's failure to argue in district court that the letter was a formal EEOC complaint forfeited that argument).

221.3 319 F.3d 103 (3d Cir. 2003).

221.4 *Id.* at 107.

221.5 *Id.* at 108.

221.6 *Id.* at 110-11.

221.7 *Id.* at 112 (finding Chevron deference inappropriate, and no persuasive EEOC arguments for Skidmore deference).

221.8 *Id.* at 116.

221.9 *Id.* at 116.

221.10 317 F.3d 339 (D.C. Cir. 2003).

221.11 *Id.* at 344, citing 42 U.S.C. § 12112 (d).

221.12 *Id.* at 344.

[2] Time Limits

Page 553, add after last paragraph:

In *Flannery v. Recording Industry Association of America*,[226.1] the court of appeals, reversing the district court, held that the 300-day period for filing a charge of ADA discrimination began to run, not on the date that the employee was told informally that he would have to be terminated because "his health was bad," but on a later date when he was formally terminated. The earlier conversation concluded with an agreement to keep the plaintiff "on and see how things went."[226.2] "Requiring employees like Mr. Flannery to file EEOC charges on the basis of ambiguous conversations regarding termination would cause a flood of false charges; litigants would be forced to file a charge at every hint of termination in order to preserve their claims."[226.3]

226.1 354 F.3d 632 (7th Cir. 2004).

226.2 *Id.* at 640.

226.3 *Id.* at 641.

[3] Scope of EEOC Charges

Page 556, add at beginning of note 244:

Russell v. TG Mo. Corp., 340 F.3d 735, 748 (8th Cir. 2003) (when plaintiff failed to check retaliation box on EEOC complaint form, and shifted her allegations as to the allegedly retaliatory employment decision, retaliation claim did not reasonably grow out of discrimination claim as to which EEOC procedures had been exhausted);

Page 558, add at end of subsection:

In *Manning v. Chevron Chemical Co.*,[252.1] the court of appeals, affirming summary judgment for the employer, held that an untimely ADA claim filed as a purported amendment to a timely race, gender, and retaliation charge was not entitled to be treated as relating back to the original charge. It reasoned that a central purpose of an employment discrimination charge is to put employers on notice of the nature of the charges against them. An untimely subsequent amendment that concerns different theories of recovery does not satisfy that standard.[252.2]

[252.1] 332 F.3d 874 (5th Cir. 2003).
[252.2] *Id.* at 878-79.

[C] Exhaustion of Title III Remedies

Page 568, add at end of subsection:

In *Harris v. P.A.M. Transport, Inc.*,[316.1] the court of appeals affirmed dismissal of ADA claims because a truck driver had failed to exhaust DOT remedies relating to determination of driver fitness, apparently based on a general rule of judicial administration "that no one is entitled to judicial relief for a supposed or threatened injury until the prescribed administrative remedy has been exhausted."[316.2] Unlike the usual case involving exhaustion of administrative remedies, the remedies that Mr. Harris was required to exhaust did not provide a determination as to his legal rights under the ADA, but rather of factual matters necessary to prove a violation of the ADA—his fitness to drive and thus to perform the duties of his position.

[316.1] 339 F.3d 635 (8th Cir. 2003).
[316.2] *Id.* at 638.

§ 9.09 SUING IN STATE COURT

Page 568, add new subsection before first paragraph:

[A] Parallel State and Federal Litigation

In *Currie v. Group Insurance Commission*,[316.1] the court of appeals held that a stay of federal litigation pending resolution of state law issues in parallel state-court litigation was appropriate.[316.2] It declined certification of state law questions to the highest state court because such certification would interfere with the normal state appellate process.[316.3]

[316.1] 290 F.3d 1 (1st Cir. 2002).
[316.2] *Id.* at 12-13.
[316.3] *Id.* at 13.

§ 9.11 ARBITRATION AND MEDIATION OF ADA CLAIMS

[C] Individual Arbitration Agreements

Page 576, add at end of first paragraph:

In *EEOC v. Luce, Forward, Hamilton & Scripps*,[357.1] the en banc Ninth Circuit, reversing the district court and overruling *Duffield v. Robertson Stephens & Co.*,[357.2] held that the ADA does not prohibit employers from requiring arbitration of all employment claims as a condition of employment. The EEOC sued on behalf of an applicant for employment, a legal secretary who was denied employment because he refused to sign an arbitration agreement. The court of appeals noted that *Gilmer* represented a shift in the Supreme Court's position in *Alexander v. Gardner Denver*.[357.3] It noted that in the "post-*Gilmer* world, our decision in *Duffield* stands alone. All of the other circuits have concluded that Title 7 does not bar compulsory arbitration agreements."[357.4] On remand, however, the court of appeals allowed the EEOC to develop further its argument that denying employment because of opposition to compulsory arbitration might be unlawful retaliation even if compulsory arbitration is permissible.[357.5]

In *Weeks v. Harden Manufacturing Corp.*,[357.6] the court of appeals held that a plaintiff's belief that requiring the arbitration of employment discrimination claims was an unlawful employment practice was not objectively reasonable, and therefore that refusing employment because of a refusal to sign agreements to arbitrate such claims did not constitute retaliation under the ADA.[357.7]

[357.1] 345 F.3d 742 (9th Cir. 2003).
[357.2] 144 F.3d 1182 (9th Cir. 1998).
[357.3] 345 F.3d at 748.
[357.4] *Id.*
[357.5] *Id.* at 754.
[357.6] 291 F.3d 1307 (11th Cir. 2002).
[357.7] *Id.* at 1312 (citing cases finding arbitration of discrimination claims to be permissible).

Page 578, add at end of section:

In *Luong v. Circuit City Stores, Inc.*,[372.1] the plaintiff brought an action in federal court for violation of the ADA. The employer successfully moved to compel arbitration, and the arbitrator found no ADA violation. The employee then filed a petition to vacate the arbitration award under § 10 of the Federal Arbitration Act.[372.2] The court of appeals, recalling that the Federal Arbitration Act does not confer subject matter jurisdiction, nevertheless found that the employee's claim that the arbitrator manifestly disregarded federal law stated a sufficient federal question to confer subject matter jurisdiction.[372.3]

The court of appeals concluded that the arbitrator did not ignore federal law, although he may have misinterpreted it. "Virtually every line of the opinion and award discussed *Toyota* and how it plays out on the facts in Luong's case. That cannot amount to 'manifest disregard of federal law.' "[372.4]

[372.1] 368 F.3d 1109 (9th Cir. 2004).
[372.2] 9 U.S.C. § 10.
[372.3] 368 F.3d at 1111.
[372.4] *Id.*

[E] Specificity of Arbitration Agreements

Page 583, add at end of section:

In *Eastern Associated Coal Corp. v. Massey,*[390.1] the court of appeals held that a collective bargaining agreement did not waive an individual employee's power to litigate a state disability discrimination complaint in court with sufficient clarity. The agreement provided, that

> neither the employer nor the union shall discriminate against any employee or with regard to the terms or availability of classified employment on the basis of race, creed, national origin, sex, age, political activity, whether intra-union or otherwise. In addition, the employer and union agree that they will adhere to the applicable provisions of the Vietnam Era Readjustment Assistance Act of 1974, the Rehabilitation Act of 1973, and the Americans with Disabilities Act.[390.2]

The court of appeals reasoned that even if the language sufficiently incorporated the ADA to obligate the employee to submit ADA claims only to arbitration, waiver of ADA claims did not waive state disability discrimination claims. "It is insufficient, then, for a waiver provision to incorporate one statute into a CBA by referring to another, independently created (though analogous) statute."[390.3]

[390.1] 373 F.3d 530 (4th Cir. 2004).
[390.2] *Id.* at 533 (quoting collective bargaining agreement).
[390.3] *Id.* at 537.

Page 587, add new subsection:

[J] Arbitration—Jurisdictional Amount

In a bizarre opinion, the Ninth Circuit denied review of an arbitration award denying ADA relief. *Vu Luong v. Circuit City Stores, Inc.*[413.1] arose when Luong was compelled to arbitrate his ADA claim. The arbitrator found that Luong was neither disabled nor regarded as disabled. Luong then filed a petition to vacate the arbitration award pursuant to Section 10 of the Federal

Arbitration Act,[413.2] premising federal jurisdiction on the Federal Arbitration Act and also diversity of citizenship with more than $75,000 in controversy. He argued that the arbitrator ignored federal law and incorrectly applied federal law.[413.3] The district court dismissed for lack of subject matter jurisdiction.

The court of appeals began its analysis with the proposition that the FAA itself does not confer federal question jurisdiction.[413.4] Then, the court of appeals rejected Luong's argument that the jurisdictional amount was to be determined by his original claim in federal court, which was dismissed incident to the order to compel arbitration, rather than the award, which was for zero dollars. The court was unpersuaded by Luong's argument that he sought to vacate the zero-dollar award and to recover a larger amount.[413.5]

The author believes that this reasoning by the court of appeals is completely irrational. Jurisdictional amount is appropriately determined, not by the value of the status quo preceding litigation, but rather by the amount sought by the plaintiff, unless there is a legal certainty he cannot recover that amount. Luong sought to recover $75,000, initially in district court, then before the arbitrator, and finally in a petition to vacate the arbitration award. Accordingly, he should have been found to have satisfied the jurisdictional amount. As Circuit Judge Kozinski, dissenting, observed,

> The rule my colleagues adopt makes no sense, as it causes the amount in controversy to turn on the arbitrator's possibly erroneous ruling, rather than the actual amount in dispute between the parties. The absurdity of the rule can be demonstrated by considering the following example: X claims Y owes him $100,000 in a contract dispute. The case is ordered to arbitration, and the arbitrator comes up with an award of $80,000. X claims he was entitled to more and petitions to have the award vacated. Under the majority's approach, the District Court would have jurisdiction. But if the arbitrator happens to award only $30,000—or nothing at all—because of same claimed legal error, the District Court would lack jurisdiction. There is no principled distinction between the two cases; if the petitioner prevails in either case, the award will be vacated and petitioner will be back in arbitration seeking his full $100,000. I can see no logic at all in letting the very award that is the fruit of the claimed error govern the amount in controversy.[413.6]

Finally, the court of appeals rejected the argument that a challenge to an arbitrator's award based on manifest disregard of federal law would support federal question jurisdiction under the Second Circuit's decision in *Greenberg v. Bear, Stearns & Co.*[413.7] The court found that Luong's petition did not assert manifest disregard of federal law but only error in applying federal law, and that was not sufficient to trigger the Greenberg exception even if the court of appeals agreed with its doctrine.[413.8]

[413.1] 356 F.3d 1188 (9th Cir. 2004).

[413.2] 9 U.S.C. § 10.

[413.3] 356 F.3d at 1190 (describing procedural history).

[413.4] *Id.* at 1191 & n.3 (noting that this is an "odd construct" because Section 10 appears to confer subject matter jurisdiction).

[413.5] 356 F.3d at 1193-94.

[413.6] *Id.* at 1196, 1198 (Kozinski, J., dissenting).

[413.7] *Id.* at 1194-95 (citing Greenberg v. Bear, Stearns & Co., 220 F.3d 22, 27 (2d Cir. 2000)).

[413.8] *Id.* at 1195.

§ 9.12 SUPPLEMENTAL JURISDICTION

Page 589, add at end of section:

In *Treglia v. Town of Manlius*,[425.1] the court of appeals reversed the district court's dismissal of a state discrimination claim based on its dismissal of an ADA claim. The court of appeals noted that New York law defines disability more broadly than federal law and that the district court lacked the power to dismiss the supplemental state claim while federal claims remained in the case; the state claim did not predominate over the federal retaliation claim and did not raise novel or complex issues of state law.[425.2]

[425.1] 313 F.3d 713 (2d Cir. 2002).

[425.2] *Id.* at 723.

§ 9.14 CONGRESSIONAL PROCEDURES

Page 593, add note 475.1 reference at end of section and new note 475.1 text:

[475.1] See also § 5.02.

§ 9.16 STATUTES OF LIMITATIONS

Page 596, add following note 502 reference:

In *Ballard v. Rubin*,[502.1] the court of appeals held that the applicable statute of limitations for a Rehabilitation Act claim was the Missouri statute of limitations for personal injury lawsuits.[502.2]

In *Henrickson v. Potter*,[502.3] the court of appeals affirmed summary judgment for the United States Postal Service as a defendant, finding that the ADA does not permit actions against federal employers and that the employee's Rehabilitation Act claim was time barred because he failed to contact an EEO counselor within 45 days of the alleged discriminatory act.[502.4] The court rejected the plaintiff's argument that the postal service's refusal to purchase a chair the plaintiff claimed he needed to mitigate symptoms of carpal tunnel syndrome was not a continuing violation but a single employment action.[502.5]

[502.1] 284 F.3d 957 (8th Cir. 2002).

[502.2] *Id.* at 962-63.

502.3 327 F.3d 444 (5th Cir. 2003).
502.4 *Id.* at 447 (citing 29 C.F.R. § 1614.105(a)(1), establishing 45-day time limit).
502.5 *Id.* at 447.

Page 597, add at end of note 505:

Gaona v. Town & Country Credit, 324 F.3d 1050, 1056 (8th Cir. 2003) (approving use of Minnesota's six-year personal injury statute of limitations under ADA).

Page 600, add at end of section:

In *Craig v. Missouri Department of Health*,[530.1] the Missouri Supreme Court held that state disability law claims related back to the filing of an original ADA claim which was dismissed on Eleventh Amendment grounds after removal to federal court. It therefore held that the plaintiff was allowed to litigate her state claims in state court although her state claims were untimely if considered in isolation.[530.2]

In *Martin v. Alamo Community College District*,[530.3] the plaintiff received a right to sue letter from the EEOC and filed suit within the 90-day period. On the same day she filed suit, the EEOC mailed a notice of reconsideration, reopening its investigation. After receiving the notice of reconsideration, the plaintiff elected not to make service on the defendant, awaiting the outcome of the investigation. The district court dismissed the first suit without prejudice. Ultimately, the EEOC issued another right to sue letter, after which the employee initiated a second action in district court. Under EEOC rules, if an employee has not already filed suit based on a right to sue letter, a reconsideration notice vitiates the right to sue under the first letter. If suit has already been commenced, the original right to sue letter remains in effect. The court of appeals, reversing the district court, concluded that the defendant failed to establish that the notice of reconsideration was issued before the first suit was filed and, accordingly, that litigation of the ADA claim was not time barred.[530.4]

530.1 80 S.W.3d 457 (Mo. 2002).
530.2 *Id.* at 461.
530.3 353 F.3d 409 (5th Cir. 2003).
530.4 *Id.* at 413.

§ 9.17 DISCOVERY

[A] Consideration of Nature of Claim

Page 601, add after carryover paragraph:

In *French v. Hawaii Pizza Hut, Inc.*,[534.1] the Hawaii Supreme Court reversed, for abuse of discretion, a trial court order limiting an ADA plaintiff's discovery too narrowly. It held that the plaintiff was entitled to production of documents related to other personnel to determine whether there was a pattern with respect to treatment of employees who returned to work after suffering physical impairments.

[534.1] 99 P.3d 1046 (Haw. 2004).

[B] Videotape Depositions and Evidence

Page 603, add to note 543:

Demonstrative evidence is considered further in § 9.19[B].

Page 606, add new subsections:

[C] Discovery Sanctions

In *Maynard v. Nygren*,[558.1] the court of appeals reversed dismissal of an ADA lawsuit as a sanction for discovery abuse by the plaintiff, remanding for reconsideration of the willfulness of the withholding of a crucial document.[558.2] It also ordered the district court to reconsider monetary sanctions imposed on plaintiff's counsel.[558.3] In a subsequent appeal,[558.4] the court of appeals affirmed dismissal as a sanction for discovery violations by the plaintiff—failing to turn over a document and then lying about it.[558.5]

[558.1] 332 F.3d 462 (7th Cir. 2003).
[558.2] *Id.* at 469.
[558.3] *Id.* at 471.
[558.4] 372 F.3d 890 (7th Cir. 2004).
[558.5] *Id.* at 892.

[D] Rule 35 Examinations

Rule 35 of the Federal Rules of Civil Procedure allows a court to order that a party "submit to a physical or mental examination by a suitably licensed or certified examiner" when good cause is shown.[558.4]

Case law is split on whether a party subjected to examination under Rule 35 is entitled to have an attorney present during the examination.[558.5]

In *Fox v. Gates Corp.*,[558.6] the district court declined a request for a Rule 35 examination of an ADA plaintiff. The court held that the plaintiff had not asserted a separate cause of action for intentional or negligent infliction of emotional distress, did not allege a specific mental or psychiatric injury or disorder, and did not claim unusually severe emotional distress. Nor did she offer expert testimony in support of her claim for emotional distress damages and concede that her mental condition was "in controversy" within the meaning of Rule 35(a) of the Federal Rules of Civil Procedure. Thus, concluded the district court, the plaintiff had not placed her mental condition "in controversy," and the defendant failed to show any other good cause for examination.[558.7]

In *Sarko v. Penn-Dell Directory Co.*,[558.8] the district court ordered a limited psychiatric examination of an ADA plaintiff, finding that the plaintiff had alleged and the defendant contested only the alleged long-term impact of plaintiff's depression on her current mental state.[558.9] The plaintiff's ADA claim was premised on her allegation that she suffered from clinical depression that caused her chronic tardiness, which eventually resulted in her dismissal.

In *Casey v. Burlington Northern Railroad Co.*,[558.10] the district court granted an order that the plaintiff submit to a vocational assessment, including vocational testing, because he alleged permanent injury to his shoulder, depression, and emotional distress.

In *Morton v. Haskell Co.*,[558.11] the district court denied physical examination, while granting mental examination, of an ADA plaintiff. The plaintiff premised his ADA claim on discrimination based on plaintiff's clinical depression. The district court found that the plaintiff's physical condition had not been placed in controversy, but it found that "the crux of plaintiff's claims relate to the existence and severity of his clinical depression. Plaintiff's mental condition has thus clearly been placed in controversy since it forms the foundation for most of his claims. If the plaintiff did not suffer from this mental condition, or if it was insufficiently severe, he will not prevail on the bulk of his claims. This is clearly sufficient to place plaintiff's mental condition in controversy."[558.12]

Likewise, in *Ali v. Wang Laboratories, Inc.*,[558.13] the district court ordered mental and physical examination of an ADA plaintiff. The plaintiff had alleged joint and bone conditions constituting a statutory disability. The court found that the plaintiff's ADA claim placed his physical condition in controversy.[558.14] The court declined the plaintiff's demand that the Rule 35 order allow the presence of a court reporter, the plaintiff's wife, or recording equipment. The court's limitations on the scope of the examinations are worth setting forth verbatim as follows:

> 1. Defendant's Motion To Compel Physical and Mental Examinations of Plaintiff (Doc. # 21) is GRANTED to the extent set forth below.
>
> 2. Plaintiff shall submit to a mental examination by Dr. Ernest C. Miller and a physical examination by Dr. Michael B. Scharf. Each examination will be conducted at the respective business office of Dr. Miller and Dr. Scharf in Jacksonville, Florida during normal business hours.
>
> 3. The examinations will be conducted within 20 days after the completion of plaintiff's deposition, unless the parties otherwise mutually agree.
>
> 4. The mental examination will focus upon the matters alleged by plaintiff in his Complaint and/or deposition and the mental and emotional

injury and damages resulting from the misconduct alleged of defendant. Defendant shall provide Dr. Miller with the appropriate portion of plaintiff's answers to interrogatories, deposition, and such other documents as it deems appropriate. The examination will include the routine procedures for such an examination. Plaintiff has requested that it also include the Minnesota Multiphasic Personality Inventory examination. Dr. Miller may administer this test, but the Court will not require it. A copy of any resulting report will be provided to plaintiff's counsel.

5. The physical examination will focus upon the injuries alleged by plaintiff in his Complaint and/or deposition and the existence and severity of the injuries and plaintiff's physical capabilities. Defendant shall provide Dr. Scharf with the appropriate portion of plaintiff's answers to interrogatories, deposition, and such other documents as it deems appropriate. The examination will include the routine procedures for such an examination. A copy of any resulting report will be provided to plaintiff's counsel.[558.15]

[558.4] Fed. R. Civ. P. 35(a).

[558.5] *See* Galieti v. State Farm Mut. Auto Ins. Co., 154 F.R.D. 262, 263-64 (D. Colo. 1994) (citing cases for various approaches and requiring former employee to submit to unsupervised psychiatric examination); Hertenstein v. Kimberly Home Health Care, Inc., 189 F.R.D. 620, 630 (D. Kan. 1999) (reviewing cases suggesting why attorneys should not be present at examination and denying request to permit non-attorney third party or recording device to be present during examination).

[558.6] 179 F.R.D. 303 (D. Colo. 1998).

[558.7] *Id.* at 307-08.

[558.8] 170 F.R.D. 127 (E.D. Pa. 1997).

[558.9] *Id* at 131.

[558.10] Civil No. 95-1056-FR, 1997 U.S. Dist. LEXIS 696; 6 Am. Disabilities Cas. (BNA) 479 (D. Or. Jan. 15, 1997).

[558.11] No. 94-976-CIV-J-20, 1995 U.S. Dist. LEXIS 21883; 5 Am. Disabilities Cas. (BNA) 272 (M.D. Fla. Sept. 12, 1995).

[558.12] *Id.* at *2.

[558.13] 162 F.R.D. 165 (M.D. Fla. 1995).

[558.14] *Id.* at 168.

[558.15] *Id.* at 169.

§ 9.18 SUMMARY JUDGMENT

Page 607, add after third full paragraph:

In *Reed v. Bennett*,[563.1] the court of appeals reversed the district court and held that a district judge may not grant summary judgment against a party based on the opposing party's failure to meet local procedural rule requirements for filing a response. Such a dismissal conflicts with Federal Rule 56 (c), which requires the moving party to bear the burden of showing that summary judgment is appropriate:[563.2]

> By failing to file a response within the time specified by the local rule, Reed waived the right to file a response or to controvert the facts asserted in the summary judgment motion. But Reed's waiver did not relieve the court of its duty to make the specific determinations required by Fed. R. Civ. P. 56 (c). A District Court properly grants summary judgment pursuant to Rule 56 only if the motion demonstrates no genuine issue of material fact exists and the movant is entitled to judgment as a matter of law. Alternatively, the court can enter judgment as a sanction if warranted. While the facts of this case likely support sanctions against the offending attorney, the District Court did not expressly consider the Meade factors prior to granting summary judgment.[563.3]

[563.1] 312 F.3d 1190 (10th Cir. 2002).
[563.2] *Id.* at 1194.
[563.3] *Id.* at 1196.

Page 608, add before first full paragraph:

In *Buie v. Quad/Graphics, Inc.*,[567.1] the court of appeals affirmed summary judgment for the employer in an ADA and FMLA claim brought by an employee with AIDS. In determining the motion for summary judgment, the trial court disregarded a portion of the plaintiff's affidavit asserting that he was subjected to disciplinary suspension almost immediately after his initial disclosure to his employer that he had AIDS, on the ground that self-serving affidavits are insufficient to defeat summary judgment. The court of appeals held that the trial court abused its discretion by refusing to consider that part of the affidavit because the affidavit met the criteria for evidence on summary judgment as it was based on personal knowledge and alleged specific facts relevant to whether the employee's rights under the ADA were violated. But the court of appeals concluded that admission of the affidavit would have not allowed a reasonable jury to find in the plaintiff's favor. Accepting that suspicious timing is a type of circumstantial evidence under the direct method of proving discriminatory intent, the court found it insufficient to support a conclusion of causation. Other evidence will show that the plaintiff was on the brink of dismissal before the employer knew he had AIDS and that he nevertheless chose to miss work without excuse and without warning. It was only when employee was rebuked for missing work that he disclosed that he had AIDS.

[567.1] 366 F.3d 496 (7th Cir. 2004).

Page 608, add at end of section:

In *Ammons v. Aramark Uniform Services, Inc.*,[569.1] the court of appeals affirmed summary judgment for the employer, after the district court struck the plaintiff's responses to the defendant employer's statement of undisputed facts in support of its motion for summary judgment. The plaintiff had failed to comply with a local rule requiring that a party contesting summary judgment identify specific facts supporting the denial and to cite specific parts of the record supporting the denial.[569.2]

[569.1] 368 F.3d 809 (7th Cir. 2004).
[569.2] *Id.* at 817.

Page 608, retitle existing heading as:

§ 9.19 EVIDENCE

Page 608, renumber existing text as [A]:

[A] Expert Testimony

Page 610, add at end of page:

In *Ammons v. Aramark Uniform Services, Inc.*,[594.1] the court of appeals affirmed summary judgment for the employer, finding no abuse of discretion in the district court's striking of expert testimony that the employee could perform the "vast majority" of essential functions associated with his job. The court found a sufficient basis for the district court's conclusion that the expert testimony was unreliable and speculative, because the expert did not review deposition testimony, acknowledged that she was unfamiliar with the machinery the plaintiff would have had to repair, and did not observe anyone repairing the machinery during a three-hour tour of the plant.[594.2]

Hoffman v. Caterpillar, Inc.[594.3] involved a one-armed employee who was denied training on a high-speed document scanner because of the employer's belief that a one-handed operator could not operate the machine at the required levels of productivity. After litigation began, the plaintiff received training on how to operate the scanner and was videotaped operating it for an eight-hour period. The district court refused to allow the plaintiff's expert to testify after the expert looked at the videotape, although the district court found that the expert had a sufficient basis from the videotape to offer an opinion regarding whether the plaintiff could run the machine at established production levels. The district court implied that such testimony could not assist the trier of fact, as required by Fed. R. Evid. 702, because the jury could reach its own conclusions based on the videotape.

The court of appeals found the reasoning persuasive and found no abuse of discretion in the exclusion of the expert testimony.[594.4] The court of appeals also found that the plaintiff had failed to meet its obligations under Fed. R. Civ. P. 26(a)(2)(B), because it failed to amend prior disclosures to include the videotape as a basis for the expert's opinion.[594.5] It found that the timing of the plaintiff's renewed request to allow the expert to testify, after an earlier order excluding the testimony, would have denied the defendant an opportunity to depose the expert on the videotape as a new basis for his opinion. Also, the defendant would have "a distressingly small amount of time to develop expert testimony to counter [the plaintiff's expert]."[594.6]

[594.1] 368 F.3d 809 (7th Cir. 2004).
[594.2] *Id.* at 816.
[594.3] 368 F.3d 709 (7th Cir. 2004).
[594.4] *Id.* at 714.
[594.5] *Id.*
[594.6] *Id.* at 715.

Page 611, add new subsections:

[B] Demonstrative Evidence

Demonstrative evidence, also considered in § 9.17[B], addressing video depositions, includes in-court demonstrations and out-of-court demonstrations presented at trial through video recordings. Americans with Disabilities Act plaintiffs may wish to introduce demonstrative evidence to support two propositions: (1) that the plaintiff is substantially impaired in performing one or more life activities, and (2) that the plaintiff is qualified to perform the essential functions of a position. They are likely to confront two types of objection from defendants. The first objection is that the proffered evidence cannot be authenticated as required by Fed. R. Evid. 901 because it does not accurately reflect reality. The second is that even if the evidence could be authenticated, its prejudicial danger outweighs its probative value and therefore it should be excluded under Fed. R. Evid. 403.

In *Trapp v. North Mississippi Medical Center*,[594.7] the Mississippi Supreme Court upheld the trial court's decision to allow the jury to view a 1-hour and 20-minute film in a personal injury case. "The film depicted various activities of Cayson, such as waking up and moving from bed to wheelchair, attaching a catheter apparatus for urination, bowel evacuation procedures in the bathroom, taking a shower, dressing, eating breakfast, brushing teeth and shaving, exercising in a standup, opening mail with his teeth, moving about the house and kitchen, driving a van, emptying a lagon of urine, getting undressed and going to bed. The narration of the film by Cayson consisted of explaining what he was doing in the film."[594.8] The Mississippi Supreme Court held that the evidence represented by the film was not unduly cumulative and that, even though it was prejudicial in the sense that it was detrimental to the defendants' position in the case, it was not introduced for the purpose of inflaming the minds of the jury.[594.9]

Similarly, in *Holmes v. Black River Electric Cooperative, Inc.*,[594.10] the South Carolina Supreme Court allowed a plaintiff whose left arm was amputated as a result of negligently maintained electrical cables near a popular fishing spot to introduce photographs of the plaintiff's injured and amputated arm. The Supreme Court of South Carolina stated:

> There is no contention that the pictures do not accurately reflect Holmes and his injuries at the time the photographs were taken. There can be no doubt but that they prejudiced the defendant's case in the sense that they were detrimental, but they showed a condition which Holmes was entitled to either describe to the jury in words or by pictures, or a combination of the two. This demonstrative evidence aided the jury in its evaluation of the injuries and pain suffered. It cannot be said that they were introduced in evidence for the sole purpose of inflaming the minds of the jury; they served the proper purpose of bringing vividly to the jurors the details of tremendous injuries. The pictures were certainly admissible as a matter of discretion by the trial judge, if not as a matter of right. We find no error.[594.11]

In decision by the Wisconsin intermediate court,[594.12] exclusion of a film depicting the plaintiff's postamputation daily living pattern was found to be error. "This was proper demonstrative evidence and the trial court erred in not allowing the jury to see the 'day in the life of' film."[594.13]

"Day in the life of" videos usually are classified as demonstrative evidence, as are photographs or charts.[594.14] "Authentication of photographic evidence requires testimony identifying the subject and verifying the fairness and accuracy of the portrayal."[594.15] "Day in the life of" videos typically are relevant under Rule 402 because they facilitate the determination of facts at issue: the limiting effect of an impairment on life activities and the plaintiff's qualification to perform essential job functions.[594.16] "Day in the life of" videos are out-of-court statements, and therefore potentially excludable under the hearsay rule. But such videos typically are allowed as long as authenticating witnesses authenticate the video and cross-examination of authenticating witnesses is allowed.[594.17] Rule 403 of the Federal Rules of Evidence allows "day in the life of" videos to be excluded if their prejudicial effect, tendency to delay the trial, or cumulative nature override their probative nature.[594.18] Few courts require notice to the defendant or presence by a defendant representative at the making of the video.[594.19] Some courts, however, have treated the making of "day in the life of" videos as similar to depositions, at which opposing parties are entitled to be present and participate through cross-examination.[594.20] One commentator suggested that "day in the life of" videos should not be excluded on the ground that they are cumulative, unless another video has already been shown. However, the same commentator urged that opposing counsel be entitled to notice and possible participation as videos are produced. In addition, the commentator urged trial judges to review videos before they are shown to the jury, to exclude any unnecessarily prejudicial portions.[594.21]

Under the Federal Rules of Evidence, a video must be relevant under Rule 401; not unduly prejudicial, confusing, or a waste of time under Rule

403; must be authenticated under Rule 901; and must qualify for admission notwithstanding the hearsay rule, consistent with Rules 801, 802, and 803.

Courts routinely admit into evidence surveillance videos offered by defendants to undercut plaintiff claims of disability:

> Courts and commentators have recognized the danger of manipulation or selective editing of surveillance videotapes, which can, for example, compress hours of uneventful surveillance into a short tape that shows a misleading period of physical activity or omits a plaintiff's reactions of pain during or extended rest after an activity.... Furthermore, the full extent of such surveillance might actually corroborate, rather than impeach, a plaintiff's testimony of injury.[594.22]

In *Duncan v. Mercy Catholic Medical Center*,[594.23] the intermediate court in Pennsylvania reversed and remanded for a new trial in a medical malpractice case in which the plaintiff was cross-examined in detail about a surveillance videotape of her performing tasks she claimed she was unable to perform. The appellate court held that the video itself was inadmissible because the defendant hospital had not disclosed it during discovery and that the challenged cross-examination had the same prejudicial effect on the jury as if the tape itself had been shown.[594.24]

In *Evan v. Estelle*,[594.25] the district court granted a motion in limine foreclosing use of a surveillance video at trial. It also held that refusal to allow discovery of the video would foreclose its use at trial. The case had been pending for some two years before the defendant disclosed, on the eve of the final pretrial conference, the existence of the video. The court also noted that even if surveillance videos qualify as work product, "most courts in deciding this issue have determined that surveillance videos are discoverable because of their nature, and the fact that a party would not be able to obtain equivalent materials, since the surveillance video itself was taken at a particular time and place that can never be replicated."[594.26]

In *Beck v. Jet Equipment & Tools, Inc.*,[594.27] the district court denied a plaintiff's motion in limine to exclude or limit the portions of a surveillance video that could be shown to the jury. It did, however, instruct the defendant to edit the tapes to highlight the most significant portions, to avoid wasting time. In contrast, in *Quinn v. Wal-Mart Stores, Inc.*,[594.28] the appellate court affirmed a refusal by the trial judge to allow surveillance videos into evidence, noting the broad discretion allowed trial courts in deciding whether to admit surveillance tapes. The appellate court noted that the video showed the plaintiff performing activities that she had not denied being able to perform, although she claimed that performing those activities caused pain. The appellate court found that:

> [T]he tapes do not fairly indicate whether Ms. Quinn did experience pain after engaging in these activities. Accordingly, showing these tapes to the

> jury without context or explanation, could, as the trial court concluded, create a prejudicial impression on the jury that outweighs any probative value that they may have to impeach Ms. Quinn's testimony. As noted by the Louisiana Supreme Court, evidence in the form of moving pictures or videotapes must be approached with great caution because they show only intervals of the activities of the subject, they do not show rest periods, and do not reflect whether the subject is suffering pain during or after the activity.[594.29]

It is accurate to characterize this basis for excluding video evidence as based on flaws in authenticity as well as prejudicial effect.

In *Sheppard v. Massey Hauling Co.*,[594.30] the intermediate appellate court in Alabama found no abuse of discretion in admitting unedited videotapes made by a workers' compensation employer's investigator after the plaintiff successfully objected to admission of edited tapes that had been disclosed to plaintiff's counsel. Because the only thing that appeared on the unedited tapes that had not appeared on the edited tapes was footage in which the plaintiff did not appear, the appellate court found no prejudice to the plaintiff of admitting the unedited tapes, even though they were not disclosed to plaintiff's counsel before trial.[594.31] Employee benefit plan administrators and workers' compensation benefits decision makers regularly consider surveillance videos in deciding whether claimants are disabled, and if so, how much. Such administrative use of video evidence is accepted by reviewing courts.[594.32]

One practitioner author suggests avoiding common pitfalls of objectionable audio, such as the plaintiff screaming in pain while undergoing therapy, questioning the plaintiff on the video, or including prejudicial backgrounds such as a crucifix above the plaintiff's bed.[594.33] He urges effective, but meticulously accurate, narration on the video by the plaintiff, a medical professional, or the plaintiff's spouse.[594.34] Allowing adverse counsel to examine the plaintiff about the video scenes during the shooting can help overcome many objections to admissibility.[594.35] Proponents of video also must be prepared to allow discovery of the conditions under which the video was shot; disclose whether scenes in the video were rehearsed; state whether special camera effects were used; and what, if anything, was edited out of the video.[594.36] Also, although defense counsel may have no right to be present at the filming, one way to ensure admission of the "day in the life of" video is to invite him or her to the filming. If opposing counsel has been given the opportunity to monitor the filming, his or her objection at trial will be significantly diluted.[594.37] Plaintiff's counsel should prepare the plaintiff appropriately to avoid damaging on-camera or off-camera mistakes in front of the adverse attorney.[594.38]

In *Eckman v. Moore*,[594.39] the Mississippi Supreme Court found videos depicting the plaintiff being engaged in physical therapy; being washed, clothed, and fed by staff; and being visited by his wife and newborn son to be typical scenes found in "day of the life of" videos that would be admissible. These were distinguished from scenes of wedding pictures and pictures of the plaintiff's stepson, and scenes showing the plaintiff in a rehabilitation center, with sounds of the plaintiff's mother sobbing and saying, "Mama loves you, Mama loves you," which were found to be highly prejudicial and cumulative.[594.40]

Improvements in technology and rapidly declining prices have placed high-quality digital video equipment within the reach of any lawyer likely to represent an ADA plaintiff. Affordable software also makes it possible for ordinary people, with a little bit of practice, to edit videos made with low-cost equipment into near-studio-quality productions. Accordingly, counsel has a choice between traditional studio approaches to producing "day in the life of" videos and doing it for themselves. When financial resources permit, a professionally produced video is far superior. However, a carefully produced amateur video is better than none at all when counsel is working hard to control costs. When an amateur production is chosen, be careful about several things. First, ensure that the finished video can be authenticated, is relevant in its entirety, and avoids features that would strengthen an opponent's argument that the video's prejudicial danger outweighs its probative value. Remember that discovery is likely to unearth information about scenes that were recorded but edited out of the final video. On technical matters, sound and lighting are as important as the action recorded. Most home videos suffer from serious defects in audio and lighting. Ensure that sound quality is good. Usually, this means wiring anyone who has a speaking role with a lapel microphone. Also make sure that lighting is done professionally. Trial and error is the best way to do this.

A directory of "day in the life of" video production vendors is available at http://www.combose.com/Society/Law/Services/Litigation/Evidence_and_Presentations/Legal_Video/.

[C] Judicial Notice

In *United States v. Hoyts Cinemas Corp.*,[594.41] the court of appeals, partially reversing summary judgment in favor of the government and against movie theater chains, nevertheless agreed that movie theaters must provide disabled patrons with nondiscriminatory viewing angles, as well as unobstructed lines of sight.[594.42] However, it also found that the district court had not justified a finding that required stadium seating rather than slope seating. It found that the district judge's reliance on judicial notice to establish the preferences of movie theater patrons did not qualify under Fed. R. Evid. 201.[594.43]

[594.7] 471 So. 2d 375 (Miss. 1985).
[594.8] *Id.* at 381.
[594.9] *Id.* at 382.
[594.10] 262 S.E.2d 875 (S.C. 1980).
[594.11] *Id.* at 878.
[594.12] Buelow v. Nierengarten, 343 N.W.2d 830 (Wis. Ct. App. 1983).
[594.13] *Id.*

[594.14] Jane A. Kalinski, *Jurors at the Movies: Day in the Life Videos as Effective Evidentiary Tool or Unfairly Prejudicial Device?*, 27 Suffolk U. L. Rev. 789, 800 (1993).

[594.15] *Id.* at 801-02.

[594.16] *Id.* at 800-01 (stating general rule and concluding that "day in the life" videos typically are relevant in personal injury cases).

[594.17] *Id.* at 806-07.

[594.18] *Id.* at 809-10 (identifying four elements for evaluation of prejudice: existence of foundation, including authentication; self-serving or other prejudicial behavior by plaintiff in video; undue impact resulting from medium; undue impact because of lack of cross-examination in video itself).

[594.19] *Id.* at 813.

[594.20] *Id.* at 814.

[594.21] *Id.* at 820-22.

[594.22] Kau v. Four Seasons Maritime, Ltd., No. Civ. A. 02-3413, 2004 WL 797728 (E.D. La. Apr. 12, 2004).

[594.23] *Id.*

[594.24] 813 A. 2d at 10.

[594.25] 203 F.R.D. 172 (M.D. Pa. 2001).

[594.26] *Id.* at 173.

[594.27] No. Civ. 99-1687, 2001 WL 512243 (E.D. La. May 14, 2001).

[594.28] 774 So. 2d 1093 (La. Ct. App. 2000).

[594.29] *Id.* at 1098 (internal citations and quotations omitted).

[594.30] 726 So. 2d 682 (Ala. Civ. App. 1998).

[594.31] *Id.* at 684-85.

[594.32] *See, e.g.*, Raithaus v. UNUM Life Ins. Co., 335 F. Supp. 2d 1098 (D. Haw. 2004) (not only was surveillance video admissible before plan administrator, it would have been unreasonable for plan administrator not to rely on video, because "a picture is worth a thousand words"; nevertheless, claimant was entitled to challenge video in declaration submitted in subsequent federal court challenge to denial of benefits); Hagberg v. Liberty Life Assurance Co., 321 F. Supp. 2d 1270, 1273 (N.D. Fla. 2004) (overturning denial of total disability benefits under ERISA plan, noting that video surveillance considered by plan administrator in some ways supported finding of disability and in some ways not; activities were limited, and excluded strenuous activity); Winter v. Hartford Life & Accident Ins. Co., 309 F. Supp. 2d 409, 415 (E.D.N.Y 2004) (finding that surveillance video was insufficient evidence to support denial of disability benefits; video was 20 minutes in duration and purported to represent 2 full days of activity, but it did not "constitute substantial evidence supporting the denial of long term disability benefits" in the face of other evidence, including expert testimony that claimant was disabled); Lagge v. Corsica Co-op., 677 N.W.2d 569, 575 (S.D. 2004) (no error for workers' compensation tribunal to exclude from evidence surveillance video not disclosed in discovery or prehearing order); Osbun v. Auburn Foundry, Inc., 293 F. Supp. 2d 863, 870 (N.D. Ind. 2003) (finding termination of disability benefits based only on videotape arbitrary and capricious, because video evidence that claimant can perform light physical tasks for 1.5 hours over 2 days falls far short of demonstrating that claimant was capable of sustaining a job; video did not show how long claimant could perform tasks, whether he could perform them on daily basis, or how much pain he endured in the process).

[594.33] John Farell Fay, *Video Trial Exhibits*, 11-Mar Utah B.J. 10, 11 (1998) [hereinafter "Fay"].

[594.34] *Id.*

[594.35] *Id.*

[594.36] Fay at 12.

[594.37] *Id.*

[594.38] *Id.*

[594.39] 876 So. 2d 975 (Miss. 2004).

[594.40] *Id.* at 984.

[594.41] 380 F.3d 558 (1st Cir. 2004).

594.42 *Id.* at 567.
594.43 *Id.* at 570.

§ 9.21 JURY TRIALS

Page 611, add new subsection before first paragraph:

[A] Judge and Jury Roles

In *Bristol v. Board of County Commissioners*,[596.1] the court of appeals held that the first two elements of the statutory disability definition—existence of an impairment and impact on major life activity—are questions for the court and not for the jury. In contrast, the third question—whether the impairment substantially limits a major life activity—is a jury question.[596.2] It reversed the district court for concluding that all three steps of the analysis should be decided by the court.[596.3]

596.1 281 F.3d 1148 (10th Cir. 2002).
596.2 *Id.* at 1157-58.
596.3 *Id.* at 1159.

Page 615, add new subsection following carryover paragraph:

[B] Pretrial Orders

In *Philip v. Ford Motor Co.*,[628.1] the court of appeals affirmed a district court's refusal to consider an expanded list of substantially limited major life activities, including sleeping and sexual relations, 18 months after discovery had been closed. The court found that a district court may exclude from evidence at trial any matter that was not properly disclosed in compliance with a pretrial order, and that once discovery has closed, a district court has discretion on whether or not to reopen it.[628.2]

628.1 328 F.3d 1020 (8th Cir. 2003).
628.2 *Id.* at 1024.

§ 9.22 INJUNCTIONS

Page 618, add before first full paragraph:

In *Rodde v. Bonta*,[650.1] the court of appeals affirmed a preliminary injunction against closing a hospital that provided special services to disabled Medicaid patients based on a record that the services would not be available elsewhere. The court found that the closure "would deny certain disabled individuals meaningful access to government-provided services because of their unique needs, while others would retain access to the same class of services."[650.2] The evidence showed that before the decision to close the hospital, the county had consolidated specialized services for the disabled at that hospital. The court found that the lower court did not abuse its discretion in concluding that the balance of interests favored the plaintiff, because while the county's interest in balancing its budget was strong, the court found that the county currently had a surplus and that its calculations of savings resulting from closing the hospital failed to consider the increased cost of serving disabled patients at other facilities.[650.3]

[650.1] 357 F.3d 988 (9th Cir. 2004).
[650.2] *Id.* at 998.
[650.3] *Id.* at 999.

Page 618, add at end of page:

In *Keirnan v. Utah Transit Authority*,[654.1] the court of appeals agreed with the district court that a wheelchair-bound plaintiff had shown that the first three factors for a preliminary injunction favored the plaintiff, in her claim that a rule change by the state transit authority (excluding oversized wheelchairs such as the plaintiff's from paratransit services) violated Title II of the ADA:

> The first factor, that "[she] will suffer irreparable injury unless the injunction issues," has been demonstrated by Appellant in her briefs and at the hearing. She will lose the ability to attend religious services and medical appointments. She will also lose contact with friends and family. Appellant and other paratransit riders affected by the service change will be incapable of living their lives in the independent fashion to which they have become accustomed. Additionally, because Appellant is not alleging intentional discrimination or out-of-pocket expenses, damages might not be available should a court later find in her favor on the merits.
>
> The second factor, that "the threatened injury... outweighs whatever damage the proposed injunction may cause the opposing party," also supports Appellant's position. Surely Appellant will suffer a great deal more at the loss of her independence than UTA will suffer in continuing to provide service to Appellant and others as it has done for years. Additionally, while UTA stresses linkage concerns, UTA has offered no documented information regarding the severity of these concerns. Furthermore, this is UTA's sole offer of negative impact on it if a preliminary injunction were to issue.
>
> * * *
>
> The third factor, which takes into account the public interest, also weighs in Appellant's favor. A preliminary injunction would simply maintain the status quo pending a final determination on the merits. Because UTA has been providing this service without any documented detriment to the public, we fail to see how a temporary extension would harm the

> public interest in any capacity. Appellee is unable to point to anything adverse to the public interest should the preliminary injunction issue.[654.2]

The court of appeals agreed, however, with the district court that there was no reasonable expectation of success on the merits, even under the more lenient standard for probability of success when the first three requirements for injunctive relief tilt in the plaintiff's favor; "the mov[ant] need only show questions going to the merit so serious, substantial, difficult, and doubtful, as to make them a fair ground for litigation."[654.3] It held that the DOT regulation requiring that only common wheelchairs be transported was entitled to deference.[654.4]

In *Jones v. City of Monroe*,[654.5] the court of appeals affirmed denial of a preliminary injunction sought by a plaintiff with multiple sclerosis to compel a municipality to provide a free all-day parking space. The court of appeals stepped through the traditional requirements for preliminary injunctive relief, and concluded that the district court had permissibly concluded that the plaintiff failed to establish sufficient likelihood of success on the merits:

> When considering a motion for preliminary injunction, the district court should consider four factors: (1) whether the moving party has a strong likelihood of success on the merits; (2) whether the moving party will suffer irreparable injury without the injunction; (3) whether the issuance of the injunction would cause substantial harm to others; and (4) whether the public interest would be served by issuance of the injunction. The four considerations applicable to preliminary injunction decisions are factors to be balanced, not prerequisites that must be met. Moreover, a district court is not required to make specific findings concerning each of the four factors used in determining a motion for preliminary injunction if fewer factors are dispositive of the issue.
>
> * * *
>
> In the one-hour parking area specifically addressed by Jones, Monroe is offering the benefit of free short-term parking to individuals who wish to transact retail or other business in the downtown business district. The short-term, one-hour nature of the benefit is designed to help downtown businesses by making parking spaces in close proximity to them more readily available. Monroe quite logically has determined that downtown shopping and other downtown business activities are discouraged when patrons cannot easily obtain parking places close to their destination. All-day parking in the current one-hour spaces would thus have a negative impact on downtown businesses.
>
> In specific locations a short distance away from the one-hour parking, Monroe has also provided the benefit of free long-term, all-day parking to all individuals who come downtown, for whatever reason. While the all-day parking is not provided for the specific benefit of individuals who work downtown, they are free to use it.

> Access to the one-hour and all-day parking places is facially neutral. The one-hour limit applies to individuals with disabilities and those without disabilities. Similarly, both disabled and able-bodied persons may park in all-day parking. Both one-hour and all-day parking areas have spaces for disabled and nondisabled individuals. The parking limitations do not affect disabled and nondisabled individuals differently in any respect. Thus, the district court did not err in determining that Jones was not excluded from parking benefits offered by Monroe."[654.6]

Judge Cole dissented, arguing that "for Jones to be able to benefit from Monroe's parking program, she needs to be able to have access to the locations which non-disabled individuals can access from these parking lots."[654.7]

[654.1] 339 F.3d 1217 (10th Cir. 2003).
[654.2] *Id.* at 1220-21 (internal citations omitted).
[654.3] *Id.* at 1221 (internal quotations omitted).
[654.4] *Id.* at 1222-23 (quoting and citing 49 C.F.R. § 37.165(b)).
[654.5] 341 F.3d 474 (6th Cir. 2003).
[654.6] *Id.*
[654.7] 341 F.3d at 484 (Cole, J., dissenting).

§ 9.23 DAMAGES AND OTHER REMEDIES

[A] Generally

Page 619, add as first paragraph:

In *Kramer v. Banc of America Securities, LLC*,[663.1] the court of appeals held that compensatory and punitive damages are not available for retaliation claims under the ADA. The court reasoned that the 1991 Civil Rights Act, which expanded the remedies theretofore available under Title VII, identified only Sections 102 and Sections 102(b)(5) of the ADA as bases for compensatory and punitive damages because specific inclusion of those claims impliedly excluded claims under other sections of the ADA.[663.2]

[663.1] 355 F.3d 961 (7th Cir. 2004).
[663.2] *Id.* at 965.

[C] Front Pay

Page 622, add at end of subsection:

In *Ollie v. Titan Tire Corp.*,[672.1] the court of appeals affirmed an award of front pay based on a higher-paid tire builder position, rather than on a lower-paid forklift driver position as the employer preferred. The court rejected a cross-appeal by the plaintiff, who claimed that he should have received more than two years of front pay. The court reasoned that two years was sufficient for the relatively young plaintiff to achieve a comparable position.[672.2]

672.1 336 F.3d 680 (8th Cir. 2003).
672.2 *Id.* at 688.

[D] Punitive Damages

Page 623, add at beginning of note 681:

Ollie v. Titan Tire Corp., 336 F.3d 680, 689 (8th Cir. 2003) (affirming district court's vacation of punitive damages award; evidence showed mistaken interpretation of physician's report by employer, but not malice or evil intent);

Page 625, add at end of subsection:

In *Salitros v. Chrysler Corp.*,[690.1] the court of appeals affirmed judgment on a jury verdict awarding $100,000 in punitive damages, $445,516 in front pay and attorneys' fees of $128,268 on a claim of retaliation for exercising ADA rights. Punitive damages were warranted because of evidence that a manager said that he was going to teach the plaintiff a lesson not to file EEOC charges and not to protest work assignments he thought exceeded his medical restrictions.[690.2] The court of appeals also rejected the argument that punitive damages were unavailable because the jury made no award of compensatory damages.[690.3] It held that the award of front pay serves the purpose of compensating the plaintiff for economic losses.[690.4]

690.1 306 F.3d 562 (8th Cir. 2002).
690.2 *Id.* at 570.
690.3 *Id.* at 574.
690.4 *Id.* at 575.

[E] Compensatory Damages

Page 625, add new subsection heading before text:

[1] Generally

Page 626, add new subsection following carryover paragraph:

[2] Mitigation

The usual rule that a plaintiff seeking compensatory damages must mitigate damages applies under the ADA. In *Albert V. Smith's Food & Drug Centers, Inc.*,[698.1] the court of appeals held that an ADA claimant failed to mitigate by refusing an employer's offer of reemployment in a position she had previously sought. The court rejected her argument that the offer was a mere litigation tactic and that a period of seven days within which to decide on the offer was too short.[698.2]

[698.1] 356 F.3d 1242 (10th Cir. 2004).
[698.2] *Id.* at 1253-54.

[F] Damages Under Titles II and III

Page 627, add after penultimate paragraph:

In *Lovell v. Chandler*,[711.1] the court of appeals concluded that explicitly excluding disabled persons from an expansion of Hawaii's Medicaid program satisfied the "deliberate indifference" standard for award of compensatory damages.[711.2]

[711.1] 303 F.3d 1039 (9th Cir. 2002).
[711.2] *Id.* at 1057.

[G] Attorneys' Fees and Sanctions

[1] Generally

Page 631, add after extract:

In *Shott v. Rush-Presbyterian-St. Luke's Medical Center*,[731.1] the court of appeals reversed the district court, holding that plaintiff's counsel was not entitled to attorney's fees for time spent in the first trial of an ADA case because the plaintiff's unreasonable trial strategy necessitated the ordering of a new trial. "Shott's presentation of the evidence in a way that confused the jury and her opposition to jury instructions that may have alleviated some of the confusion—along with the District Court's specific finding that a second trial was necessary because of Shott's unreasonable strategy—leads us to this conclusion. We simply do not think it appropriate to award a litigant attorney's fees for a trial that was voided by her unreasonable strategy."[731.2] The court concluded: "We see no problem, however, with awarding fees for the work done in preparation for [the first] trial because it is likely that this work benefited the second trial as well."[731.3]

[731.1] 338 F.3d 736 (7th Cir. 2003).
[731.2] *Id.* at 742.
[731.3] *Id.* at 742-43.

Page 632, add following carryover paragraph:

In *Richard S. v. Department of Developmental Services*,[734.1] the court of appeals reversed the district court and held that ADA Title II plaintiffs who obtained a settlement agreement after they filed suit could collect attorneys' fees, distinguishing the Supreme Court's decision in *Buchanan Board and Care Home, Inc. v. West Virginia Department of Health and Human Resources*,[734.2] which eliminated the "catalyst theory" of attorneys' fees.[734.3] However, the court of appeals affirmed the district court in its conclusion that the plaintiffs were not entitled to attorneys' fees for their efforts to modify language in a permanent injunction granted to the interveners.[734.4]

In *Armstrong v. Davis*,[734.5] the court of appeals allowed attorneys' fees to counsel for prisoners who prevailed on their ADA claims. Among other things, it allowed fees for defending an appeal on another case presenting identical issues and held that the Prisoners Litigation Reform Act did not limit the award of attorneys' fees because attorneys' fees were authorized directly under the ADA.[734.6]

In *Barrios v. California Interscholastic Federation*,[734.7] the court of appeals rejected a conclusion that a $10,000 settlement award did not qualify the plaintiff as a prevailing party for purposes of an attorneys' fee award.[734.8]

In *Race v. Toledo-Davila*,[734.9] the court of appeals held that obtaining a preliminary injunction accompanied by a trial court statement that it did not address the merits of plaintiff's claim, failed to qualify the plaintiff for attorneys' fees.

In *American Disability Association, Inc. v. Chmielarz*,[734.10] the court of appeals held that judicial approval of a settlement agreement incident to its approval of voluntary dismissal of suit sufficiently changed the relationship of the parties, thereby qualifying the plaintiff for attorneys' fees.[734.11]

[734.1] 317 F.3d 1080 (9th Cir. 2003).

[734.2] 532 U.S. 598 (2001).

[734.3] 317 F.3d at 1086 (distinguishing *Buchanan*).

[734.4] *Id.* at 1089 (attorneys' fees might be available if interveners had sided with defendant, but in this case intervener sided with plaintiff).

[734.5] 318 F.3d 965 (9th Cir. 2003).

[734.6] *Id.* at 974, citing 42 U.S.C. § 12205.

[734.7] 277 F.3d 1128 (9th Cir. 2002).

[734.8] *Id.* at 1135.

[734.9] 291 F.3d 857 (1st Cir. 2002).

[734.10] 289 F.3d 1315 (11th Cir. 2002).

[734.11] *Id.* at 1320.

[2] Fees for Defendants and Sanctions

Page 634, add at end of subsection:

In *Sanglap v. LaSalle Bank, FSB*,[755.1] the court of appeals affirmed a district court's denial of attorney's fees to a defendant bank on an ADA claim. The bank argued that the claim against it was baseless, because the bank did not know of the plaintiff's epilepsy until after it closed his account for having seizures in the bank. The court of appeals held that there was sufficient basis to bring the lawsuit:

> The problem with [the defendant's] argument is that liability for disability discrimination does not require professional understanding of the plaintiff's condition. It is enough to show that the defendant knew of symptoms raising an inference that the plaintiff was disabled.... Most people who observe

> someone suffer frequent seizures will assume that a disability of some sort is to blame. Likewise, although LaSalle could not have been expected to know that Sanglap was particularly susceptible to severe emotional distress, bank employees did observe his seizures and could have inferred from their observations that he had epilepsy or another disabling condition. Sanglap's pursuit of his ADA claim therefore was not unreasonable, so the District Court acted well within its discretion in denying the request for fees.[755.2]

[755.1] 345 F.3d 515 (7th Cir. 2003).
[755.2] *Id.* at 520 (internal citations omitted).

Page 634, add new subsection:

[H] Reinstatement

In *Dilley v. Supervalu, Inc.*,[755.1] the court of appeals, reversing the district court, held that an employee's failure to mitigate by looking for jobs with other employers was immaterial to his claim for reinstatement.[755.2]

[755.1] 296 F.3d 958 (10th Cir. 2002).
[755.2] *Id.* at 967-68.

§ 9.24 PRECLUSION

[A] Generally

Page 636, add at end of subsection:

In *Nowak v. St. Rita High School*,[765.1] the Illinois Supreme Court held that a federal judgment rejecting an ADA claim because the plaintiff could not show he was qualified did not have preclusive effect in subsequent state court litigation asserting breach of tenure contract and promissory estoppel. Dismissing pendent state claims was not an adjudication on the merits, and the plaintiff remained free to assert them in state court.[765.2]

[765.1] 757 N.E.2d 471 (Ill. 2001).
[765.2] *Id.* at 479-80 (citing and interpreting Restatement (Second) of Judgment § 26(1) (1982)).

[D] "Splitting" Claims

Page 643, add at beginning of subsection:

In *Davila v. Delta Airlines, Inc.*,[790.1] the court of appeals affirmed dismissal of an ADA suit on *res judicata* grounds. The plaintiff, an airline pilot, had been dismissed for allegedly committing fraud in applying for and receiving disability payments from Delta Airlines. He protested the dismissal under the Railway Labor Act, and a "System Board of Adjustment" (an arbitration panel) rejected the grievance. The district court, affirmed by the court of appeals, declined to review the arbitration decision. He then filed an ADA claim in state court, which was removed to federal court, where it was dismissed on *res judicata* grounds. The plaintiff argued that *res judicata* did not bar his claims because the dismissal of the challenge to the arbitration award was not on the merits but based on a finding of lack of jurisdiction, and that he could not have asserted his ADA claim at the same time as the earlier lawsuit because he did not yet have a right to sue letter.[790.2]

The court of appeals rejected the idea that ADA plaintiffs may split their claims on the grounds of the timing of a right to sue letter. It identified at least three other circuits agreeing with that approach.[790.3] It also noted that the ADA claim shared "precisely the same transactional basis as the claim he advanced before the system board, i.e., his termination."[790.4] It found more serious grounds for analysis in the plaintiff's claim that the dismissal of the earlier lawsuit was not on the merits but on jurisdictional grounds. Although the first court had used jurisdictional language, the court of appeals found that the decision actually was on the merits. "In other words, it is not that the court found that it lacked the power to hear Davila's claim; it is simply that the court found those claims to be unpersuasive."[790.5]

[790.1] 326 F.3d 1183 (11th Cir. 2003).

[790.2] *Id.* at 1187.

[790.3] *Id.* at 1187 (citing earlier Eleventh Circuit opinion, Jang v. United Techs. Corp., 206 F.3d 1147, 1149 (11th Cir. 2000) (citing Heyliger v. State Univ. & Community College Sys., 126 F.3d 849, 855-56 (6th Cir. 1997) (noting that plaintiff had duty to request right to sue letter and amend state complaint); Brzostowski v. Laidlaw Waste Sys., Inc., 49 F.3d 337, 339 (7th Cir. 1995); Woods v. Dunlop Tire Corp., 972 F.2d 36, 41 (2d Cir. 1992) (suggesting stay pending completion of Title VII administrative proceeding, or amendment after obtaining right to sue letter)).

[790.4] 326 F.3d at 1188.

[790.5] *Id.* at 1189.

Page 643, add at end of section:

The plaintiff in *Mitchell v. Chapman*[793.1] complained of disability discrimination when he was denied a transfer to his old letter carrier position with modification of the mechanism for carrying his mail pouch necessary to relieve chronic neck pain. He failed to file with the EEOC within the 45-day limitation period, so when he sued on his claim, his case was dismissed for failure to file timely. Subsequently, he filed another lawsuit, reasserting violations of the Rehabilitation Act and the ADA, along with additional civil rights claims. The district court in the second lawsuit dismissed the claims as precluded by the first judgment. On appeal, the plaintiff conceded that his second ADA and Rehabilitation Act claims were barred, but argued that individual-capacity claims against certain other employees and his FMLA claim were not barred. The court of appeals accepted this argument, and held that because the time limitations applicable to his Rehabilitation Act claim did not apply to the FMLA, and because the individual-capacity lawsuits were distinct from the earlier official-capacity lawsuits, he could litigate with respect to those claims notwithstanding the earlier judgment.[793.2]

793.1 343 F.3d 811 (6th Cir. 2003).
793.2 *Id.* at 825.

[F] Law of the Case

Page 644, add at end of section:

In *Williams v. Thomson Corp.*,[805.1] the court of appeals affirmed summary judgment for the former employer and held that the transfer of a case from one district court to another did not represent the law of the case on the timeliness of an ADA action in federal court. A transfer order is an interlocutory order, and "the doctrine of law of the case is applicable only to final judgments, not to interlocutory orders."[805.2] This pronouncement as to interlocutory orders is questionable, but the outcome is probably right because it is not clear that the transferring court explicitly considered the timeliness of the suit.

805.1 383 F.3d 789 (8th Cir. 2004).
805.2 *Id.* at 791 (quoting Murr Plumbing, Inc. v. Scherer Bros. Fin. Servs. Co., 48 F.3d 1066, 1070 (8th Cir. 1995)).

§ 9.25 APPELLATE REVIEW

Page 645, add new subsection heading before text:

[A] Generally

Page 646, add new subsection following second full paragraph:

[B] Timing of Appeals

In *Garcia-Velazquez v. Frito Lay Snacks Caribbean*,[815.1] the court of appeals dismissed an appeal, finding that the 30-day period for filing a notice of appeal runs, not from the filing of a Fed. R. Civ. P. 59(e) motion to alter or amend the judgment, but rather from the entry of the judgment itself. The Rule 59(e) motion did not count in the particular case to toll the period for filing the appeal because that motion was not timely filed. The court of appeals rejected the argument that New Year's Eve should have been counted as a legal holiday under Fed. R. Civ. P. 6(a) because the clerk's office was closed for business on that day by order of the Chief Judge, and an individual in the clerk's office allegedly told the appellants that New Year's Eve would count as a holiday for purposes of computing the 30-day period for appeal.

815.1 358 F.3d 6 (1st Cir. 2004).

Volume 2

CHAPTER 14
EARLY PRETRIAL PLANNING, MOTIONS FOR SUMMARY JUDGMENT, AND SUPPORTING MEMORANDA

Page 120, add new section:

§ 14.04 PLANNING EVIDENCE FOR AMPUTEE CASES

Litigating ADA claims by amputees is particularly challenging. Amputation is undeniably permanent, and most ordinary people would consider someone who has lost an arm or a leg undeniably "disabled," in comparison with claimants who have less visible physical impairments. But recent case law suggests that amputees face particular challenges because of the requirement that qualification as "disabled" be determined after considering how the claimant functions with corrective measures, including prostheses. Amputees may prove themselves out of court if they go too far in showing how well they can perform with their prostheses. An amputee who tries to show that he can perform essential job functions by offering evidence that he participates in sports, for example, risks a finding that he is not disabled at all, under the statute.[17]

Counsel representing an amputee—particularly a young one—should anticipate that the defendant will turn evidence of the following against the plaintiff:

- That the amputee walks well, with slight, or no, limp
- That the amputee participates in foot races
- That the amputee bicycles
- That the amputee plays golf
- That the amputee participates in other challenging sports, such as rock climbing

Even if the amputee himself or herself does not offer evidence of such high functioning, counsel must anticipate that it will be discovered through depositions of the plaintiff.

It is essential, even at the pleading stage, for amputee counsel to allege—and be prepared to prove—that despite high levels of performance in athletic endeavors, the amputee nevertheless is significantly impaired in performance of daily life activities. For example, counsel should ensure that the discovery record shows:

- Difficulties driving a manual transmission car
- Difficulties bathing
- Difficulties associated with irritation of the residual limb, requiring the amputee to forego the prosthesis for a period of time, walking on crutches
- Actual or perceived difficulties with sexual partners

But, just as counsel for an amputee does not want to prove the client out of court because of a determination that the client is not statutorily disabled, counsel must be attentive to the need to show that the amputee can perform the essential functions of the position sought. In this regard counsel should carefully question the amputee client as to experienced difficulties in:

- Sitting for extended periods of time. An AK amputee has to sit on a rigid socket.
- Walking on uneven ground
- How often the prosthesis must be removed, and what happens then in terms of performing job functions
- Ability to drive vehicles, not only automobiles but also vehicles that are designed for operators with two normal feet
- Ability to climb
- Ability to stand for extended periods of time

Once such limitations with potential impact on job performance have been identified, counsel and client must develop a litigation strategy to overcome likely employer arguments that the client is not qualified to perform essential job functions, including assessment of reasonable accommodation, while also using these limitations to buttress the record establishing statutory disability.

In preparing the amputee's case, counsel may find helpful information available from the following websites: *http://www.amputee-coalition.org; http://www.abovekneeamputee.com; http://www.amputee.ca; http://www.activeamp.org; http://www.amputee-online.com/amputee/onyerbike.html; http://www.ampedriders.com; http://www.mtbamputee.com; http://www.ampsurf.com; http://www.m3racer.com; http://www.1footloose.com; http://members.shaw.ca/oneski; http://www.cameronclapp.com; http://www.onelegtim.com.*

Discussion boards on many of the websites provide a means of finding expert witnesses and fact witnesses who can reinforce the plaintiff's testimony about the impact of amputation and the level of function possible with a good prosthesis.

Hoffman v. Caterpillar, Inc.[18] offers a useful and concrete illustration of evidentiary missteps in proving that a one-armed plaintiff could operate a high-speed document scanner at production levels required by the employer. The district court entered judgment on a jury verdict for the employer after the jury viewed a videotape of the plaintiff operating the machine in question. The court of appeals affirmed the judgment, among other things, rejecting the plaintiff's argument on appeal that the district court abused its discretion because it allowed the plaintiff only four hours of training and four-and- one-half days of practice on the high-speed scanner before taking an eight-hour videotaped test, instead of a two-week period of training, the denial of which had given rise to the ADA lawsuit. "At a pretrial conference ... [the plaintiff] not only expressly agreed to these particular conditions, but also stated that if the District Court would allow an in-court demonstration in front of the jury, [the plaintiff] could operate the machine without any training, and that in any case, two weeks of training was unnecessary."[19] The court of appeals also found no abuse of discretion in the exclusion of an expert witness proffered by the plaintiff.[20]

Sections 9.17[B] and 9.19[B] offer suggestions to counsel on using video recordings and other demonstrative evidence, which are likely to be particularly effective in amputee cases in proving statutory disability, as well as qualification for essential functions.

[17] *See* § 3.03[OO].

[18] 368 F.3d 709 (7th Cir. 2004).

[19] *Id.* at 716 n.5.

[20] This part of the court's opinion is considered in § 9.19[A] of this supplement.

CHAPTER 18
PREVENTIVE MATERIALS

§ 18.21 ARBITRATION AGREEMENT

Page 393, add at end of section:

In *EEOC v. Luce, Forward, Hamilton & Scripps*,[68.1] the en banc Ninth Circuit, overruling earlier Ninth Circuit case law, held that requiring an employee to sign the following arbitration agreement as a condition of employment did not violate the Civil Rights Act of 1991:

> In the event of any dispute or claim between you and the firm (including employees, partners, agents, successors and assigns), including but not limited to claims arising from or related to your employment or the termination of your employment, we jointly agree to submit all such disputes or claims to confidential binding arbitration, under the Federal Arbitration Act. Any arbitration must be initiated within 180 days after the dispute or claim first arose, and will be heard before a retired State or Federal judge in the county containing the firm office in which you were last employed. The law of the State in which you last worked will apply.[68.2]

[68.1] 345 F.3d 742 (9th Cir. 2003).
[68.2] *Id.* at 745.

Page 782, add new Appendix G (note: this supersedes the version on the CD-ROM accompanying Volume 2 of the Fourth Edition):

APPENDIX G

ACCESSIBILITY GUIDELINES FOR BUILDINGS AND FACILITIES

The full text of the ADA Accessibility Guidelines for Buildings and Facilities (ADAAG), as amended through September 2002, can be found at *http://www.access-board.gov/adaag/html/adaag.htm#2. GENERAL.*

The following materials, as reprinted from the The Access Board's website *http://www.access-board.gov/indexes/accessindex.htm,* give an overview of the background and revisions to the ADAAG.

About this Edition of ADAAG

http://www.access-board.gov/adaag/html/intro.htm

The Americans with Disabilities Act (ADA) is a landmark law that protects the civil rights of persons with disabilities. It prohibits discrimination on the basis of disability in employment, State and local government services, transportation, public accommodations, commercial facilities, and telecommunications. To ensure access to the built environment, the ADA requires the establishment of design criteria for the construction and alteration of facilities covered by the law. These requirements, which were developed by the Access Board, are known as the **ADA Accessibility Guidelines** (ADAAG).

ADAAG serves as the basis for standards used to enforce the design requirements of the ADA. These standards are maintained by the **U.S. Department of Justice** (DOJ) and the **U.S. Department of Transportation** (DOT). It is these standards that the public is required to follow. Regulations issued from these agencies provide important information on using and applying the standards.

As originally published in July 1991, ADAAG addressed places of public accommodation and commercial facilities in the private sector. This reprint of ADAAG includes supplements issued by the Access Board that cover:

- state and local government facilities (1998)
- building elements designed for children's use (1998)
- play areas (2000)
- recreation facilities (2002)

These four supplements add new specifications to the guidelines and also revise existing provisions. They have not yet been incorporated into the DOJ and DOT standards and thus are not enforceable at this time. However, they provide helpful guidance in providing access to the various types of facilities they cover.

This document reflects existing ADAAG provisions. The Access Board is in the process of **updating** its accessibility guidelines for buildings and facilities covered by the ADA and the ABA. When a final rule is issued it will be available on the Board's website and through the Federal Register.

SUPPLEMENTS AND REVISIONS TO ADAAG (1993–2002)

Automated Teller Machines (1993)

The Board revised specifications for automated teller machines pertaining to clear floor space (4.35.2) and control heights (4.35.3). These changes are reflected in the enforceable standards.

Detectable Warnings (1994–2001)

ADAAG requires detectable warnings, a distinctively textured surface detectable by cane and underfoot, on the surface of curb ramps to provide a tactile cue for persons with vision impairments of their approach to streets (4.7.7). They are also required at hazardous vehicular areas (4.29.5), reflecting pools (4.29.6), and the edges of boarding platforms in transit facilities (10.3.1(8)). The Board temporarily suspended these requirements (except those applicable to boarding platforms) in 1994 due to concerns raised about the technical specifications, the availability of complying products, maintenance issues such as snow and ice removal, usefulness, and safety. DOJ and DOT joined the Board in this action, which effectively removed the requirement from the enforceable standards. The suspension, which was further extended, expired on July 26, 2001. The requirements for detectable warnings at curb ramps and other areas are again part of ADAAG and the enforceable standards.

State and Local Government Facilities (1998)

ADAAG, as originally published, addressed private sector facilities (places of public accommodation and commercial facilities). The Board added supplements that cover occupancies specific to the state and local government sectors. These include new occupancy sections on judicial, legislative, and regulatory facilities (Section 11) and detention and correctional facilities (Section 12). In addition, various provisions were revised or added for application to state and local government facilities generally:

- new definitions for terms used in the supplements (3.5)
- new general exceptions (4.1.1(5)(b)) and exceptions for elevators and platform lifts (4.1.3(5) exceptions 1, 4(e), and 5)
- revised scoping provisions for entrances (4.1.3(8)) and public telephones with TTYs (4.1.3(17)(c))
- new requirements for sales and service counters (7.2(3)) and airport security screening devices (10.4.1(8))

- new advisory material that clarifies provisions in the supplements (appendix)

These changes are not yet reflected in the enforceable standards.

Building E lements Designed for Children's Use (1998)

ADAAG, like most other accessibility guidelines, provided specifications based only on adult dimensions. The Board added alternate specifications based on children's dimensions that can be used where certain building elements are designed specifically for children's use. These alternate specifications address:

- drinking fountains (4.15.5)
- water closets (4.16.1 and 4.16.7)
- toilet stalls (4.17.1 and 4.17.7)
- lavatories (4.19.1 and 4.19.2) and sinks (4.25.3)
- fixed or built-in seating and tables (4.32.1 and 4.32.5)

Advisory information was added to the appendix that addresses children's reach ranges (A4.2.5 and A4.2.6), handrails at ramps and stairs (A4.8.5 and A4.9.5), water closets and toilet stalls (A4.16.7 and A4.17.7), mirrors (A4.19.6) and storage and controls (A4.25.3 and A4.27.3).

These changes are not yet reflected in the enforceable standards.

Play Areas (2000) and Recreation Facilities (2002)

A new occupancy section was added to address various types of recreation facilities (Section 15). This section covers access to amusement rides (15.1), boating facilities (15.2), fishing piers and platforms (15.3), golf courses (15.4), miniature golf courses (15.5), play areas (15.6), exercise equipment, bowling lanes, and shooting facilities (15.7), and swimming pools, wading pools and spas (15.8). In addition, existing sections of the guidelines were supplemented by the addition of:

- references to industry standards used in the new guidelines (2.3)
- definitions for terms used in the new provisions (3.5)
- general exceptions (4.1.1(5)(b)(iv-vii))
- provisions and exceptions for accessible routes (4.1.2(2)(b), 4.1.2(3) exception, 4.1.2(4) exceptions 1 and 2; and 4.1.3(1)(b), 4.1.3(2) exception, 4.1.3(3) exceptions 1 and 2, 4.1.3(5) exception 4(f))
- scoping provisions for lockers (4.1.3(12)(c))
- an exception for exercise equipment (4.1.3(13), exception)

- supplementary scoping provisions for team and player seating areas (4.13(19)(c))
- scoping and technical provisions for locker rooms (4.1.3(21), 4.35.1, and 4.35.4) and saunas and steam rooms (4.1.3(22) and 4.36)
- technical provisions for benches (4.37)
- advisory material that clarifies various provisions (appendix)

These changes are not yet reflected in the enforceable standards.

Revision of ADA and ABA Accessibility Guidelines

http://www.access-board.gov/ada-aba/status.htm

The Board's guidelines issued under the **Americans with Disabilities Act** (ADA) *http://www.access-board.gov/about/ADA.htm* and the **Architectural Barriers Act** (ABA) *http://www.access-board.gov/about/ABA.htm* are to be completely updated and revised. The ADA Accessibility Guidelines (ADAAG) cover the construction and alteration of facilities in the private sector (places of public accommodation and commercial facilities) and the public sector (state and local government facilities). The accessibility guidelines issued under the ABA primarily address facilities in the Federal sector and others designed, built, altered, or leased with Federal funds. The guidelines under both laws are being updated together in one rule that contains three parts: a scoping document for ADA facilities, a scoping document for ABA facilities, and a common set of technical criteria that the scoping sections will reference. As a result, the requirements for both ADA and ABA facilities will be made more consistent. The rule also includes new scoping and technical provisions for accessible housing that derive from requirements for "Type A" dwelling units contained in the 1998 edition of the ICC/ANSI A117.1 standard, "Accessible and Usable Buildings and Facilities."

Current Status: On April 2, 2002, the Board published a notice indicating that it was placing in the docket for public review a draft of the final guidelines revising the ADA and ABA Act Accessibility Guidelines.

What's Next: The Board will submit the final guidelines to the Office of Management and Budget (OMB) for review and clearance. OMB has 90 days for its review. Once cleared by OMB, the guidelines will be published in final form. Other Federal departments responsible for the standards used to enforce the ADA and ABA must then similarly modify their standards so that they are consistent with the updated guidelines. Until then, the current standards remain in effect. On August 8, 2000, the Department of Transportation published a notice *http://www.access-board.gov/ada-aba/dot.htm* to update its ADA standards based on the Board's proposed guidelines.

Background: The Board established an advisory committee to conduct a complete review of ADAAG and to recommend changes. The **ADAAG Review Advisory Committee** *http://www.access-board.gov/ada-aba/CommList.htm* consisted of 22 members representing the design and construction industry, the building code community, State and local governments entities, and people with disabilities. The committee was charged with reviewing ADAAG in its entirety and making recommendations for updating ADAAG so that it remains consistent with technological developments and changes in model codes and national standards and continues to meet the needs of people with disabilities. The committee developed a comprehensive set of recommendations that address substantive changes to ADAAG scoping provisions and technical requirements as well as its format and numbering system. Cited as an outstanding example of reinventing government, the Committee and the Board received the Vice Presidential Hammer Award in July 1996. The Board's proposal will be largely based on the committee's final report, **Recommendations for a New ADAAG** *http://www.access-board.gov/ada-aba/commrept.htm.*

On November 16, 1999, a **proposed rule** *http://www.access-board.gov/ada-aba/guidenprm.htm* was published in the *Federal Register* for public comment. The deadline for comments was May 15, 2000 (extended from March 15). The Board held public hearings on the proposal in **Los Angeles**, CA (January 31, 2000) and **Arlington**, VA (March 13, 2000) during the comment period. Over 2,500 **comments** were received on the proposal. **Summary of proposed rule** *http://www.access-board.gov/ada-aba/ruleoverview.htm*

Rulemaking History:

- September 14, 1994, Board creates the ADAAG Review Advisory Committee
- July 10, 1996, ADAAG Review Advisory Committee submits its report to the Board
- March 11, 1998, Board adopts a plan to combine revision of ADAAG with revision of ABA Accessibility Guidelines, which cover Federally funded facilities
- March 10, 1999, Board approves a proposed rule
- September 3, 1999, Board submits proposed rule to the Office of Management and Budget for clearance
- November 16, 1999, Proposed rule is published in the *Federal Register*
- January 31, 2000, Board holds public hearing on proposed rule in Los Angeles, CA
- March 13, 2000, Board holds public hearing on proposed rule in Arlington, VA
- May 15, 2000, Deadline for public comments on the proposed rule; over 2,500 comments received
- October 24 and 25, 2000, the Board holds information meetings on ATMs, reach ranges, and captioning
- April 2, 2002, the Board places in the docket for public review a draft of the final guideline

TABLE OF CASES

References are to sections in both the main volume and in the supplement.

B

C

D

E

F

G

H

K

L

M

N

O

P

T

U

V

W

X

Y

Z

TABLE OF STATUTES

References are to sections in both the main volume and in the supplement.

AMERICANS WITH DISABILITIES ACT

Act §	*U.S. Code Citation*	*Text §*
	42 U.S.C. §§ 12101–12213	1.01, 2.01, 3.01, 4.01, 5.01, 6.01, 7.01, 8.01, 9.01, 10.01,10.02[A], 11.01, 12.01, 13.01, 14.01, 15.01[A], 16.01[A], 17.01[A], 18.01
	42 U.S.C. § 12101	5.07[E]
	42 U.S.C. § 12101(a)(3)	6.03[A]
	42 U.S.C. § 12101(b)(4)	5.20, 9.04[H]
3(2)	42 U.S.C. § 12102(2)	3.02
3(2)(A)	42 U.S.C. § 12102(2)(A)	3.02[A], 3.02[A][2], 3.03[A], 3.05
	42 U.S.C. § 12102(2)(A)	3.02[C][2]
3(2)(B)	42 U.S.C. § 12102(2)(B)	3.02[B], 3.03[G], 3.08
	42 U.S.C. § 12102(2)(B)	3.02[C][2]
3(2)(C)	42 U.S.C. § 12102(2)(C)	3.02[A][2], 3.02[C], 3.04, 4.11[B][4][b]
	42 U.S.C. § 12102(2)(C)	3.02[C][2]
12(7)	42 U.S.C. § 12101(7)	1.07[B]
101–107	42 U.S.C. §§ 12111–12117	1.01, 2.03, 3.01, 4.01, 5.01, 6.01, 8.01, 9.01, 10.01, 10.02[A], 12.03[A], 16.01[B][7], 17.01[B][2], 18.04[B][6]
101(2)	42 U.S.C. § 12111(2)	4.02[A]

Act §	*U.S. Code Citation*	*Text §*
	42 U.S.C. § 12111(2)	5.20, 9.04[H]
101(3)	42 U.S.C. § 12111(3)	4.10[C]
101(4)	42 U.S.C. § 12111(4)	4.02[B]
101(5)	42 U.S.C. § 12111(5)	2.03
101(5)(A)	42 U.S.C. § 12111(5)(A)	4.02[C]
101(5)(B)	42 U.S.C. § 12111(5)(B)	4.02[C], 8.01
101(6)	42 U.S.C. § 12111(6)	1.03, 4.13
101(7)	42 U.S.C. § 12111(7)	1.03
	42 U.S.C. § 12111(7)	5.20, 9.04[H]
101(8)	42 U.S.C. § 12111(8)	3.06, 3.06[D], 4.05[D], 16.01[B][7]
101(9)	42 U.S.C. § 12111(9)	4.05[A], 4.05[B][5], 4.10[B][1], 18.08[B][9]
101(9)(B)	42 U.S.C. § 12111(9)(B)	4.06[B][23], 4.06[B][27]
101(10)	42 U.S.C. § 12111(10)	4.10[B][1], 4.10[C], 18.08[B][9]
101(10)(B)(ii)	42 U.S.C. § 12111(10)(B)(ii)	4.10[B][1]
101(10)(B)(iii)	42 U.S.C. § 12111(10)(B)(iii)	4.10[B][1]
102	42 U.S.C. § 12112	3.02, 18.08[B][9]
102(a)	42 U.S.C. § 12112(a)	4.03[F], 4.03[I], 4.03[H][2], 4.11[B][1], 5.26, 9.04[G], 9.08[B], 18.04[B][6], 18.08[B][9]
	42 U.S.C. § 12112(a)	5.20, 9.04[H]
102(b)	42 U.S.C. § 12112(b)	18.04[B][6]
102(b)(1)	42 U.S.C. § 12112(b)(1)	4.03[A], 4.03[J], 8.11,17.01[B][10]
102(b)(2)	42 U.S.C. § 12112(b)(2)	4.03[D], 4.16[B]
102(b)(3)	42 U.S.C. § 12112(b)(3)	4.03[C], 4.05[D], 4.11[B][3]
102(b)(3)(A)	42 U.S.C. § 12112(b)(3)(A)	4.06[B][11]
102(b)(4)	42 U.S.C. § 12112(b)(4)	3.11, 4.03[E]

Act §	*U.S. Code Citation*	*Text §*
102(b)(5)	42 U.S.C. § 12112(b)(5)	4.03[E], 4.05[A], 4.05[C],4.10[B][1], 4.11[B][4][b], 8.11
102(b)(5)(A)	42 U.S.C. § 12112(b)(5)(A)	4.03[A], 4.03[E], 4.05[B][5],4.10[B][1], 12.03[A]
	42 U.S.C. § 12112(b)(5)(A)	3.02[A][3]
102(b)(5)(B)	42 U.S.C. § 12112(b)(5)(B)	4.03[A]
102(b)(6)	42 U.S.C. § 12112(b)(6)	4.03[G][1], 4.05[D]
102(b)(7)	42 U.S.C. § 12112(b)(7)	4.03[G][1], 8.11
102(c)	42 U.S.C. § 12112(c)	4.14, 18.07[B]
	42 U.S.C. § 12112(c)	3.07
102(c)(1)	42 U.S.C. § 12112(c)(1)	4.03[H][1]
102(c)(1)(A)	42 U.S.C. § 12112(c)(1)(A)	18.04[B][6]
102(c)(1)(B)	42 U.S.C. § 12112(c)(1)(B)	18.04[B][6]
102(c)(2)(A)	42 U.S.C. § 12112(c)(2)(A)	4.03[H][1], 18.10
102(c)(2)(B)	42 U.S.C. § 12112(c)(2)(B)	4.03[H][1], 18.10
102(c)(3)(A)	42 U.S.C. § 12112(c)(3)(A)	4.03[H][1]
102(c)(3)(B)	42 U.S.C. § 12112(c)(3)(B)	4.03[H][1], 18.10
102(c)(3)(B)(i)	42 U.S.C. § 12112(c)(3)(B)(i)	4.03[H][1]
102(c)(3)(B)(ii)	42 U.S.C. § 12112(c)(3)(B)(ii)	4.03[H][1]
102(c)(3)(B)(iii)	42 U.S.C. § 12112(c)(3)(B)(iii)	4.03[H][1]
102(c)(3)	42 U.S.C. § 12112(c)(3)	4.03[H][1]
102(c)(3)(C)	42 U.S.C. § 12112(c)(3)(C)	4.03[H][1]
102(c)(4)(A)	42 U.S.C. § 12112(c)(4)(A)	4.03[H][1]
102(c)(4)(B)	42 U.S.C. § 12112(c)(4)(B)	4.03[H][1], 4.03[H][2]
102(c)(4)(B)	42 U.S.C. § 12112(d)	4.03[H][2], 4.03[H][3]
	42 U.S.C. § 12112(d)(2)	4.03[H][2], 5.07[E]
	42 U.S.C. § 12112(d)(3)	5.07[E]
	42 U.S.C. § 12112(d)(3)(B)	4.03[H][2]
	42 U.S.C. § 12112(d)(3)(C)	4.03[H][2]
	42 U.S.C. § 12112(d)(4)	4.03[H][2], 5.07[E]
	42 U.S.C. § 12112(d)(4)(A)	4.03[H][2]
103	42 U.S.C. § 12113	3.04, 4.10[A]
103(a)	42 U.S.C. § 12113(a)	4.10[A], 14.02[B][3]
103(b)	42 U.S.C. § 12113(b)	2.05, 3.04, 4.10[A], 4.10[C], 14.02[B][3]

Act §	*U.S. Code Citation*	*Text §*
	42 U.S.C. § 12113(c)(2)	4.15
103(d)	42 U.S.C. § 12113(d)	3.04, 4.10[C]
104	42 U.S.C. § 12114	1.01, 4.13, 5.17
104(a)	42 U.S.C. § 12114(a)	3.12, 4.13
104(b)	42 U.S.C. § 12114(b)	3.12
	42 U.S.C. § 12114(b)(2)	4.13
	42 U.S.C. § 12114(b)(3)	3.12, 4.13
104(c)	42 U.S.C. § 12114(c)	3.12, 4.13
	42 U.S.C. § 12114(c)(2)	4.13
104(c)(3)	42 U.S.C. § 12114(c)(3)	3.12
	42 U.S.C. § 12114(c)(4)	4.11[B][5]
104(c)(5)	42 U.S.C. § 12114(c)(5)	3.12, 4.13
104(d)	42 U.S.C. § 12114(d)	4.13
104(d)(2)	42 U.S.C. § 12114(d)(2)	3.12
	42 U.S.C. § 12114(e)	4.13
105	42 U.S.C. § 12115	4.16[G]
106	42 U.S.C. § 12116	9.03
107	42 U.S.C. § 12117	2.07, 9.08[a][1], 17.01[B][10]
107(a)	42 U.S.C. § 12117(a)	4.02[D], 5.02, 9.02, 9.16, 17.01[B][2], 17.01[B][8], 18.23[B][3]
	42 U.S.C. § 12117(a)	5.20, 9.04[H]
	42 U.S.C. § 12117(b)	8.02[A]
108	42 U.S.C. § 12117	1.05, 2.03, 4.02[C]
201–246	42 U.S.C. §§ 12131–12165	1.01, 2.05, 3.01, 5.01, 6.02[A], 7.01, 8.01, 9.01, 11.01, 17.02[B][4]
201(1)	42 U.S.C. § 12131(1)	5.01, 8.01
	42 U.S.C. § 12131(1)(A)–(B)	9.04[A]
	42 U.S.C. § 12131(2)	4.04, 5.07[E], 5.09[C]
202	42 U.S.C. § 12132	3.02, 4.14, 5.04, 5.07[D], 5.08[A], 5.09[D], 5.09[K], 5.09[L], 5.09[M],

Act §	*U.S. Code Citation*	*Text §*
		5.26, 7.02, 9.04[A]
	42 U.S.C. § 12132	5.20, 9.04[H]
203	42 U.S.C. § 12133	9.02, 9.14, 9.16, 9.22, 9.23[F], 17.01[B][10]
	42 U.S.C. § 12133	5.20, 9.04[H]
204	42 U.S.C. § 12134	5.05, 9.06, 9.23[G][1]
	42 U.S.C. § 12141(1)	7.02
221(2)	42 U.S.C. § 12141(2)	7.01, 7.02
221(3)	42 U.S.C. § 12141(3)	7.02
222(a)	42 U.S.C. § 12142(a)	7.02, 7.08
222(b)	42 U.S.C. § 12142(b)	7.02, 7.08
222(b)(7)	42 U.S.C. § 12142(b)(7)	7.02
222(c)	42 U.S.C. § 12142(c)	7.02
222(c)(1)	42 U.S.C. § 12142(c)(1)	7.08
222(c)(2)(A)	42 U.S.C. § 12142(c)(2)(A)	7.08
223	42 U.S.C. § 12143	7.02
223(b)	42 U.S.C. § 12143(b)	7.02
223(c)(1)	42 U.S.C. § 12143(c)(1)	7.02
223(d)	42 U.S.C. § 12143(d)	7.02
223(e)	42 U.S.C. § 12143(e)	7.02
224	42 U.S.C. § 12144	7.02
226	42 U.S.C. § 12146	7.02
227(a)	42 U.S.C. § 12147(a)	7.02
227(b)(2)(A)	42 U.S.C. § 12147(b)(2)(A)	7.02
227(b)(2)(B)	42 U.S.C. § 12147(b)(2)(B)	7.02
	42 U.S.C. § 12148	7.02
228(a)(2)	42 U.S.C. § 12148(a)(2)	7.02
228(a)(3)	42 U.S.C. § 12148(a)(3)	7.02
	42 U.S.C. § 12148(b)	7.02
229	42 U.S.C. § 12149	7.05
	42 U.S.C. § 12162	7.02
242(2)(a)	42 U.S.C. § 12162(a)	7.02
242(b)	42 U.S.C. § 12162(b)	7.02
242(e)	42 U.S.C. § 12162(e)	7.02
244	42 U.S.C. § 12164	7.05

Act §	*U.S. Code Citation*	*Text §*
301–310	42 U.S.C. §§ 12181–12189	1.01, 2.05, 3.01, 4.14, 6.01, 7.01, 8.01, 9.01, 11.01, 12.03[A], 18.24
301(a)	42 U.S.C. § 12181(a)	1.05, 6.11
301(b)	42 U.S.C. § 12181(b)	1.05, 6.11
301(c)	42 U.S.C. § 12181(c)	1.05, 6.11
301(2)	42 U.S.C. § 12181(2)	6.01, 9.06
301(3)	42 U.S.C. § 12181(3)	7.02, 7.04
301(4)	42 U.S.C. § 12181(4)	7.02, 7.04
301(5)	42 U.S.C. § 12181(5)	7.04
301(6)	42 U.S.C. § 12181(6)	8.01
301(7)	42 U.S.C. § 12181(7)	6.02[A], 8.01
	42 U.S.C. § 12181(7)	5.04, 9.06
301(7)(F)	42 U.S.C. § 12181(7)(F)	9.04[K]
301(7)(G)	42 U.S.C. § 12181(7)(G)	7.02
301(7)	42 U.S.C. § 12181(7)(I)	6.02[A]
301(9)	42 U.S.C. § 12181(9)	6.03[D][4]
301(9)(A)	42 U.S.C. § 12181(9)(A)	6.03[D][4]
301(9)(B)	42 U.S.C. § 12181(9)(B)	6.03[D][4]
301(9)(C)	42 U.S.C. § 12181(9)(C)	6.03[D][4]
301(9)(D)	42 U.S.C. § 12181(9)(D)	6.03[D][4]
301(10)	42 U.S.C. § 12181(10)	7.01, 7.02
301(11)	42 U.S.C. § 12181(11)	7.02
302	42 U.S.C. § 12182	5.02, 5.09[D], 6.02[A], 6.03[A], 6.04[D], 6.04[E], 7.02
302(a)	42 U.S.C. § 12182(a)	3.02, 6.02[A], 6.03[A], 6.04[D], 6.12
	42 U.S.C. § 12182(a)	6.02[D]
302(b)(1)	42 U.S.C. § 12182(b)(1)	6.12
302(b)(1)(A)(i)	42 U.S.C. § 12182(b)(1)(A)(i)	6.03[A]
302(b)(1)(A)(ii)	42 U.S.C. § 12182(b)(1)(A)(ii)	6.03[A]
302(b)(1)(A)(iii)	42 U.S.C. § 12182(b)(1)(A)(iii)	6.03[A]
302(b)(1)(B)	42 U.S.C. § 12182(b)(1)(B)	6.03[A]
302(b)(1)(C)	42 U.S.C. § 12182(b)(1)(C)	6.03[A]
302(b)(1)(D)	42 U.S.C. § 12182(b)(1)(D)	6.03[A]

Act §	*U.S. Code Citation*	*Text §*
302(b)(1)(E)	42 U.S.C. § 12182(b)(1)(E)	6.03[A]
302(b)(2)	42 U.S.C. § 12182(b)(2)	6.12
302(b)(2)(A)(i)	42 U.S.C. § 12182(b)(2)(A)(i)	6.03[A], 12.03[A]
302(b)(2)(A)(ii)	42 U.S.C. § 12182(b)(2)(A)(ii)	6.01, 6.03[A], 6.03[B], 6.04[B], 12.03[A]
302(b)(2)(A)(iii)	42 U.S.C. § 12182(b)(2)(A)(iii)	6.01, 6.03[C][1], 6.03[C][3], 6.04[A], 6.04[C], 12.03[A]
302(b)(2)(A)(iv)	42 U.S.C. § 12182(b)(2)(A)(iv)	6.01, 6.03[D][1], 6.03[D][4], 9.22, 12.03[A]
302(b)(2)(A)(v)	42 U.S.C. § 12182(b)(2)(A)(v)	6.01, 6.03[D][4], 12.03[A]
302(b)(2)(B)	42 U.S.C. § 12182(b)(2)(B)	7.02, 7.04
302(b)(2)(C)	42 U.S.C. § 12182(b)(2)(C)	7.02, 7.04
302(b)(2)(C)(ii)	42 U.S.C. § 12182(b)(2)(C)(ii)	7.04
302(b)(2)(D)	42 U.S.C. § 12182(b)(2)(D)	7.02, 7.04
302(b)(3)	42 U.S.C. § 12182(b)(3)	6.04[E]
303	42 U.S.C. § 12183	6.02[A], 6.03[E], 6.12, 9.02, 9.22
303(a)	42 U.S.C. § 12183(a)	9.22
303(a)(1)	42 U.S.C. § 12183(a)(1)	6.01, 6.03[E], 6.10[B], 7.02
303(a)(2)	42 U.S.C. § 12183(a)(2)	6.03[E]
303(b)	42 U.S.C. § 12183(b)	6.03[E]
	42 U.S.C. § 12183(b)(3)	6.04[E]
304	42 U.S.C. § 12184	6.03[J], 6.13, 7.02, 7.03
304(a)	42 U.S.C. § 12184(a)	6.03[I]
304(b)(1)	42 U.S.C. § 12184(b)(1)	6.03[I]
304(b)(2)(C)	42 U.S.C. § 12184(b)(2)(C)	6.03[I]
304(b)(3)	42 U.S.C. § 12184(b)(3)	6.03[I], 7.02
304(c)	42 U.S.C. § 12184(c)	6.03[I]
306	42 U.S.C. § 12186	7.05
306(a)	42 U.S.C. § 12186(a)	6.12
306(a)(1)	42 U.S.C. § 12186(a)(1)	6.12

Act §	*U.S. Code Citation*	*Text §*
306(a)(2)(B)(iii)	42 U.S.C. § 12186(a)(2)(B)(iii)	6.12
306(a)(2)(C)	42 U.S.C. § 12186(a)(2)(C)	6.12
306(b)	42 U.S.C. § 12186(b)	6.12
306(c)	42 U.S.C. § 12186(c)	6.12
306(d)(1)	42 U.S.C. § 12186(d)(1)	6.12
307	42 U.S.C. § 12187	6.02[B]
308	42 U.S.C. § 12188	17.01[B][10]
	42 U.S.C. § 12188(a)	9.14
308(a)(1)	42 U.S.C. § 12188(a)(1)	6.08, 9.02, 9.04[E], 9.16, 9.22, 9.23[G][1]
	42 U.S.C. § 12188(a)(1)	9.05
308(a)(2)	42 U.S.C. § 12188(a)(2)	6.08, 9.02, 9.22
	42 U.S.C. § 12188(b)	7.06
308(b)(1)(A)(i)	42 U.S.C. § 12188(b)(1)(A)(i)	6.08, 9.02
308(b)(1)(A)(ii)	42 U.S.C. § 12188(b)(1)(A)(ii)	6.03[E], 6.08, 9.02
308(b)(1)(B)	42 U.S.C. § 12188(b)(1)(B)	6.08, 9.02, 9.04[E], 9.23[F]
308(b)(2)	42 U.S.C. § 12188(b)(2)	9.22
308(b)(2)(C)	42 U.S.C. § 12188(b)(2)(C)	6.08, 9.02
308(b)(4)	42 U.S.C. § 12188(b)(4)	6.08, 9.02
309	42 U.S.C. § 12189	6.03[G]
310(6)	42 U.S.C. § 12181(6)	8.01
	47 U.S.C. §§ 151–613	7.01
	47 U.S.C. § 153	7.16
	47 U.S.C. § 153(10)	7.16
	47 U.S.C. § 223	7.16
	47 U.S.C. § 223(e)(6)	7.16
	47 U.S.C. § 223(h)(1)(B)	7.16
401	47 U.S.C. § 225	1.01, 2.01, 2.08, 3.01, 4.01, 5.01, 6.01, 7.01, 7.09, 7.11, 7.15, 7.16, 8.01, 9.01, 9.03, 10.01, 10.02[A], 11.01, 12.01, 13.01, 14.01, 15.01[A], 16.01[A], 17.01[A], 18.01
401(a)(1)	47 U.S.C. § 225(a)(1)	7.10, 7.16

Act §	*U.S. Code Citation*	*Text §*
401(b)	47 U.S.C. § 225(b)	7.16
401(b)(2)	47 U.S.C. § 225(b)(2)	7.15
401(c)	47 U.S.C. § 225(c)	7.16
401(d)	47 U.S.C. § 225(d)	7.09, 7.16
	47 U.S.C. § 225(d)(2)	7.09
	47 U.S.C. § 228	7.16
	47 U.S.C. § 230(b)	7.16
	47 U.S.C. § 230(e)	7.16
	47 U.S.C. § 230(e)(2)	7.16
	47 U.S.C. § 610 *et seq.*	7.15
	47 U.S.C. § 610(a)	7.15
	47 U.S.C. § 610(c)	7.15
402	47 U.S.C. § 711	1.01, 2.01, 2.08, 3.01, 5.01, 4.01, 6.01, 7.01, 7.11, 7.16, 8.01, 9.01, 9.03, 10.01, 10.02[A], 11.01, 12.01, 13.01, 14.01, 15.01[A], 16.01[A], 17.01[A], 18.01
501	42 U.S.C. § 12201	8.02[A]
501–514	42 U.S.C. §§ 12201–12213	1.01, 5.20, 6.07, 7.17
501(a)	42 U.S.C. § 12201(a)	6.14
501(b)	42 U.S.C. § 12201(b)	1.01, 6.08, 9.02, 9.15
	42 U.S.C. § 12201(b)	1.07[A], 5.25, 6.14
501(c)	42 U.S.C. § 12201(c)	4.14
	42 U.S.C. § 12201(c)	4.14
501(c)(3)	42 U.S.C. § 12201(c)(3)	4.14
	42 U.S.C. § 12201(c)(3)	4.14
502	42 U.S.C. § 12202	1.01
503	42 U.S.C. § 12203	6.03[A]
	42 U.S.C. § 12203	1.01, 4.03[K], 5.20, 5.20, 6.07, 9.04[H]
503(a)	42 U.S.C. § 12203(a)	4.03[K]
	42 U.S.C. § 12203(a)	4.03[E], 5.20, 9.04[H]
503(b)	42 U.S.C. § 12203(b)	4.03[K]

Act §	*U.S. Code Citation*	*Text §*
	42 U.S.C. § 12203(b)	4.03[E], 4.03[K]
	42 U.S.C. § 12203(c)	4.03[E], 5.20, 9.04[H]
504	42 U.S.C. § 12204	8.13
	42 U.S.C. § 12204	6.10[A]
504(a)	42 U.S.C. § 12204(a)	6.12
504(b)	42 U.S.C. § 12204(b)	6.12
	42 U.S.C. § 12205	1.08, 9.23[G][1]
506(a)(1)	42 U.S.C. § 12206(a)(1)	6.13
506(c)(1)	42 U.S.C. § 12206(c)(1)	6.13
506(c)(2)(C)	42 U.S.C. § 12206(c)(2)(C)	6.13
506(c)(3)	42 U.S.C. § 12206(c)(3)	6.13
506(d)	42 U.S.C. § 12206(d)	6.13
506(e)	42 U.S.C. § 12205	9.23[G][1]
506(e)	42 U.S.C. § 12206(e)	6.13
509	42 U.S.C. § 12209	4.02[C]
	42 U.S.C. § 12210	2.05, 4.13, 5.17
	42 U.S.C. § 12210(d)(1)	4.13
510(b)	42 U.S.C. § 12210(b)	5.17
510(c)	42 U.S.C. § 12210(c)	4.13
	42 U.S.C. § 12211	3.02
511(a)	42 U.S.C. § 12211(a)	3.13
511(b)	42 U.S.C. § 12211(b)	3.13
	42 U.S.C. § 12212	8.10, 9.11[C]
	42 U.S.C. § 12213	18.27

OTHER UNITED STATES CODE PROVISIONS

2 U.S.C.

§ 1301(3)	2.02, 4.02[D], 5.02, 9.14
§ 1301(9)	2.02, 4.02[D], 5.02, 9.14
§ 1302	4.02[D], 5.02
§ 1302(a)(3)(10)	4.02[D], 5.02
§ 1311	4.02[D], 5.02
§ 1311(a)(3)	4.02[D], 5.02
§ 1311(b)(3)	4.02[D], 5.02, 9.14
§ 1331(a)	9.14
§ 1331(c)	9.14
§ 1331(d)	9.14
§ 1331(d)(1)	9.14
§ 1331(d)(4)	9.14

42 U.S.C.

REHABILITATION ACT

CODE OF FEDERAL REGULATIONS

17 C.F.R.

28 C.F.R.

29 C.F.R.

36 C.F.R.

38 C.F.R.

41 C.F.R.

42 C.F.R.

§ 37.165(b)	7.05, 9.22
§ 440.240	5.09[L]

45 C.F.R.

§§ 84.1–84.61	8.08
§ 84.2	8.04[A]
§ 84.3(I)(A)	8.01
§ 84.3(I)(B)	8.01
§ 84.3(j)(i)–(ii)	8.01
§ 84.11	8.04[A], 8.04[B]
§ 84.11(c)	4.16[B]
§ 84.12	4.06[B][27], 8.04[A], 8.08
§ 84.12(b)(1)	4.05[A]
§ 84.12(c)	4.10[B][1]
§ 84.13	8.04[A], 8.11
§ 84.14	8.04[A]

47 C.F.R.

§§ 64.601–64.608	2.08
§ 64.601(7)	7.09
§ 64.601(8)	7.10
§ 64.601(9)	7.12
§ 64.603	7.09, 7.10
§ 64.604(a)(1)	7.11
§ 64.604(a)(2)	7.10
§ 64.604(a)(3)	7.10
§ 64.604(b)(1)	7.12
§ 64.604(b)(2)	7.11, 7.12
§ 64.604(b)(4)	7.10
§ 64.604(b)(5)	7.09, 7.12
§ 64.604(c)(4)	7.10
§ 64.604(c)(4)(ii)	7.14
§ 64.605	7.10
§ 64.605(d)(4)(i)	7.13
§ 68.3	7.15

49 C.F.R.

pt. 27	2.08, 6.03[J], 7.05
pts. 37–38	7.05
pt. 37	2.08
pt. 37, sub. C	7.06
§ 37.3	3.02, 7.03, 7.05

FEDERAL RULES OF APPELLATE PROCEDURE

FEDERAL RULES OF CIVIL PROCEDURE

FEDERAL RULES OF CRIMINAL PROCEDURE

FEDERAL RULES OF EVIDENCE

STATE STATUTES AND RULES

California

Illinois

Kentucky

Maryland

Massachusetts

Missouri

Nevada

New Jersey

N.J. Stat. Ann. § 10:5-5(q)	4.11[B][4][b]

New York

N.Y. Civ. Prac. L. & R. art. 50-B	5.07[B]

Pennsylvania

42 Pa. Cons. Stat. Ann. § 8302	9.04[L]
Pa. R. Civ. P. 1020	9.15

Washington

Wash. Admin. Code § 162-22-050(3)	4.06[B][8]
Wash. Rev. Code § 49.60.181(1)	4.06[B][8]

West Virginia

W. Va. Code § 5-11-1	8.14
W. Va. Code § 55-2-12	9.16

INDEX

References are to sections in both the main volume and the supplement.

E

F

G

H

N

O

P

Q

R

S

U

V

W